STORMWATCH
Post Human Division
BOOK TWO

Writer: Christos Gage

Artist: Matthew Dow Smith (#5)
Andy Smith (#8-12)

Colors: David Baron

Letters: Pat Brosseau (#5, 8)
Travis Lanham (#9-10)
Phil Balsman (#11)
Steve Wands (#12)

Jim Lee, Editorial Director
John Nee, Senior VP—Business Development
Ben Abernathy, Editor
Kristy Quinn, Assistant Editor
Ed Roeder, Art Director
Paul Levitz, President & Publisher
Georg Brewer, VP—Design & DC Direct Creative
Richard Bruning, Senior VP—Creative Director
Patrick Caldon, Executive VP—Finance & Operations
Chris Caramalis, VP—Finance
John Cunningham, VP—Marketing
Terri Cunningham, VP—Managing Editor
Alison Gill, VP—Manufacturing
David Hyde, VP—Publicity
Hank Kanalz, VP—General Manager, WildStorm
Paula Lowitt, Senior VP—Business & Legal Affairs
MaryEllen McLaughlin, VP—Advertising & Custom Publishing
Gregory Noveck, Senior VP—Creative Affairs
Sue Pohja, VP—Book Trade Sales
Steve Rotterdam, Senior VP—Sales & Marketing
Cheryl Rubin, Senior VP—Brand Management
Jeff Trojan, VP—Business Development, DC Direct
Bob Wayne, VP—Sales

STORMWATCH: P.H.D. Book Two published by WildStorm Productions. 888 Prospect St. #240, La Jolla, CA 92037. Compilation and sketchbook Copyright © 2008 WildStorm Productions, an imprint of DC Comics. All Rights Reserved. WildStorm and logo, StormWatch, all characters, the distinctive likenesses thereof and all related elements are trademarks of DC Comics. Originally published in single magazine form as STORMWATCH: PHD #5, 8-12 © 2007 WildStorm Productions, an imprint of DC Comics.

DC Comics, a Warner Bros. Entertainment Company.

ISBN: 978-1-4012-1678-8

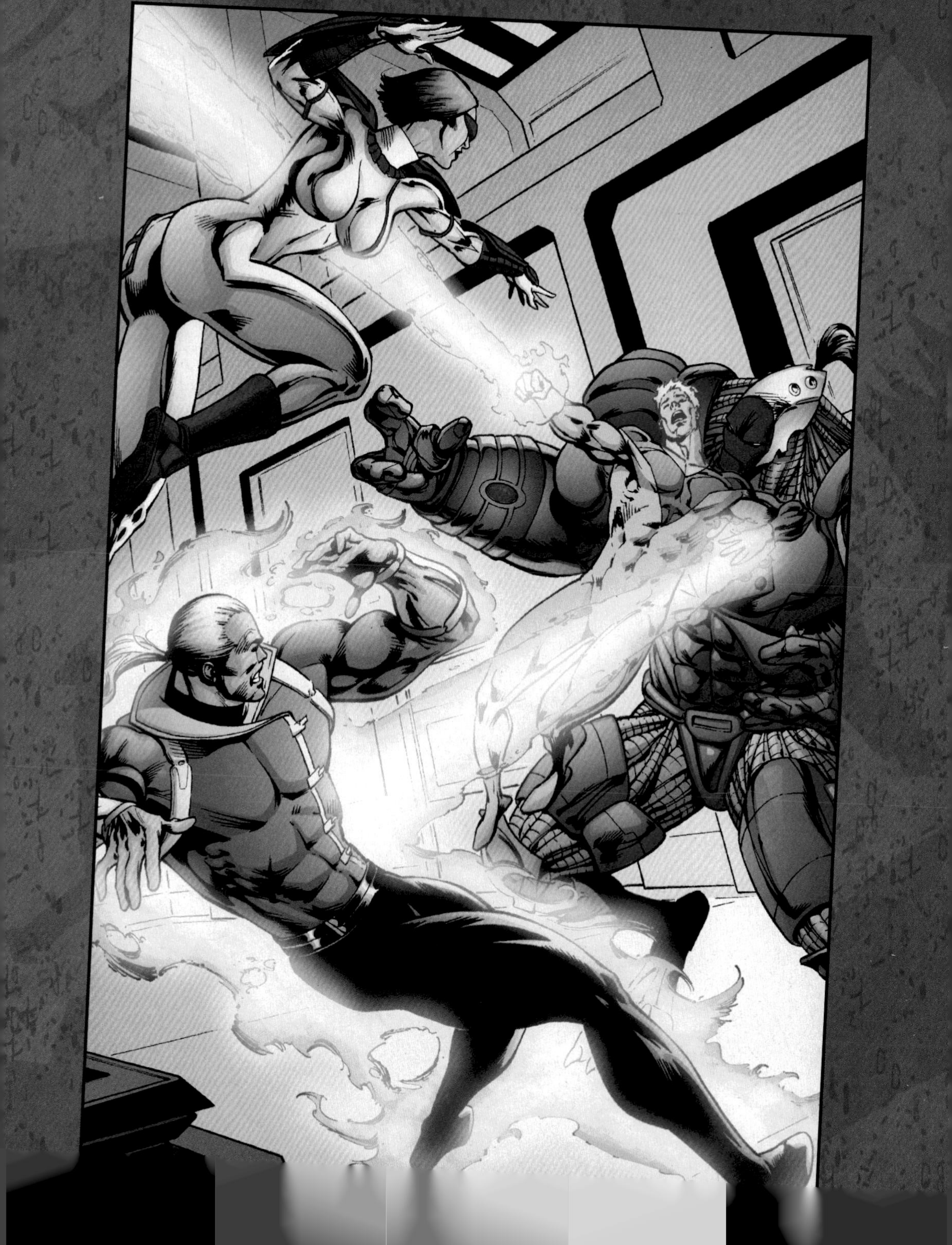

Chapter 1: Talking with the King

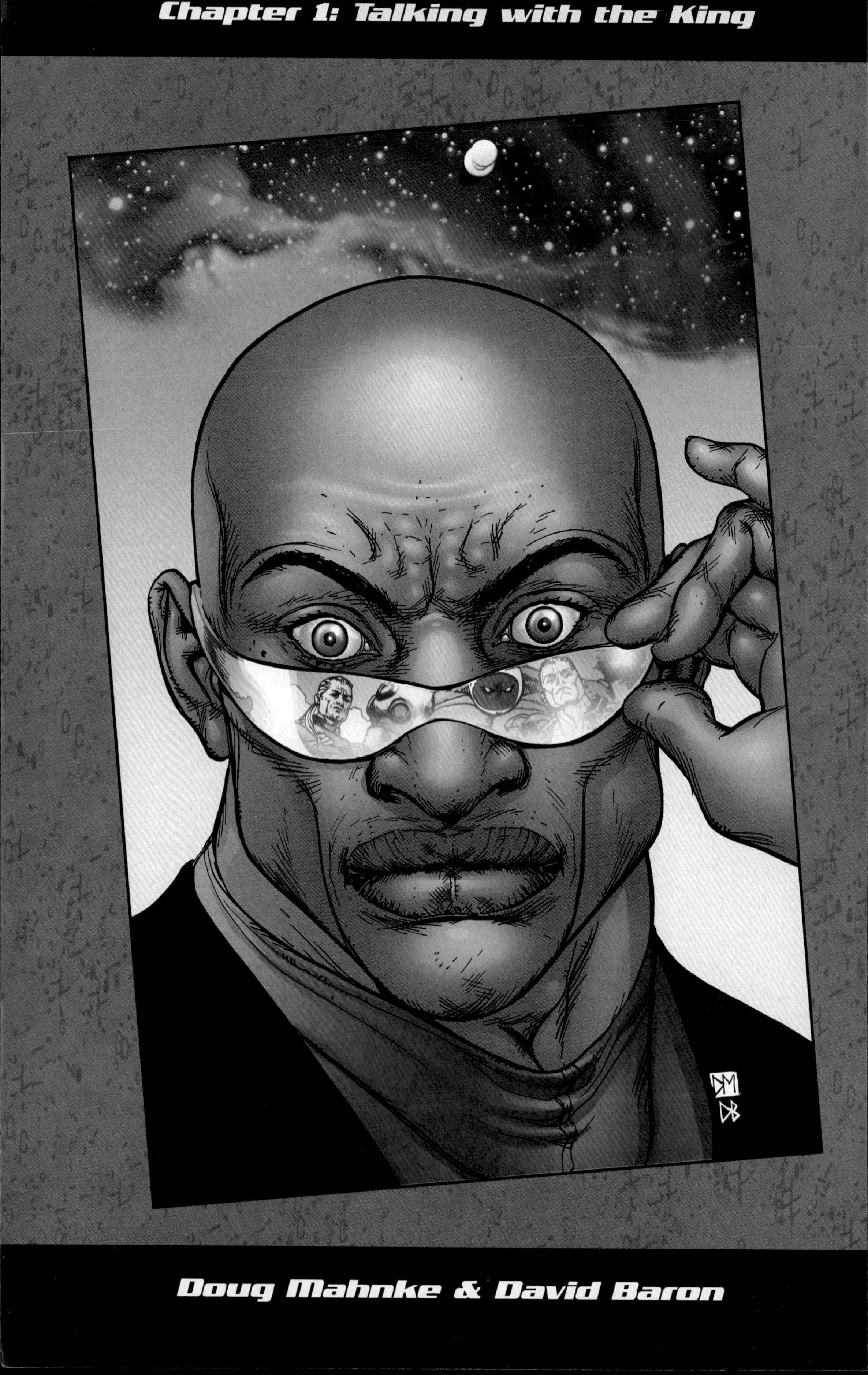

Doug Mahnke & David Baron

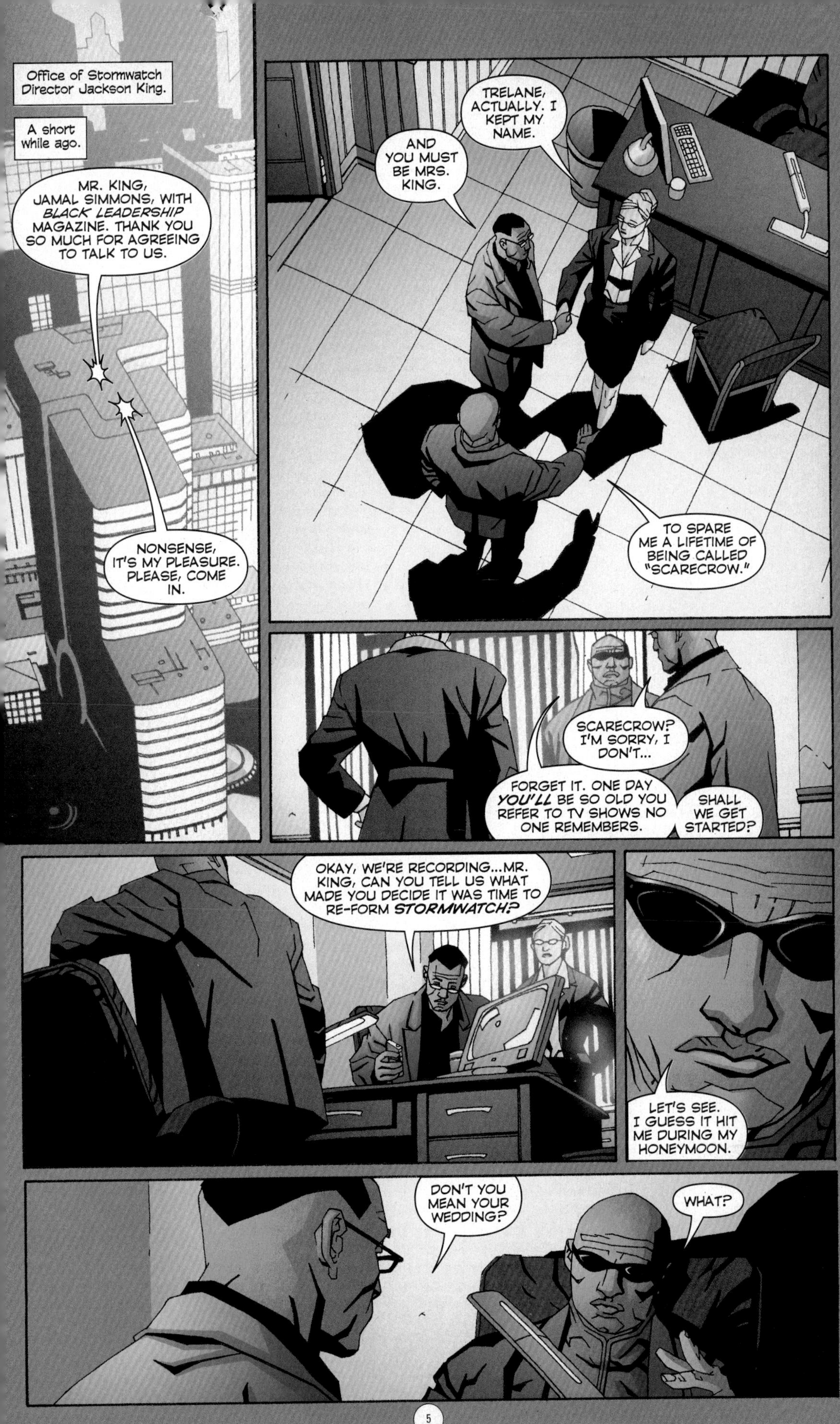

Office of Stormwatch Director Jackson King.
A short while ago.
MR. KING, JAMAL SIMMONS, WITH *BLACK LEADERSHIP* MAGAZINE. THANK YOU SO MUCH FOR AGREEING TO TALK TO US.
NONSENSE, IT'S MY PLEASURE. PLEASE, COME IN.
AND YOU MUST BE MRS. KING.
TRELANE, ACTUALLY. I KEPT MY NAME.
TO SPARE ME A LIFETIME OF BEING CALLED "SCARECROW."
SCARECROW? I'M SORRY, I DON'T...
FORGET IT. ONE DAY *YOU'LL* BE SO OLD YOU REFER TO TV SHOWS NO ONE REMEMBERS.
SHALL WE GET STARTED?
OKAY, WE'RE RECORDING...MR. KING, CAN YOU TELL US WHAT MADE YOU DECIDE IT WAS TIME TO RE-FORM *STORMWATCH?*
LET'S SEE. I GUESS IT HIT ME DURING MY HONEYMOON.
DON'T YOU MEAN YOUR WEDDING?
WHAT?

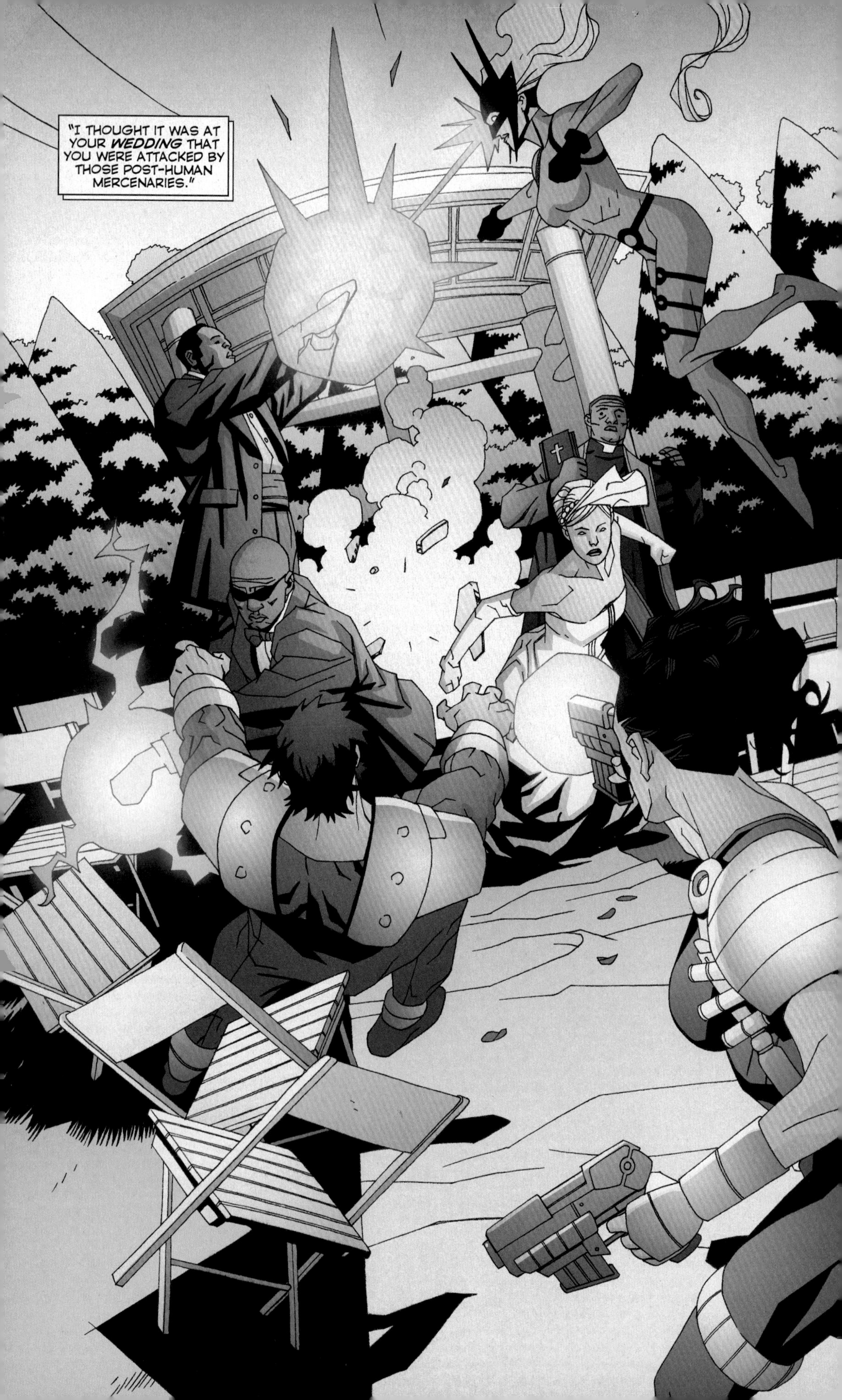
"I THOUGHT IT WAS AT YOUR *WEDDING* THAT YOU WERE ATTACKED BY THOSE POST-HUMAN MERCENARIES."

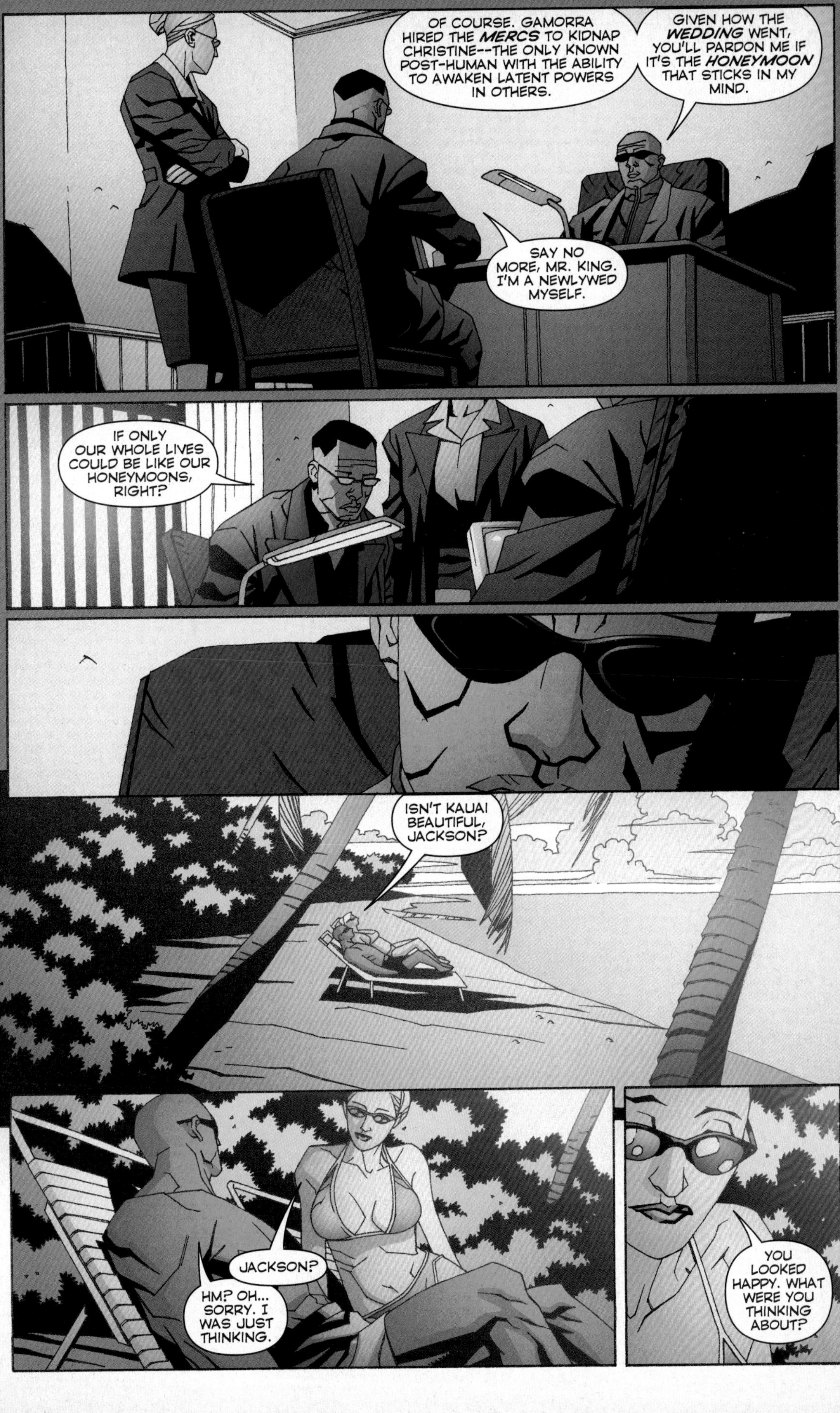
OF COURSE. GAMORRA HIRED THE MERCS TO KIDNAP CHRISTINE--THE ONLY KNOWN POST-HUMAN WITH THE ABILITY TO AWAKEN LATENT POWERS IN OTHERS.
GIVEN HOW THE WEDDING WENT, YOU'LL PARDON ME IF IT'S THE HONEYMOON THAT STICKS IN MY MIND.
SAY NO MORE, MR. KING. I'M A NEWLYWED MYSELF.
IF ONLY OUR WHOLE LIVES COULD BE LIKE OUR HONEYMOONS, RIGHT?
ISN'T KAUAI BEAUTIFUL, JACKSON?
JACKSON?
HM? OH... SORRY. I WAS JUST THINKING.
YOU LOOKED HAPPY. WHAT WERE YOU THINKING ABOUT?

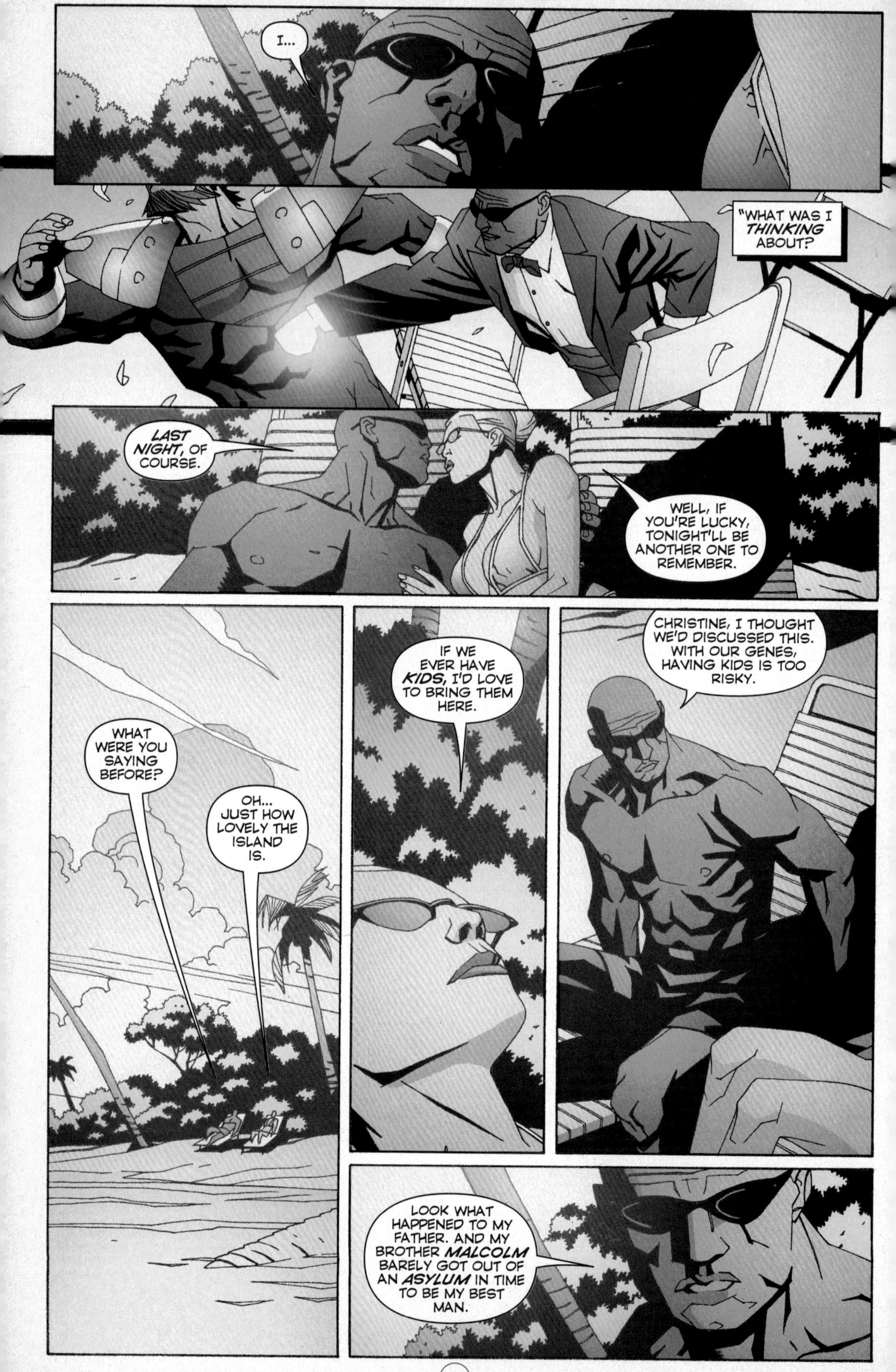
I...
"WHAT WAS I THINKING ABOUT?
LAST NIGHT, OF COURSE.
WELL, IF YOU'RE LUCKY, TONIGHT'LL BE ANOTHER ONE TO REMEMBER.
WHAT WERE YOU SAYING BEFORE?
OH... JUST HOW LOVELY THE ISLAND IS.
IF WE EVER HAVE KIDS, I'D LOVE TO BRING THEM HERE.
CHRISTINE, I THOUGHT WE'D DISCUSSED THIS. WITH OUR GENES, HAVING KIDS IS TOO RISKY.
LOOK WHAT HAPPENED TO MY FATHER. AND MY BROTHER MALCOLM BARELY GOT OUT OF AN ASYLUM IN TIME TO BE MY BEST MAN.

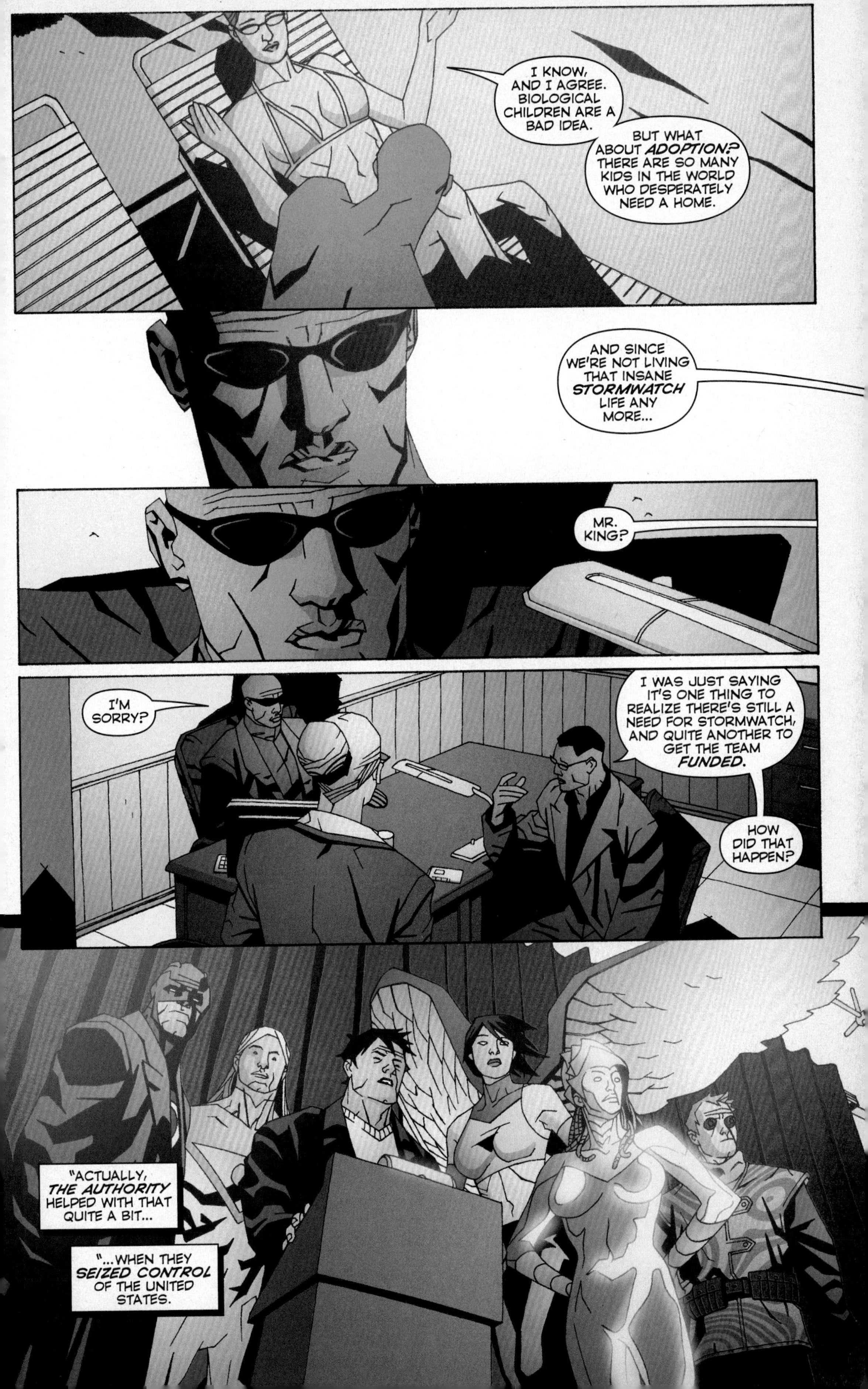
I KNOW, AND I AGREE. BIOLOGICAL CHILDREN ARE A BAD IDEA.
BUT WHAT ABOUT ADOPTION? THERE ARE SO MANY KIDS IN THE WORLD WHO DESPERATELY NEED A HOME.
AND SINCE WE'RE NOT LIVING THAT INSANE STORMWATCH LIFE ANY MORE...
MR. KING?
I'M SORRY?
I WAS JUST SAYING IT'S ONE THING TO REALIZE THERE'S STILL A NEED FOR STORMWATCH, AND QUITE ANOTHER TO GET THE TEAM FUNDED.
HOW DID THAT HAPPEN?
"ACTUALLY, THE AUTHORITY HELPED WITH THAT QUITE A BIT...
"...WHEN THEY SEIZED CONTROL OF THE UNITED STATES.

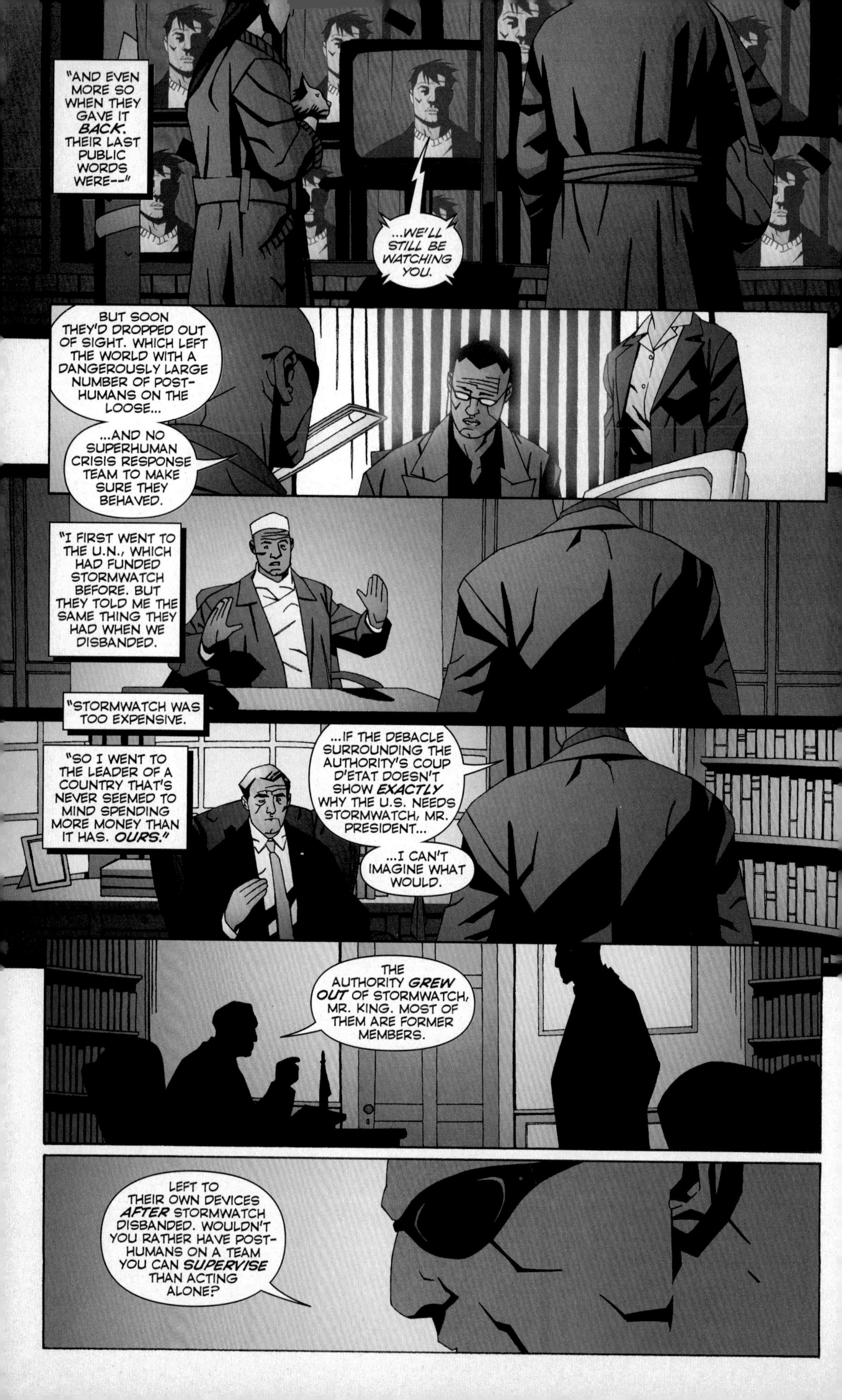

"AND EVEN MORE SO WHEN THEY GAVE IT BACK. THEIR LAST PUBLIC WORDS WERE--"
...WE'LL STILL BE WATCHING YOU.
BUT SOON THEY'D DROPPED OUT OF SIGHT. WHICH LEFT THE WORLD WITH A DANGEROUSLY LARGE NUMBER OF POST-HUMANS ON THE LOOSE...
...AND NO SUPERHUMAN CRISIS RESPONSE TEAM TO MAKE SURE THEY BEHAVED.
"I FIRST WENT TO THE U.N., WHICH HAD FUNDED STORMWATCH BEFORE. BUT THEY TOLD ME THE SAME THING THEY HAD WHEN WE DISBANDED.
"STORMWATCH WAS TOO EXPENSIVE.
"SO I WENT TO THE LEADER OF A COUNTRY THAT'S NEVER SEEMED TO MIND SPENDING MORE MONEY THAN IT HAS. OURS."
...IF THE DEBACLE SURROUNDING THE AUTHORITY'S COUP D'ETAT DOESN'T SHOW EXACTLY WHY THE U.S. NEEDS STORMWATCH, MR. PRESIDENT...
...I CAN'T IMAGINE WHAT WOULD.
THE AUTHORITY GREW OUT OF STORMWATCH, MR. KING. MOST OF THEM ARE FORMER MEMBERS.
LEFT TO THEIR OWN DEVICES AFTER STORMWATCH DISBANDED. WOULDN'T YOU RATHER HAVE POST-HUMANS ON A TEAM YOU CAN SUPERVISE THAN ACTING ALONE?

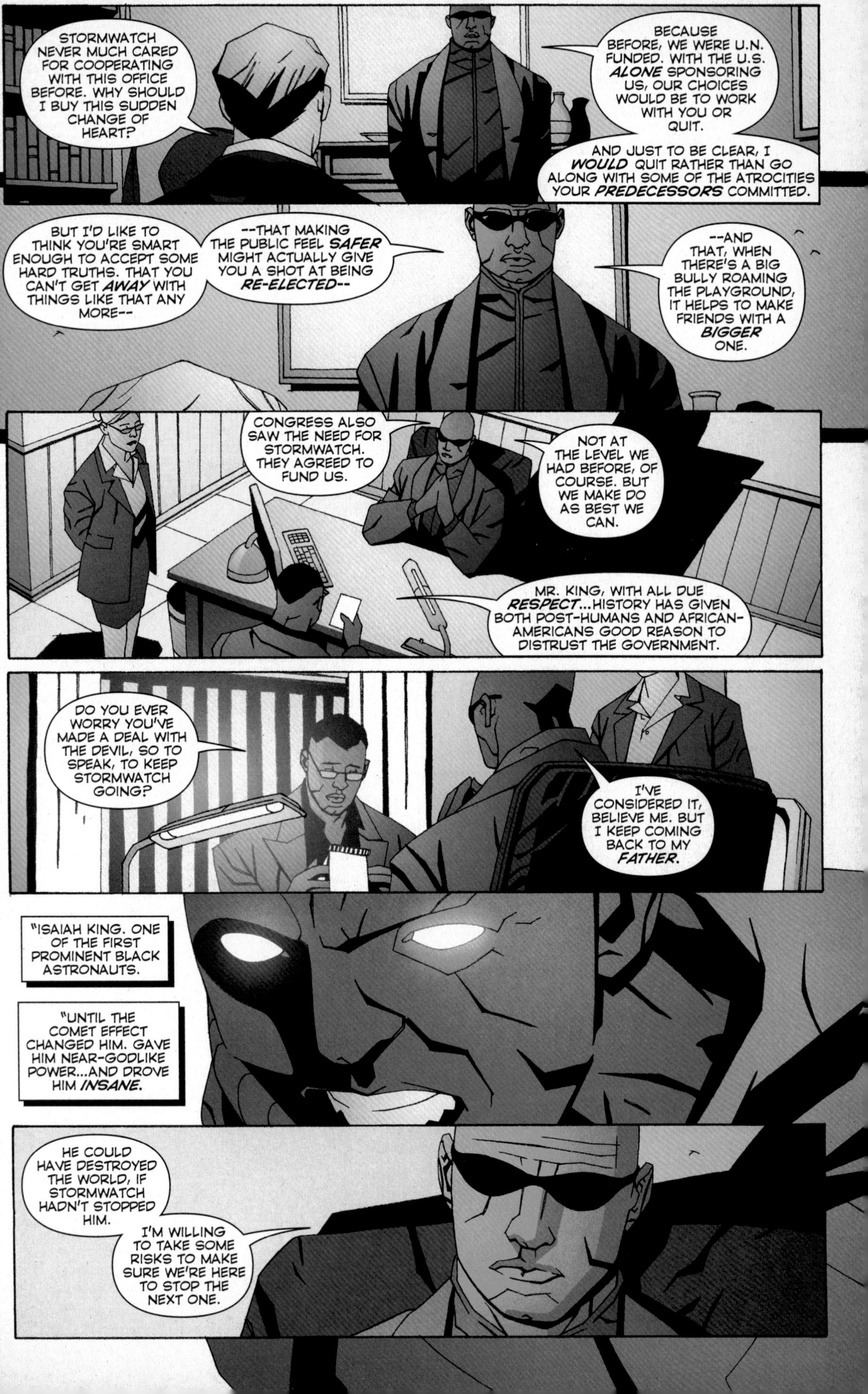
STORMWATCH NEVER MUCH CARED FOR COOPERATING WITH THIS OFFICE BEFORE. WHY SHOULD I BUY THIS SUDDEN CHANGE OF HEART?
BECAUSE BEFORE, WE WERE U.N. FUNDED. WITH THE U.S. ALONE SPONSORING US, OUR CHOICES WOULD BE TO WORK WITH YOU OR QUIT.
AND JUST TO BE CLEAR, I WOULD QUIT RATHER THAN GO ALONG WITH SOME OF THE ATROCITIES YOUR PREDECESSORS COMMITTED.
BUT I'D LIKE TO THINK YOU'RE SMART ENOUGH TO ACCEPT SOME HARD TRUTHS. THAT YOU CAN'T GET AWAY WITH THINGS LIKE THAT ANY MORE--
--THAT MAKING THE PUBLIC FEEL SAFER MIGHT ACTUALLY GIVE YOU A SHOT AT BEING RE-ELECTED--
--AND THAT, WHEN THERE'S A BIG BULLY ROAMING THE PLAYGROUND, IT HELPS TO MAKE FRIENDS WITH A BIGGER ONE.
CONGRESS ALSO SAW THE NEED FOR STORMWATCH. THEY AGREED TO FUND US.
NOT AT THE LEVEL WE HAD BEFORE, OF COURSE. BUT WE MAKE DO AS BEST WE CAN.
MR. KING, WITH ALL DUE RESPECT...HISTORY HAS GIVEN BOTH POST-HUMANS AND AFRICAN-AMERICANS GOOD REASON TO DISTRUST THE GOVERNMENT.
DO YOU EVER WORRY YOU'VE MADE A DEAL WITH THE DEVIL, SO TO SPEAK, TO KEEP STORMWATCH GOING?
I'VE CONSIDERED IT, BELIEVE ME. BUT I KEEP COMING BACK TO MY FATHER.
"ISAIAH KING. ONE OF THE FIRST PROMINENT BLACK ASTRONAUTS.
"UNTIL THE COMET EFFECT CHANGED HIM. GAVE HIM NEAR-GODLIKE POWER...AND DROVE HIM INSANE.
HE COULD HAVE DESTROYED THE WORLD, IF STORMWATCH HADN'T STOPPED HIM.
I'M WILLING TO TAKE SOME RISKS TO MAKE SURE WE'RE HERE TO STOP THE NEXT ONE.

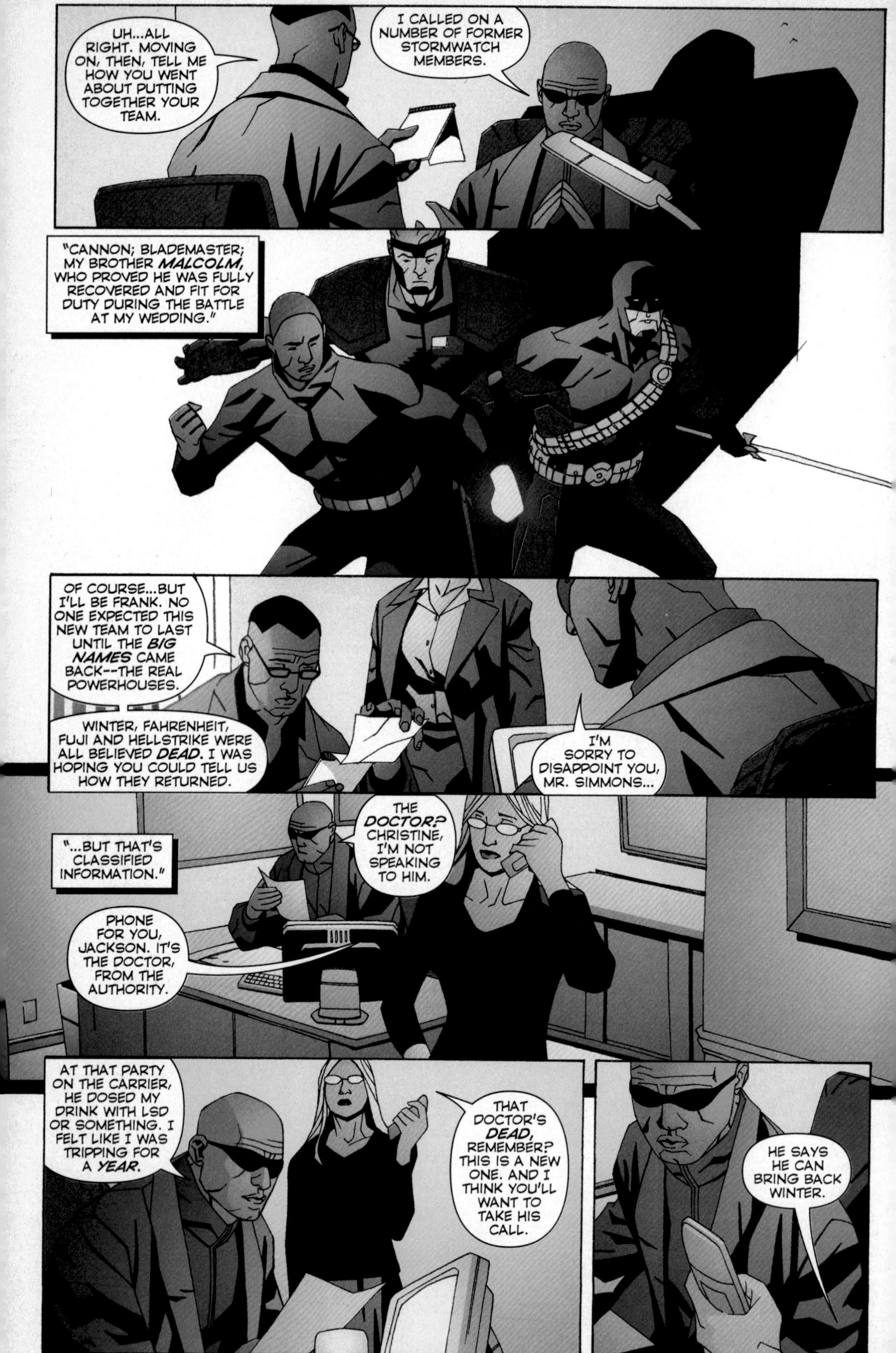
UH...ALL RIGHT. MOVING ON, THEN. TELL ME HOW YOU WENT ABOUT PUTTING TOGETHER YOUR TEAM.
I CALLED ON A NUMBER OF FORMER STORMWATCH MEMBERS.
"CANNON; BLADEMASTER; MY BROTHER MALCOLM, WHO PROVED HE WAS FULLY RECOVERED AND FIT FOR DUTY DURING THE BATTLE AT MY WEDDING."
OF COURSE...BUT I'LL BE FRANK. NO ONE EXPECTED THIS NEW TEAM TO LAST UNTIL THE BIG NAMES CAME BACK--THE REAL POWERHOUSES.
WINTER, FAHRENHEIT, FUJI AND HELLSTRIKE WERE ALL BELIEVED DEAD. I WAS HOPING YOU COULD TELL US HOW THEY RETURNED.
I'M SORRY TO DISAPPOINT YOU, MR. SIMMONS...
"...BUT THAT'S CLASSIFIED INFORMATION."
PHONE FOR YOU, JACKSON. IT'S THE DOCTOR, FROM THE AUTHORITY.
THE DOCTOR? CHRISTINE, I'M NOT SPEAKING TO HIM.
AT THAT PARTY ON THE CARRIER, HE DOSED MY DRINK WITH LSD OR SOMETHING. I FELT LIKE I WAS TRIPPING FOR A YEAR.
THAT DOCTOR'S DEAD, REMEMBER? THIS IS A NEW ONE. AND I THINK YOU'LL WANT TO TAKE HIS CALL.
HE SAYS HE CAN BRING BACK WINTER.

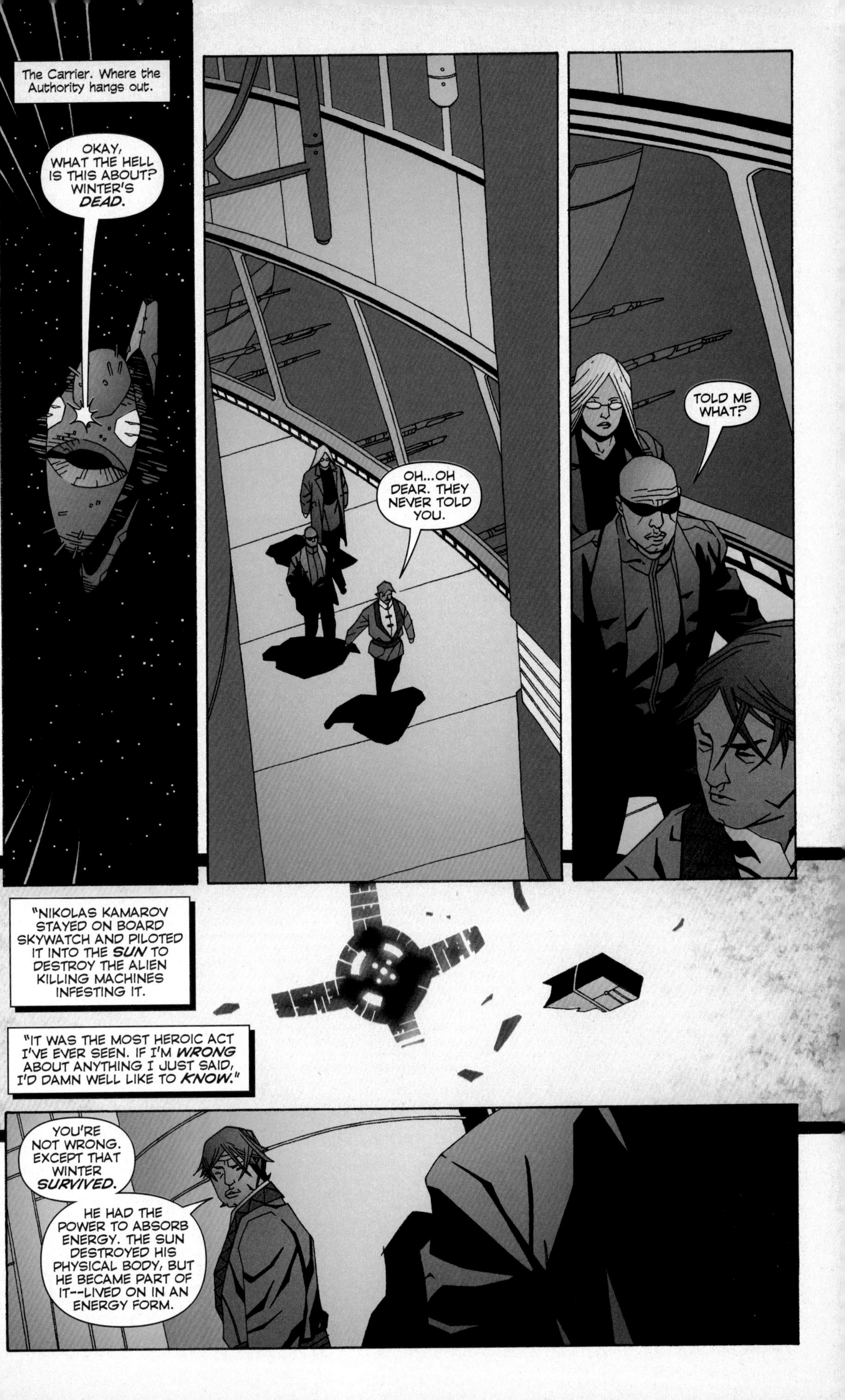
The Carrier. Where the Authority hangs out.
OKAY, WHAT THE HELL IS THIS ABOUT? WINTER'S *DEAD*.
OH...OH DEAR. THEY NEVER TOLD YOU.
TOLD ME WHAT?
"NIKOLAS KAMAROV STAYED ON BOARD SKYWATCH AND PILOTED IT INTO THE *SUN* TO DESTROY THE ALIEN KILLING MACHINES INFESTING IT.
"IT WAS THE MOST HEROIC ACT I'VE EVER SEEN. IF I'M *WRONG* ABOUT ANYTHING I JUST SAID, I'D DAMN WELL LIKE TO *KNOW*."
YOU'RE NOT WRONG. EXCEPT THAT WINTER *SURVIVED*.
HE HAD THE POWER TO ABSORB ENERGY. THE SUN DESTROYED HIS PHYSICAL BODY, BUT HE BECAME PART OF IT--LIVED ON IN AN ENERGY FORM.

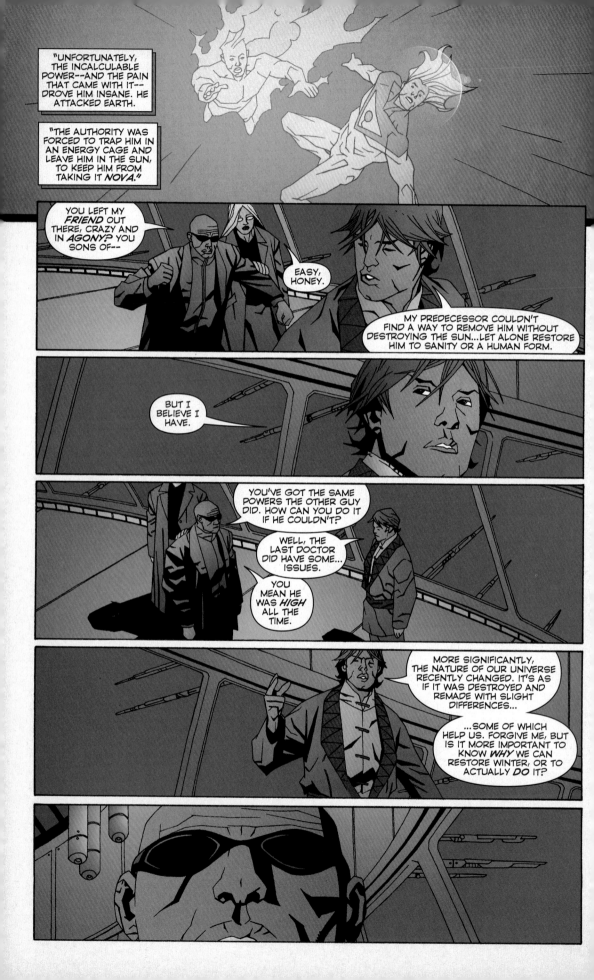

"UNFORTUNATELY, THE INCALCULABLE POWER--AND THE PAIN THAT CAME WITH IT-- DROVE HIM INSANE. HE ATTACKED EARTH.

"THE AUTHORITY WAS FORCED TO TRAP HIM IN AN ENERGY CAGE AND LEAVE HIM IN THE SUN, TO KEEP HIM FROM TAKING IT *NOVA*."

YOU LEFT MY *FRIEND* OUT THERE, CRAZY AND IN *AGONY?* YOU SONS OF--

EASY, HONEY.

MY PREDECESSOR COULDN'T FIND A WAY TO REMOVE HIM WITHOUT DESTROYING THE SUN...LET ALONE RESTORE HIM TO SANITY OR A HUMAN FORM.

BUT I BELIEVE I HAVE.

YOU'VE GOT THE SAME POWERS THE OTHER GUY DID. HOW CAN YOU DO IT IF HE COULDN'T?

WELL, THE LAST DOCTOR DID HAVE SOME... ISSUES.

YOU MEAN HE WAS *HIGH* ALL THE TIME.

MORE SIGNIFICANTLY, THE NATURE OF OUR UNIVERSE RECENTLY CHANGED. IT'S AS IF IT WAS DESTROYED AND REMADE WITH SLIGHT DIFFERENCES...

...SOME OF WHICH HELP US. FORGIVE ME, BUT IS IT MORE IMPORTANT TO KNOW *WHY* WE CAN RESTORE WINTER, OR TO ACTUALLY *DO* IT?

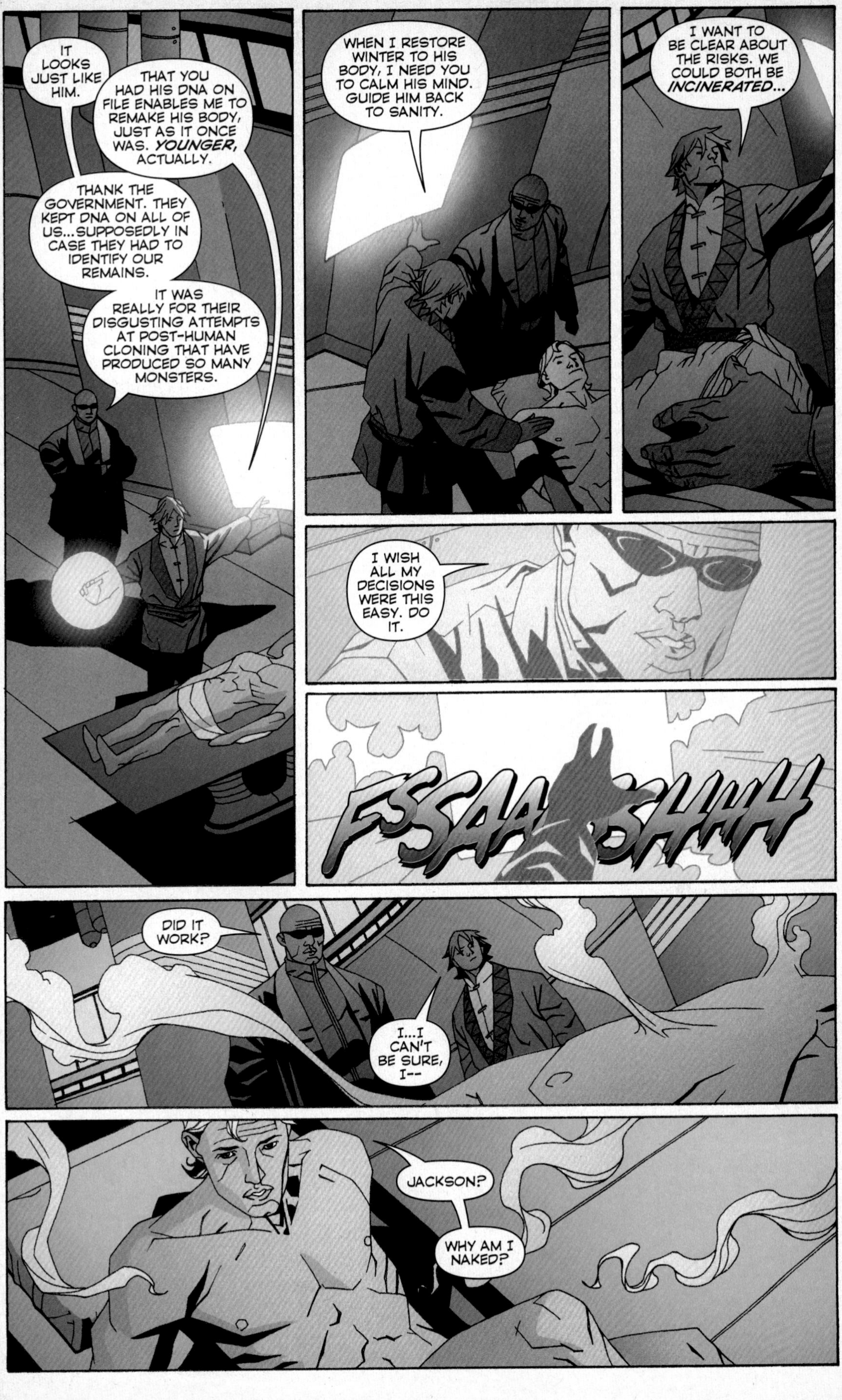

IT LOOKS JUST LIKE HIM.
THAT YOU HAD HIS DNA ON FILE ENABLES ME TO REMAKE HIS BODY, JUST AS IT ONCE WAS. YOUNGER, ACTUALLY.
THANK THE GOVERNMENT. THEY KEPT DNA ON ALL OF US...SUPPOSEDLY IN CASE THEY HAD TO IDENTIFY OUR REMAINS.
IT WAS REALLY FOR THEIR DISGUSTING ATTEMPTS AT POST-HUMAN CLONING THAT HAVE PRODUCED SO MANY MONSTERS.
WHEN I RESTORE WINTER TO HIS BODY, I NEED YOU TO CALM HIS MIND. GUIDE HIM BACK TO SANITY.
I WANT TO BE CLEAR ABOUT THE RISKS. WE COULD BOTH BE INCINERATED...
I WISH ALL MY DECISIONS WERE THIS EASY. DO IT.
FSSAAASHHH
DID IT WORK?
I...I CAN'T BE SURE, I--
JACKSON?
WHY AM I NAKED?

SON, I'VE HAD ISSUES WITH SOME OF THE THINGS THE AUTHORITY'S DONE, BUT YOU JUST MADE UP FOR ALL OF THEM.

WAIT. WAIT, I...

...THERE'S MORE.

MORE? WHAT--WHAT'S WRONG WITH YOU?

...SOMETHING LINKED TO WINTER... I CAN'T--

I DON'T KNOW WHAT IT IS, BUT IT'S COMING THROUGH AND I CAN'T STOP IT--

--UUUARRRGGGHH

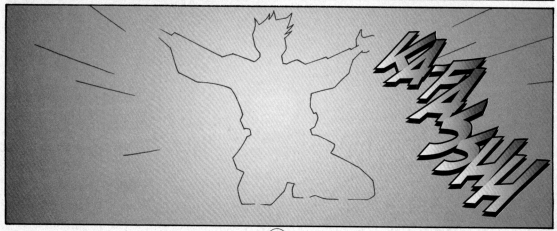

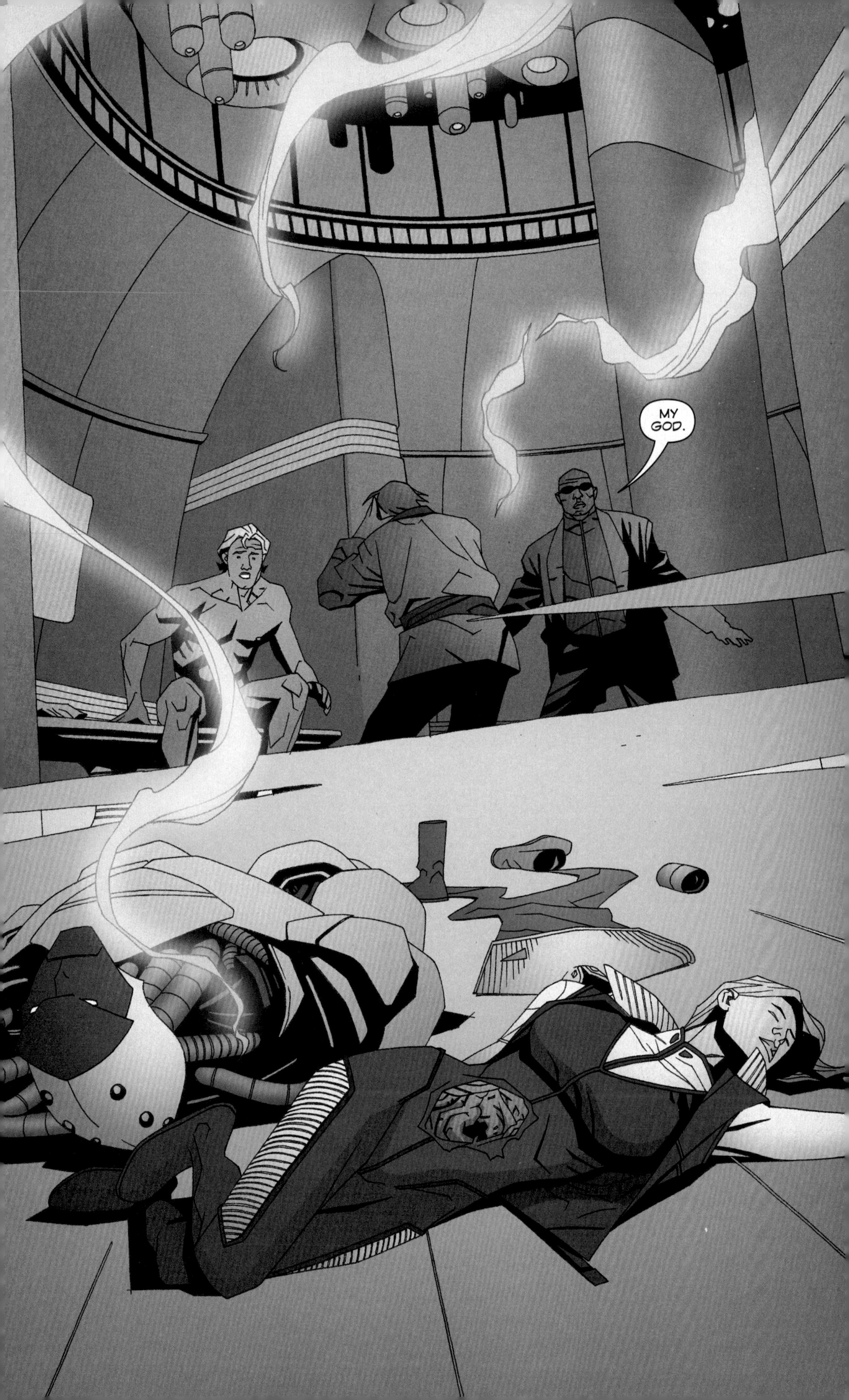
MY GOD.

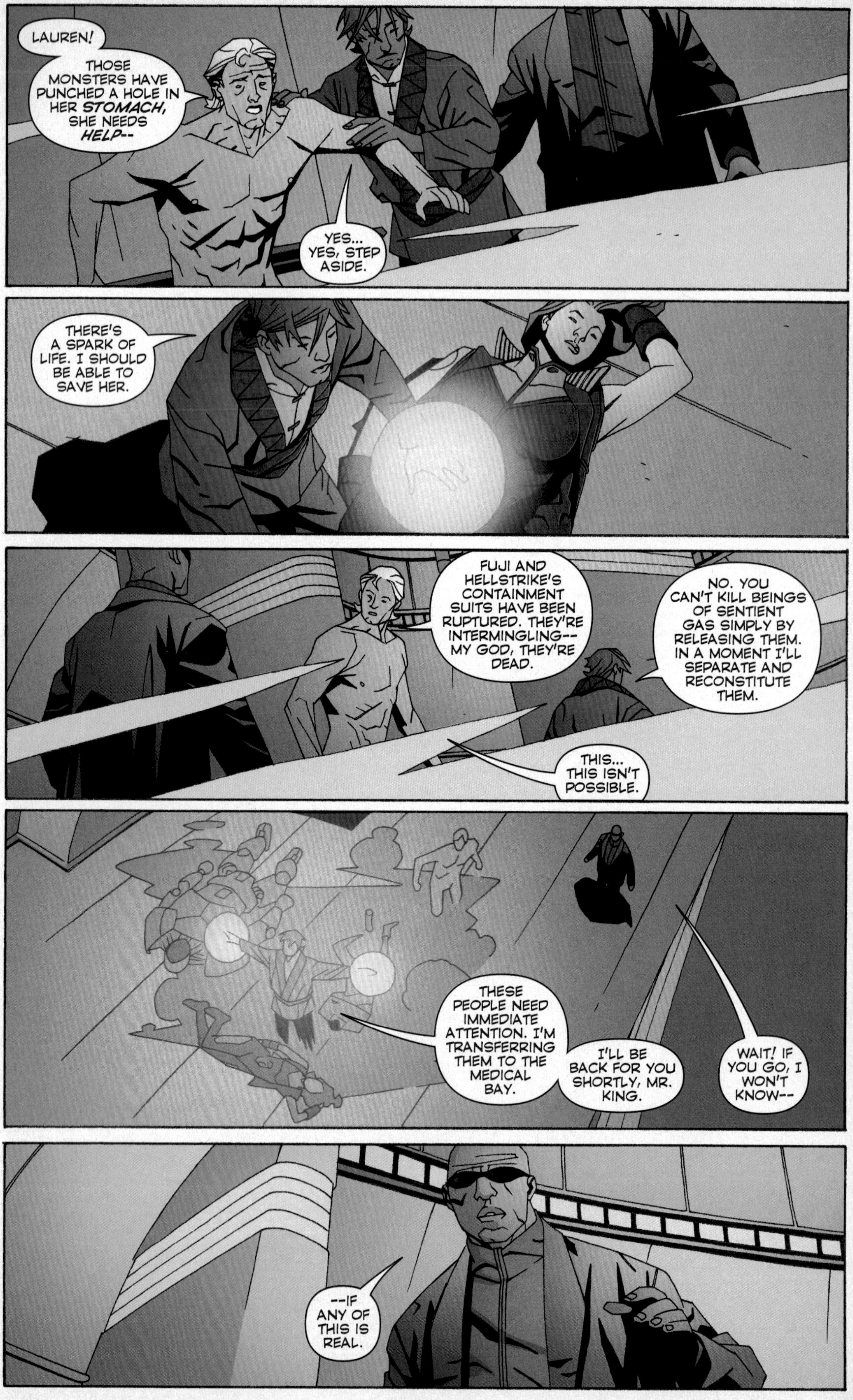
LAUREN!
THOSE MONSTERS HAVE PUNCHED A HOLE IN HER STOMACH, SHE NEEDS HELP--
YES... YES, STEP ASIDE.
THERE'S A SPARK OF LIFE. I SHOULD BE ABLE TO SAVE HER.
FUJI AND HELLSTRIKE'S CONTAINMENT SUITS HAVE BEEN RUPTURED. THEY'RE INTERMINGLING-- MY GOD, THEY'RE DEAD.
NO. YOU CAN'T KILL BEINGS OF SENTIENT GAS SIMPLY BY RELEASING THEM. IN A MOMENT I'LL SEPARATE AND RECONSTITUTE THEM.
THIS... THIS ISN'T POSSIBLE.
THESE PEOPLE NEED IMMEDIATE ATTENTION. I'M TRANSFERRING THEM TO THE MEDICAL BAY.
I'LL BE BACK FOR YOU SHORTLY, MR. KING.
WAIT! IF YOU GO, I WON'T KNOW--
--IF ANY OF THIS IS REAL.

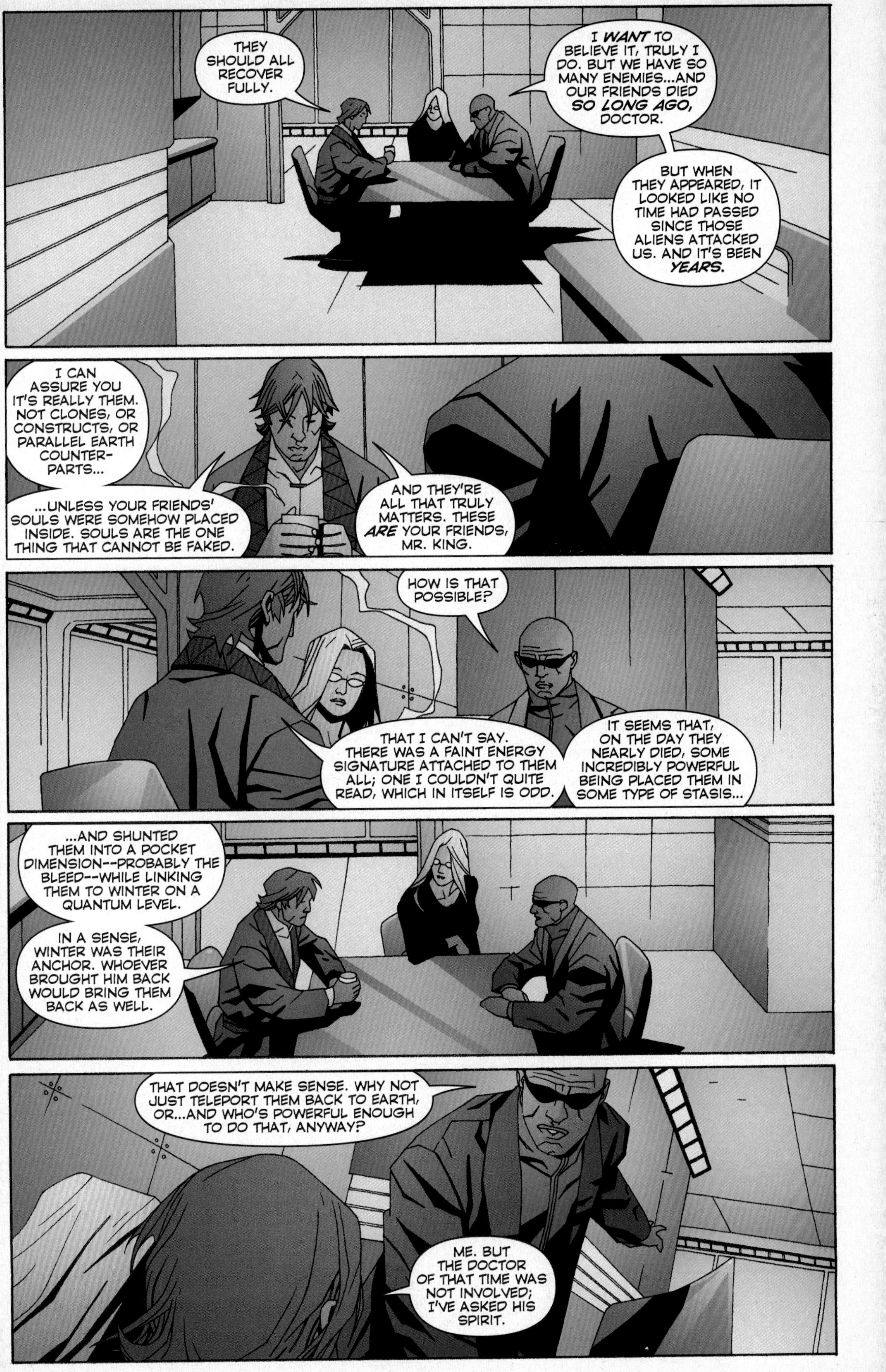
THEY SHOULD ALL RECOVER FULLY.
I *WANT* TO BELIEVE IT, TRULY I DO. BUT WE HAVE SO MANY ENEMIES...AND OUR FRIENDS DIED *SO LONG AGO*, DOCTOR.
BUT WHEN THEY APPEARED, IT LOOKED LIKE NO TIME HAD PASSED SINCE THOSE ALIENS ATTACKED US. AND IT'S BEEN *YEARS*.
I CAN ASSURE YOU IT'S REALLY THEM. NOT CLONES, OR CONSTRUCTS, OR PARALLEL EARTH COUNTER-PARTS...
...UNLESS YOUR FRIENDS' SOULS WERE SOMEHOW PLACED INSIDE. SOULS ARE THE ONE THING THAT CANNOT BE FAKED.
AND THEY'RE ALL THAT TRULY MATTERS. THESE *ARE* YOUR FRIENDS, MR. KING.
HOW IS THAT POSSIBLE?
THAT I CAN'T SAY. THERE WAS A FAINT ENERGY SIGNATURE ATTACHED TO THEM ALL; ONE I COULDN'T QUITE READ, WHICH IN ITSELF IS ODD.
IT SEEMS THAT, ON THE DAY THEY NEARLY DIED, SOME INCREDIBLY POWERFUL BEING PLACED THEM IN SOME TYPE OF STASIS...
...AND SHUNTED THEM INTO A POCKET DIMENSION--PROBABLY THE BLEED--WHILE LINKING THEM TO WINTER ON A QUANTUM LEVEL.
IN A SENSE, WINTER WAS THEIR ANCHOR. WHOEVER BROUGHT HIM BACK WOULD BRING THEM BACK AS WELL.
THAT DOESN'T MAKE SENSE. WHY NOT JUST TELEPORT THEM BACK TO EARTH, OR...AND WHO'S POWERFUL ENOUGH TO DO THAT, ANYWAY?
ME. BUT THE DOCTOR OF THAT TIME WAS NOT INVOLVED; I'VE ASKED HIS SPIRIT.

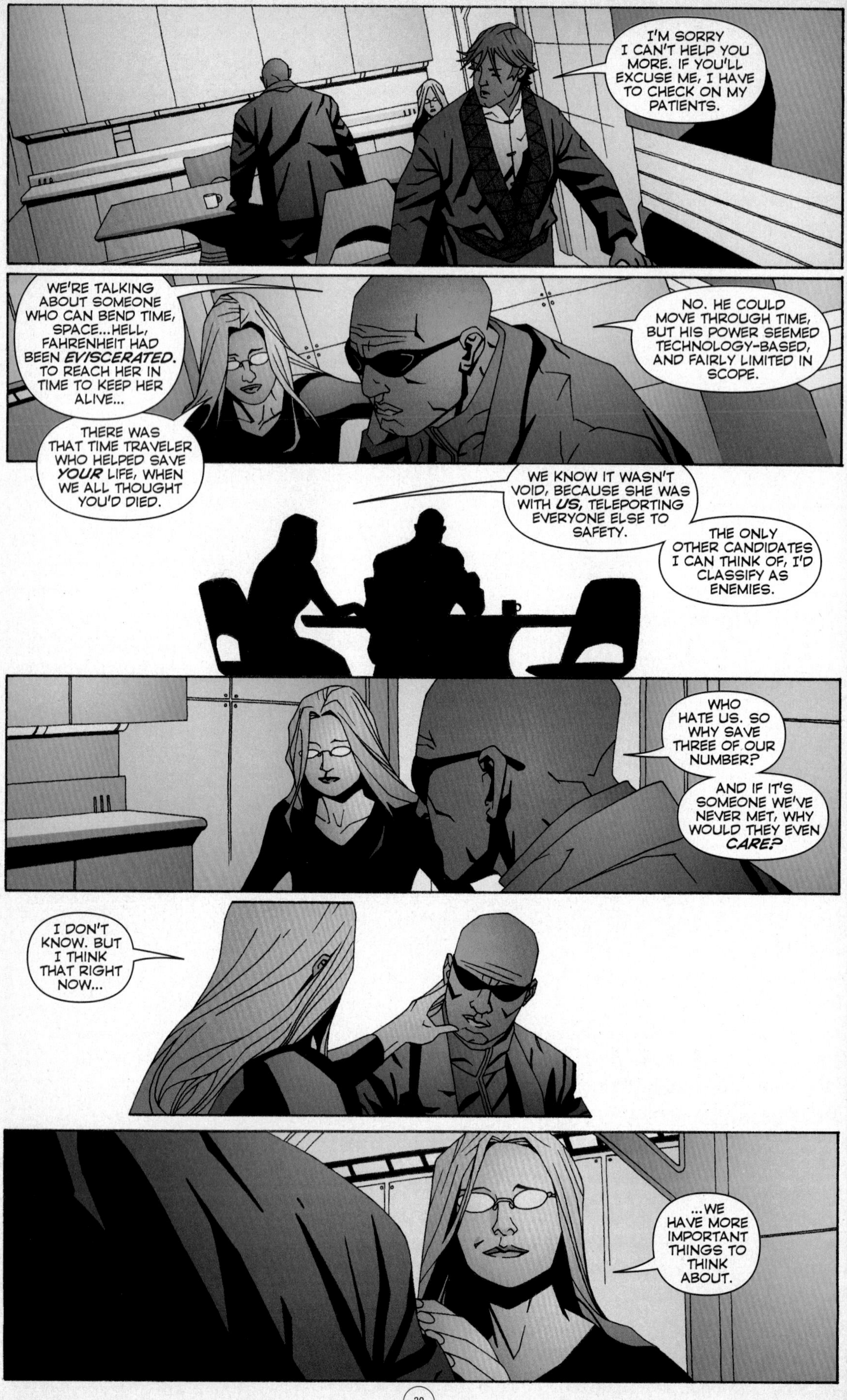
I'M SORRY I CAN'T HELP YOU MORE. IF YOU'LL EXCUSE ME, I HAVE TO CHECK ON MY PATIENTS.
WE'RE TALKING ABOUT SOMEONE WHO CAN BEND TIME, SPACE...HELL, FAHRENHEIT HAD BEEN EVISCERATED. TO REACH HER IN TIME TO KEEP HER ALIVE...
THERE WAS THAT TIME TRAVELER WHO HELPED SAVE YOUR LIFE, WHEN WE ALL THOUGHT YOU'D DIED.
NO. HE COULD MOVE THROUGH TIME, BUT HIS POWER SEEMED TECHNOLOGY-BASED, AND FAIRLY LIMITED IN SCOPE.
WE KNOW IT WASN'T VOID, BECAUSE SHE WAS WITH US, TELEPORTING EVERYONE ELSE TO SAFETY.
THE ONLY OTHER CANDIDATES I CAN THINK OF, I'D CLASSIFY AS ENEMIES.
WHO HATE US. SO WHY SAVE THREE OF OUR NUMBER?
AND IF IT'S SOMEONE WE'VE NEVER MET, WHY WOULD THEY EVEN CARE?
I DON'T KNOW. BUT I THINK THAT RIGHT NOW...
...WE HAVE MORE IMPORTANT THINGS TO THINK ABOUT.

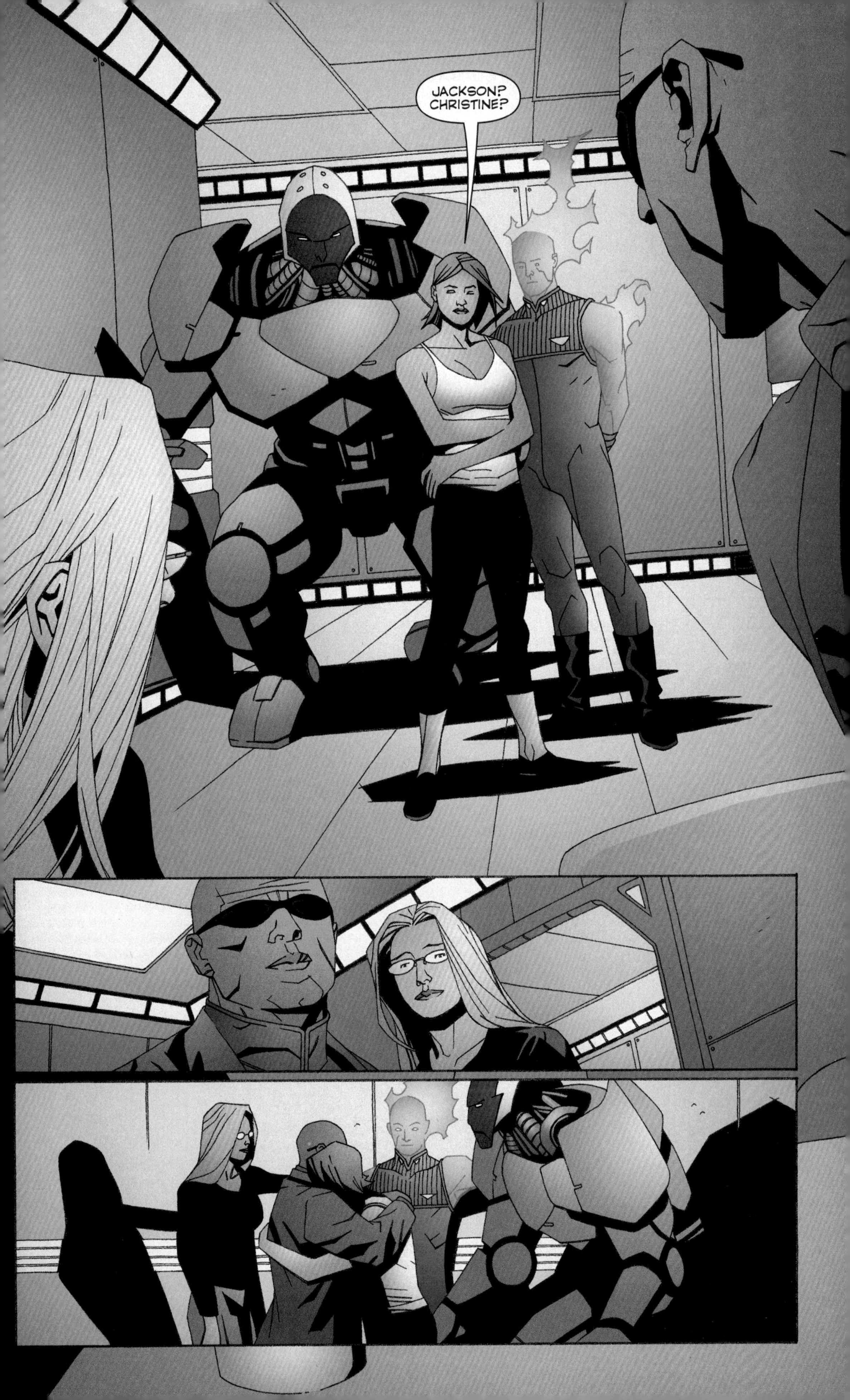
JACKSON? CHRISTINE?

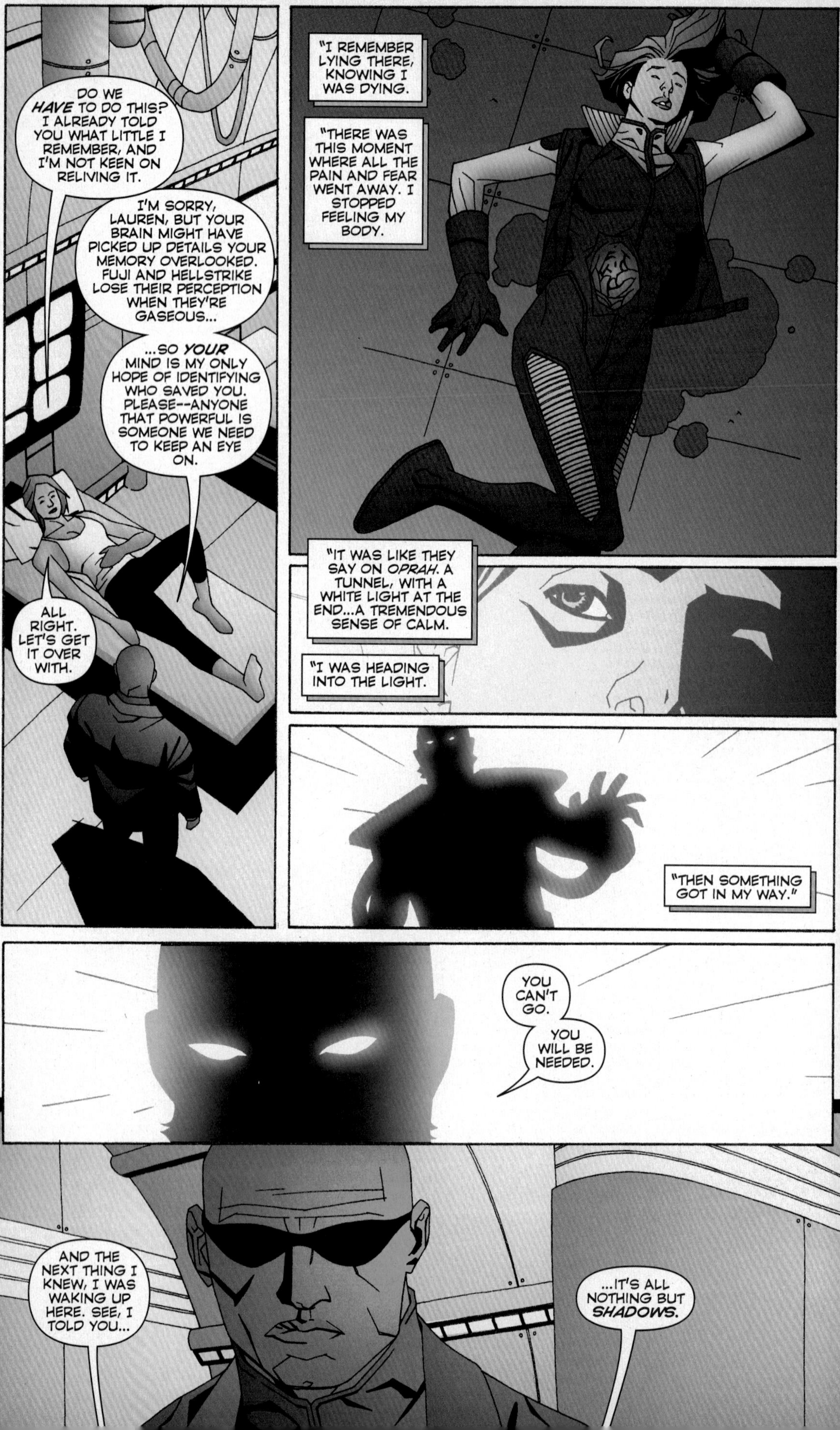

DO WE HAVE TO DO THIS? I ALREADY TOLD YOU WHAT LITTLE I REMEMBER, AND I'M NOT KEEN ON RELIVING IT.
I'M SORRY, LAUREN, BUT YOUR BRAIN MIGHT HAVE PICKED UP DETAILS YOUR MEMORY OVERLOOKED. FUJI AND HELLSTRIKE LOSE THEIR PERCEPTION WHEN THEY'RE GASEOUS...
...SO YOUR MIND IS MY ONLY HOPE OF IDENTIFYING WHO SAVED YOU. PLEASE--ANYONE THAT POWERFUL IS SOMEONE WE NEED TO KEEP AN EYE ON.
ALL RIGHT. LET'S GET IT OVER WITH.
"I REMEMBER LYING THERE, KNOWING I WAS DYING.
"THERE WAS THIS MOMENT WHERE ALL THE PAIN AND FEAR WENT AWAY. I STOPPED FEELING MY BODY.
"IT WAS LIKE THEY SAY ON OPRAH. A TUNNEL, WITH A WHITE LIGHT AT THE END...A TREMENDOUS SENSE OF CALM.
"I WAS HEADING INTO THE LIGHT.
"THEN SOMETHING GOT IN MY WAY."
YOU CAN'T GO.
YOU WILL BE NEEDED.
AND THE NEXT THING I KNEW, I WAS WAKING UP HERE. SEE, I TOLD YOU...
...IT'S ALL NOTHING BUT SHADOWS.

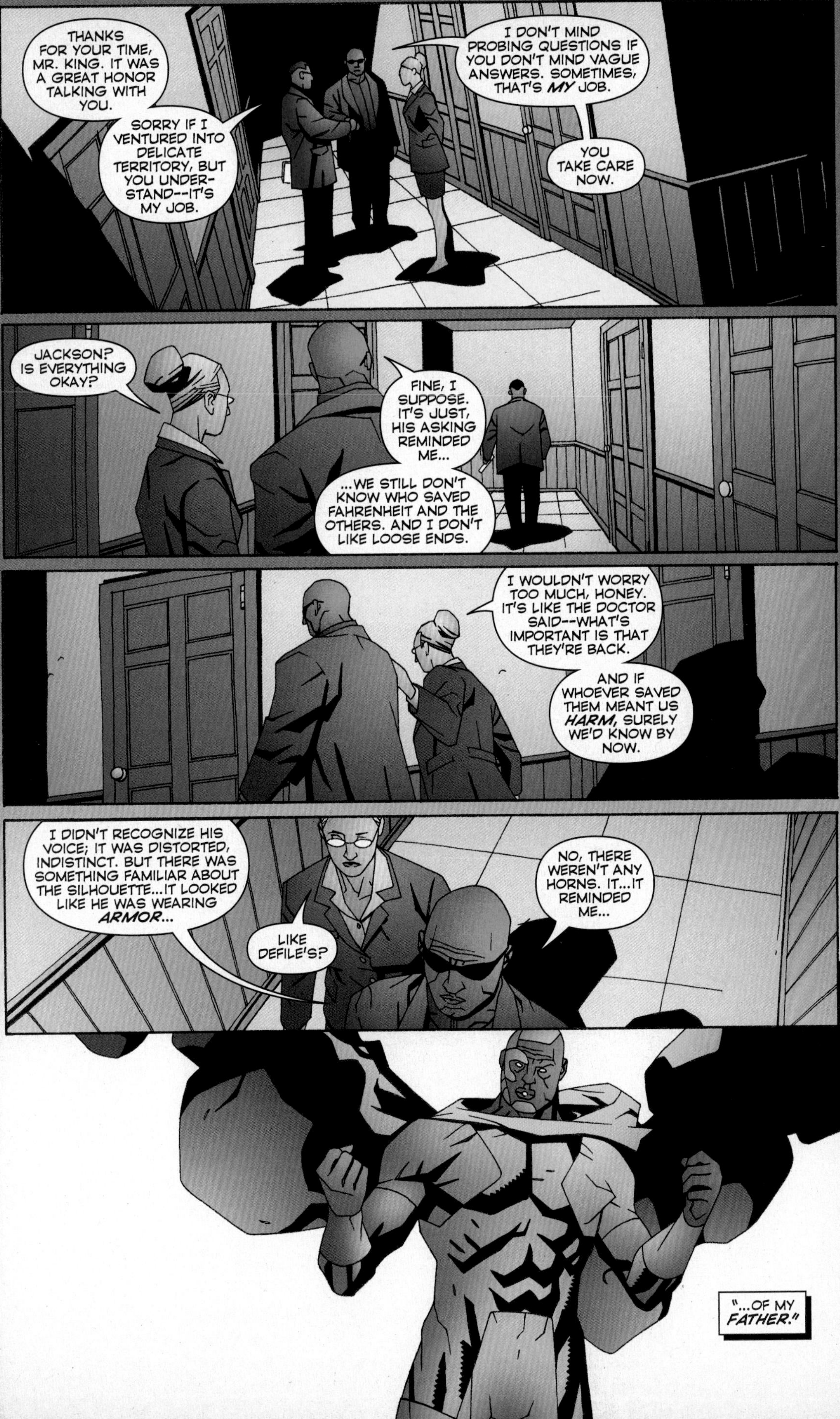
THANKS FOR YOUR TIME, MR. KING. IT WAS A GREAT HONOR TALKING WITH YOU.
SORRY IF I VENTURED INTO DELICATE TERRITORY, BUT YOU UNDER-STAND--IT'S MY JOB.
I DON'T MIND PROBING QUESTIONS IF YOU DON'T MIND VAGUE ANSWERS. SOMETIMES, THAT'S MY JOB.
YOU TAKE CARE NOW.
JACKSON? IS EVERYTHING OKAY?
FINE, I SUPPOSE. IT'S JUST, HIS ASKING REMINDED ME...
...WE STILL DON'T KNOW WHO SAVED FAHRENHEIT AND THE OTHERS. AND I DON'T LIKE LOOSE ENDS.
I WOULDN'T WORRY TOO MUCH, HONEY. IT'S LIKE THE DOCTOR SAID--WHAT'S IMPORTANT IS THAT THEY'RE BACK.
AND IF WHOEVER SAVED THEM MEANT US HARM, SURELY WE'D KNOW BY NOW.
I DIDN'T RECOGNIZE HIS VOICE; IT WAS DISTORTED, INDISTINCT. BUT THERE WAS SOMETHING FAMILIAR ABOUT THE SILHOUETTE...IT LOOKED LIKE HE WAS WEARING ARMOR...
LIKE DEFILE'S?
NO, THERE WEREN'T ANY HORNS. IT...IT REMINDED ME...
"...OF MY FATHER."

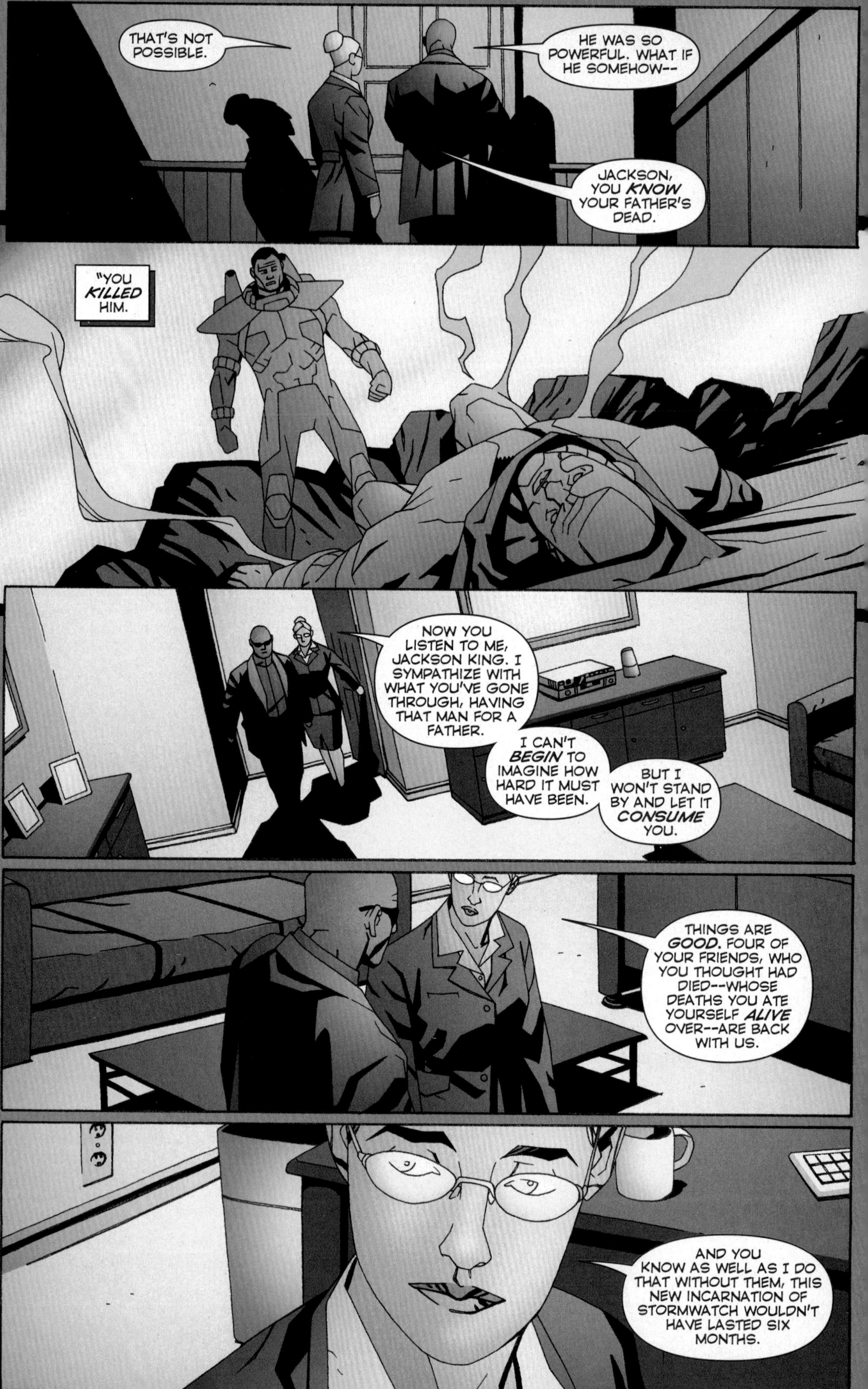

THAT'S NOT POSSIBLE.
HE WAS SO POWERFUL. WHAT IF HE SOMEHOW--
JACKSON, YOU *KNOW* YOUR FATHER'S DEAD.
"YOU *KILLED* HIM.
NOW YOU LISTEN TO ME, JACKSON KING. I SYMPATHIZE WITH WHAT YOU'VE GONE THROUGH, HAVING THAT MAN FOR A FATHER.
I CAN'T *BEGIN* TO IMAGINE HOW HARD IT MUST HAVE BEEN.
BUT I WON'T STAND BY AND LET IT *CONSUME* YOU.
THINGS ARE **GOOD.** FOUR OF YOUR FRIENDS, WHO YOU THOUGHT HAD DIED--WHOSE DEATHS YOU ATE YOURSELF *ALIVE* OVER--ARE BACK WITH US.
AND YOU KNOW AS WELL AS I DO THAT WITHOUT THEM, THIS NEW INCARNATION OF STORMWATCH WOULDN'T HAVE LASTED SIX MONTHS.

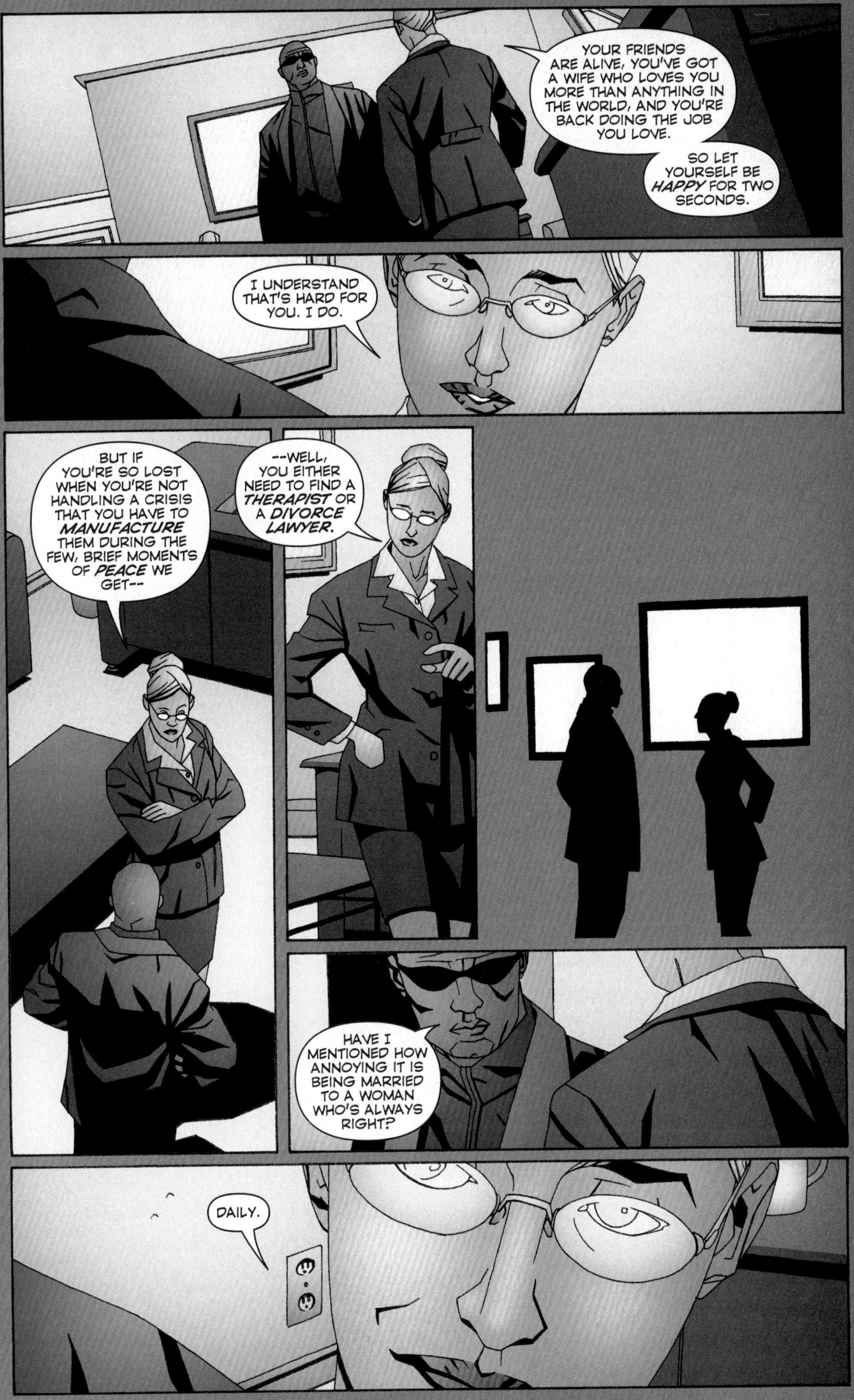

YOUR FRIENDS ARE ALIVE, YOU'VE GOT A WIFE WHO LOVES YOU MORE THAN ANYTHING IN THE WORLD, AND YOU'RE BACK DOING THE JOB YOU LOVE.
SO LET YOURSELF BE HAPPY FOR TWO SECONDS.
I UNDERSTAND THAT'S HARD FOR YOU. I DO.
BUT IF YOU'RE SO LOST WHEN YOU'RE NOT HANDLING A CRISIS THAT YOU HAVE TO MANUFACTURE THEM DURING THE FEW, BRIEF MOMENTS OF PEACE WE GET--
--WELL, YOU EITHER NEED TO FIND A THERAPIST OR A DIVORCE LAWYER.
HAVE I MENTIONED HOW ANNOYING IT IS BEING MARRIED TO A WOMAN WHO'S ALWAYS RIGHT?
DAILY.

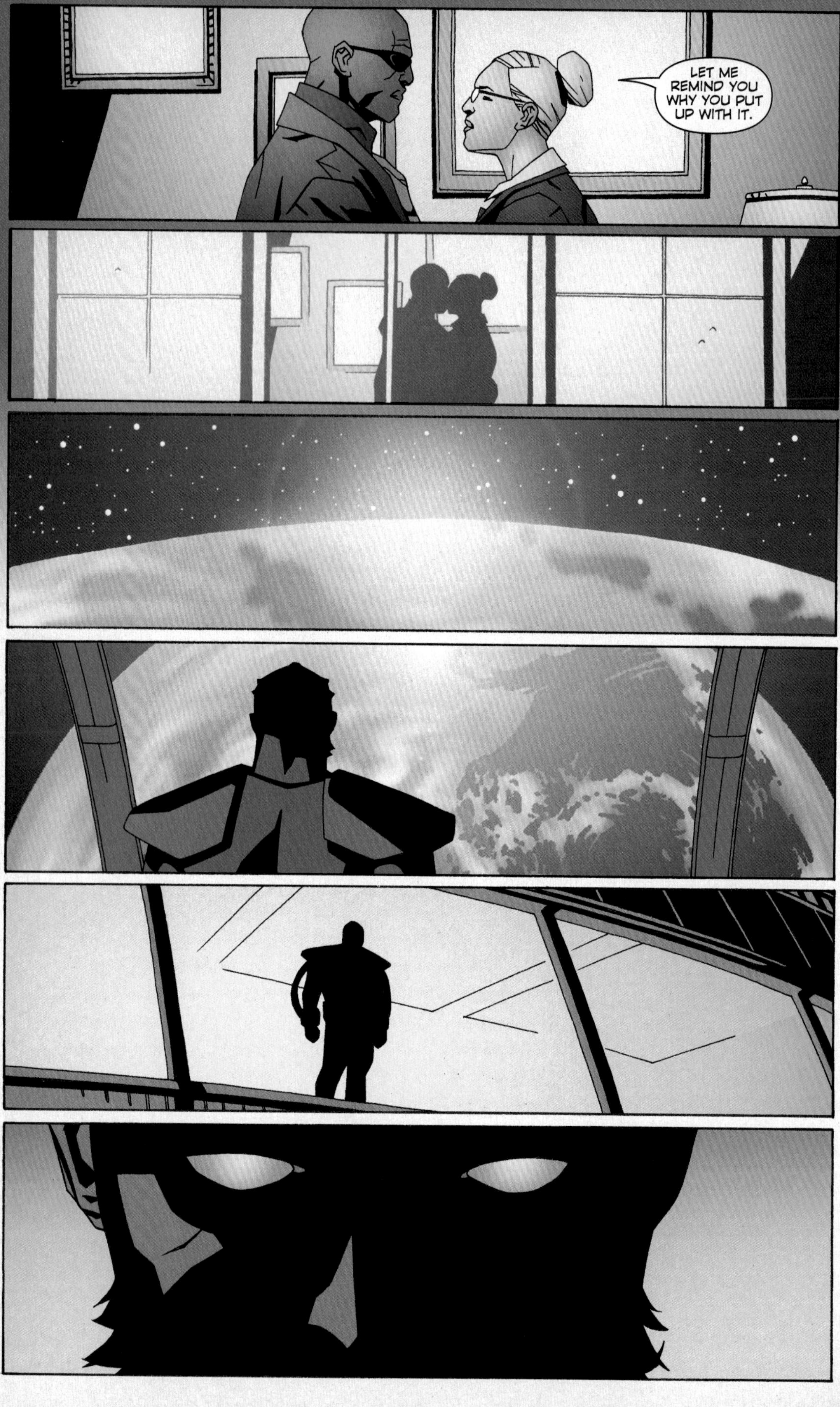
LET ME REMIND YOU WHY YOU PUT UP WITH IT.

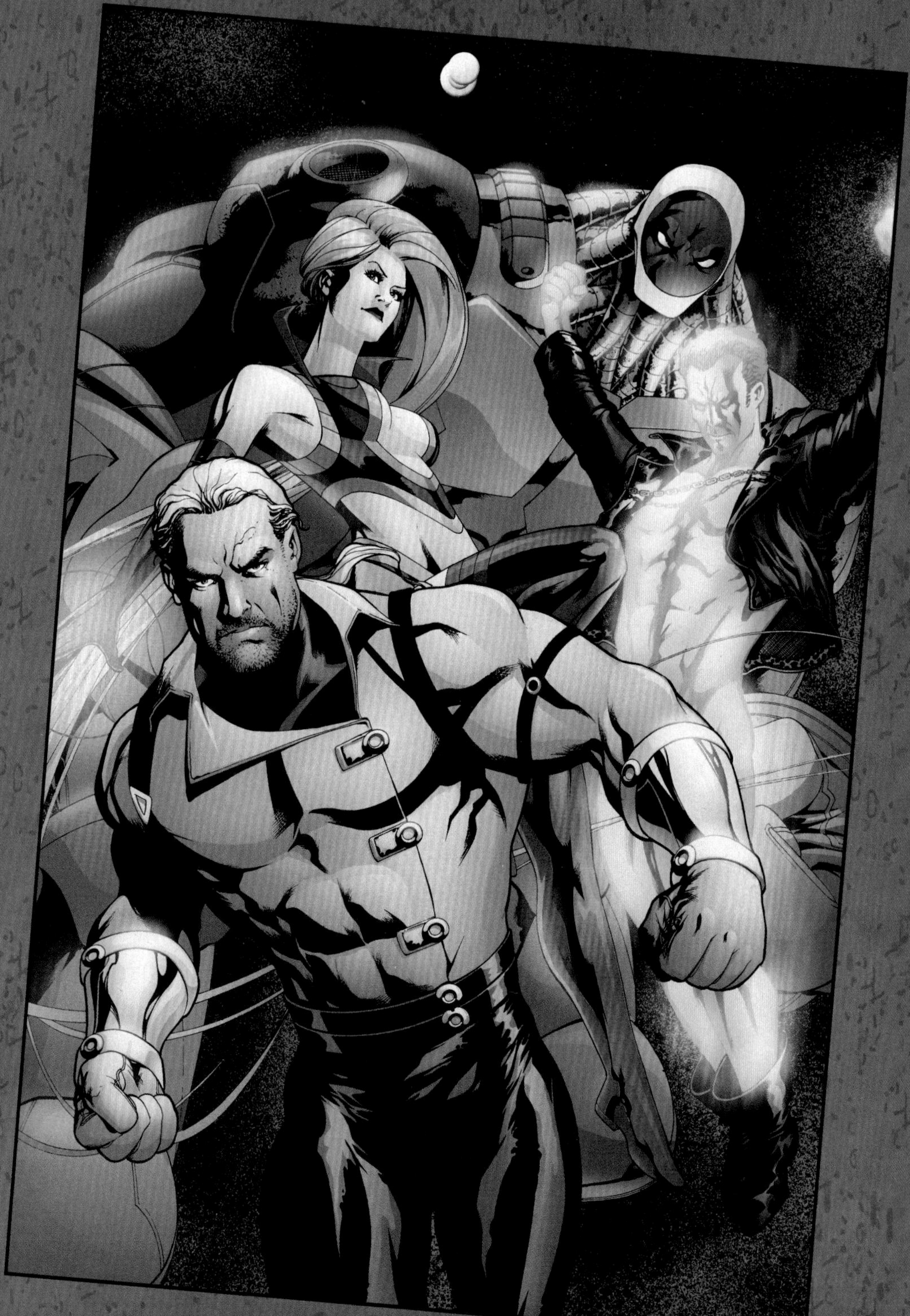

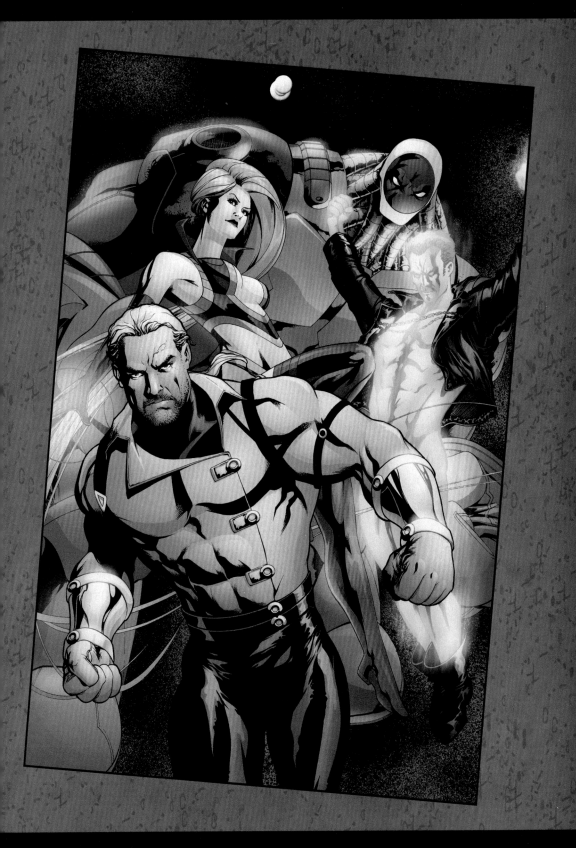

Mike McKone & Carrie Strachan

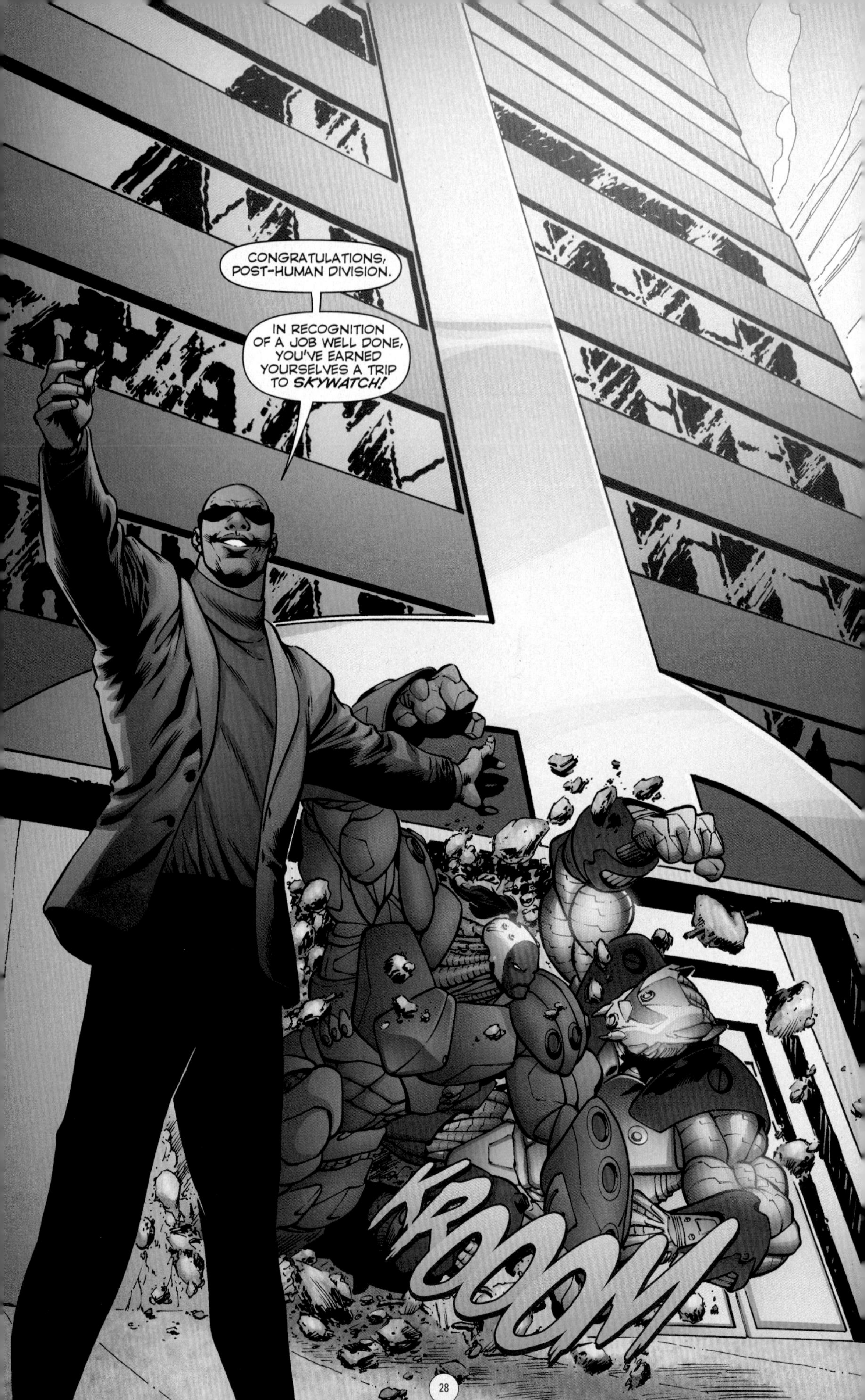
CONGRATULATIONS, POST-HUMAN DIVISION.
IN RECOGNITION OF A JOB WELL DONE, YOU'VE EARNED YOURSELVES A TRIP TO SKYWATCH!
KROOOM

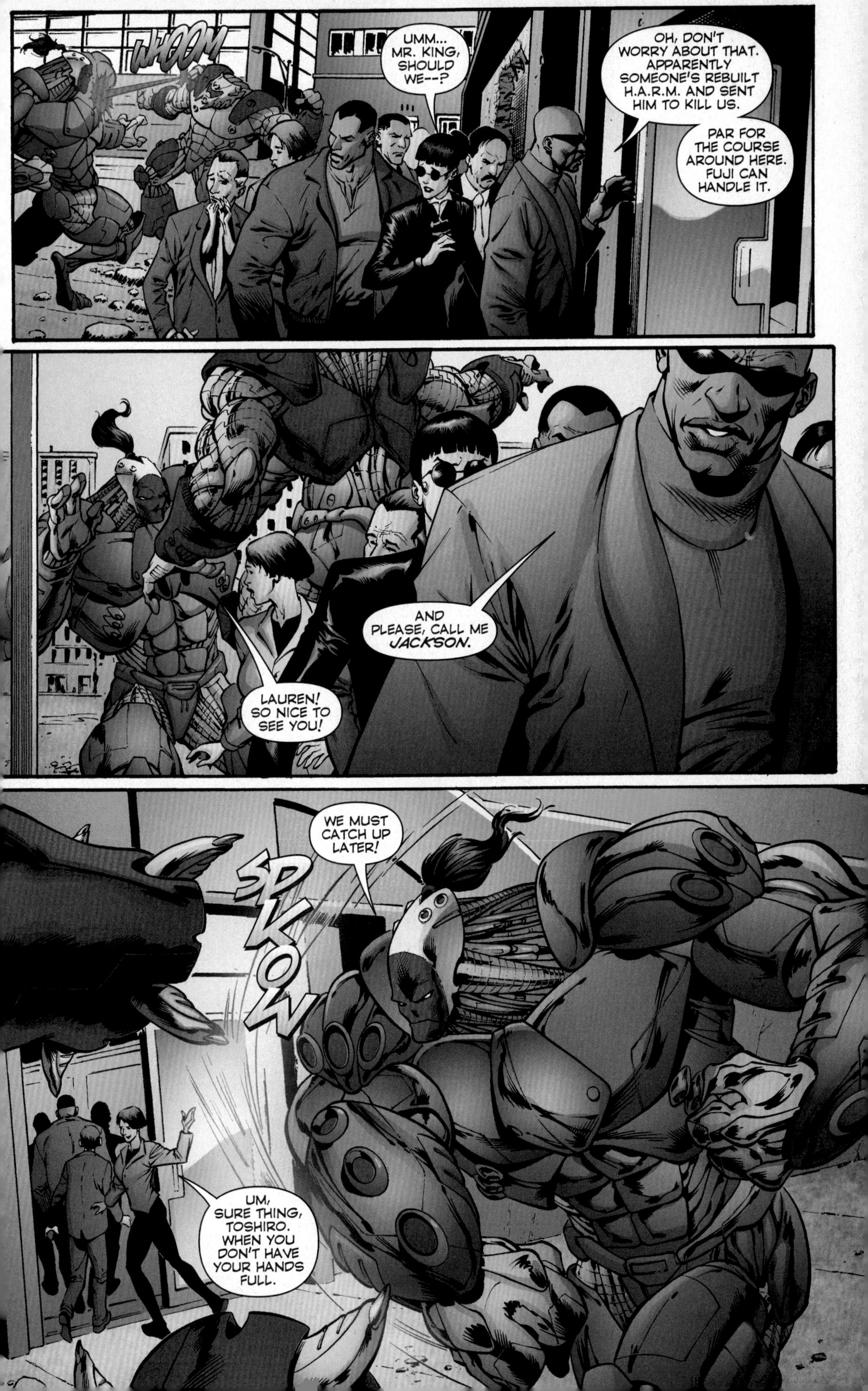
WHOOM
UMM... MR. KING, SHOULD WE--?
OH, DON'T WORRY ABOUT THAT. APPARENTLY SOMEONE'S REBUILT H.A.R.M. AND SENT HIM TO KILL US.
PAR FOR THE COURSE AROUND HERE. FUJI CAN HANDLE IT.
AND PLEASE, CALL ME JACKSON.
LAUREN! SO NICE TO SEE YOU!
WE MUST CATCH UP LATER!
SPKOW
UM, SURE THING, TOSHIRO. WHEN YOU DON'T HAVE YOUR HANDS FULL.

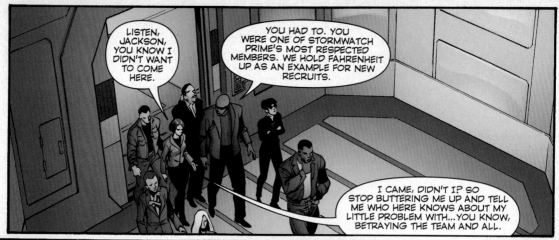

LISTEN, JACKSON, YOU KNOW I DIDN'T WANT TO COME HERE.

YOU HAD TO. YOU WERE ONE OF STORMWATCH PRIME'S MOST RESPECTED MEMBERS. WE HOLD FAHRENHEIT UP AS AN EXAMPLE FOR NEW RECRUITS.

I CAME, DIDN'T I? SO STOP BUTTERING ME UP AND TELL ME WHO HERE KNOWS ABOUT MY LITTLE PROBLEM WITH...YOU KNOW, BETRAYING THE TEAM AND ALL.

NO ONE. YOU WERE BEING MANIPULATED. IT WASN'T YOUR FAULT, SO I SAW NO NEED TO MENTION IT.

THANK HEAVEN FOR SMALL FAVORS.

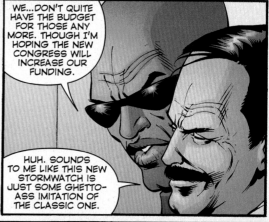

HEY, BOSS. I KIND OF EXPECTED A PLACE CALLED SKYWATCH TO BE, Y'KNOW...UP IN THE SKY.

THIS BUILDING IS NINETY STORIES TALL.

OKAY, BUT STORMWATCH IS FAMOUS FOR ITS ORBITAL SATELLITES. I THOUGHT WE WERE GOING UP ON ONE.

WE...DON'T QUITE HAVE THE BUDGET FOR THOSE ANY MORE. THOUGH I'M HOPING THE NEW CONGRESS WILL INCREASE OUR FUNDING.

HUH. SOUNDS TO ME LIKE THIS NEW STORMWATCH IS JUST SOME GHETTO-ASS IMITATION OF THE CLASSIC ONE.

IF I WERE YOU, I'D FOCUS MORE ON MAKING A GOOD IMPRESSION.

CONSIDERING YOU TRIED TO KILL MOST EVERYONE IN STORMWATCH DURING YOUR CAREER AS A SUPER-VILLAIN. AND THESE PEOPLE HAVE LONG MEMORIES.

OH, MY ACID REFLUX...

DING

HERE WE ARE, PEOPLE.

AND, SATELLITE OR NOT, I THINK YOU'LL AGREE...

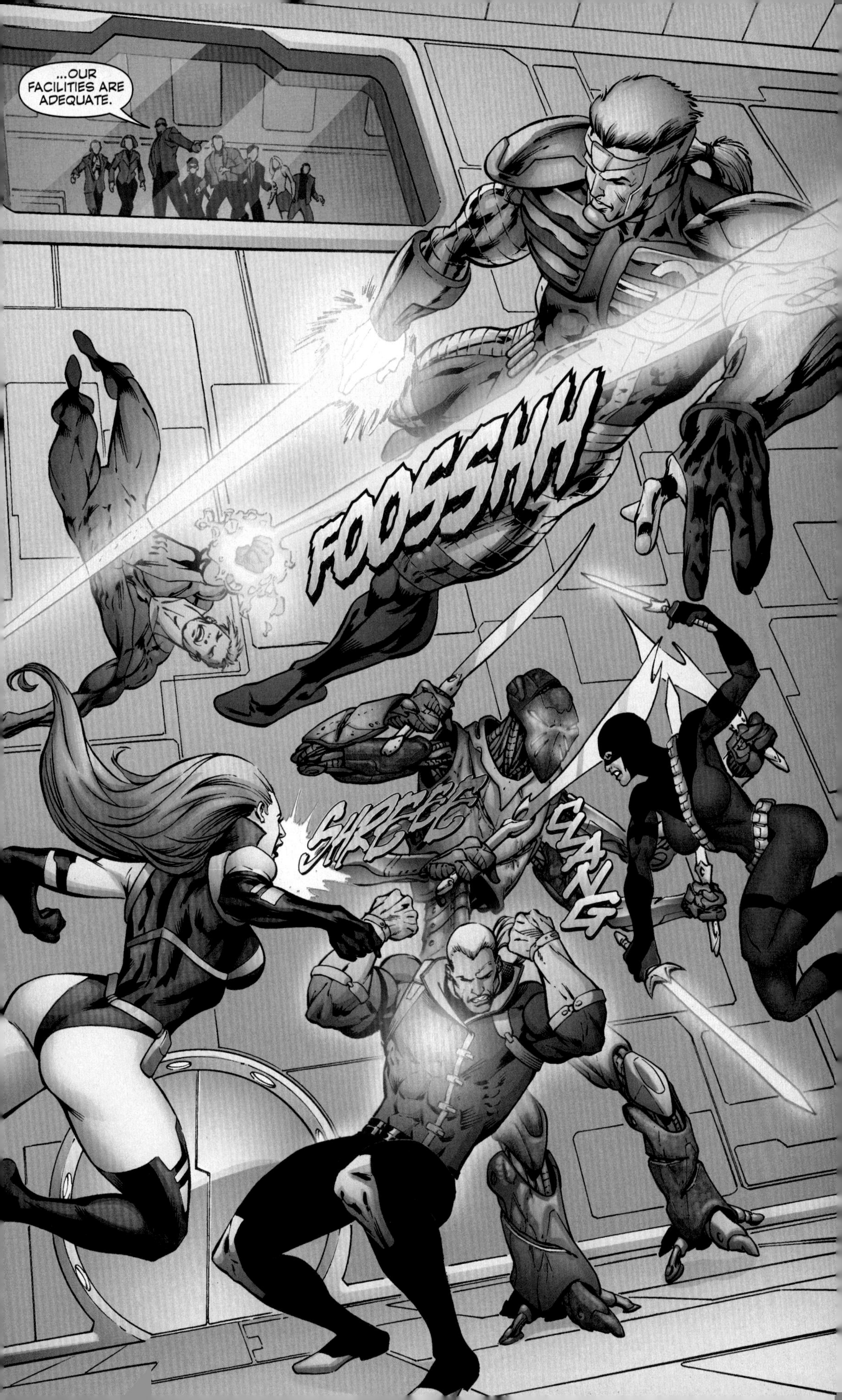
...OUR FACILITIES ARE ADEQUATE.
FOOSHH
SHREEE
CLANG

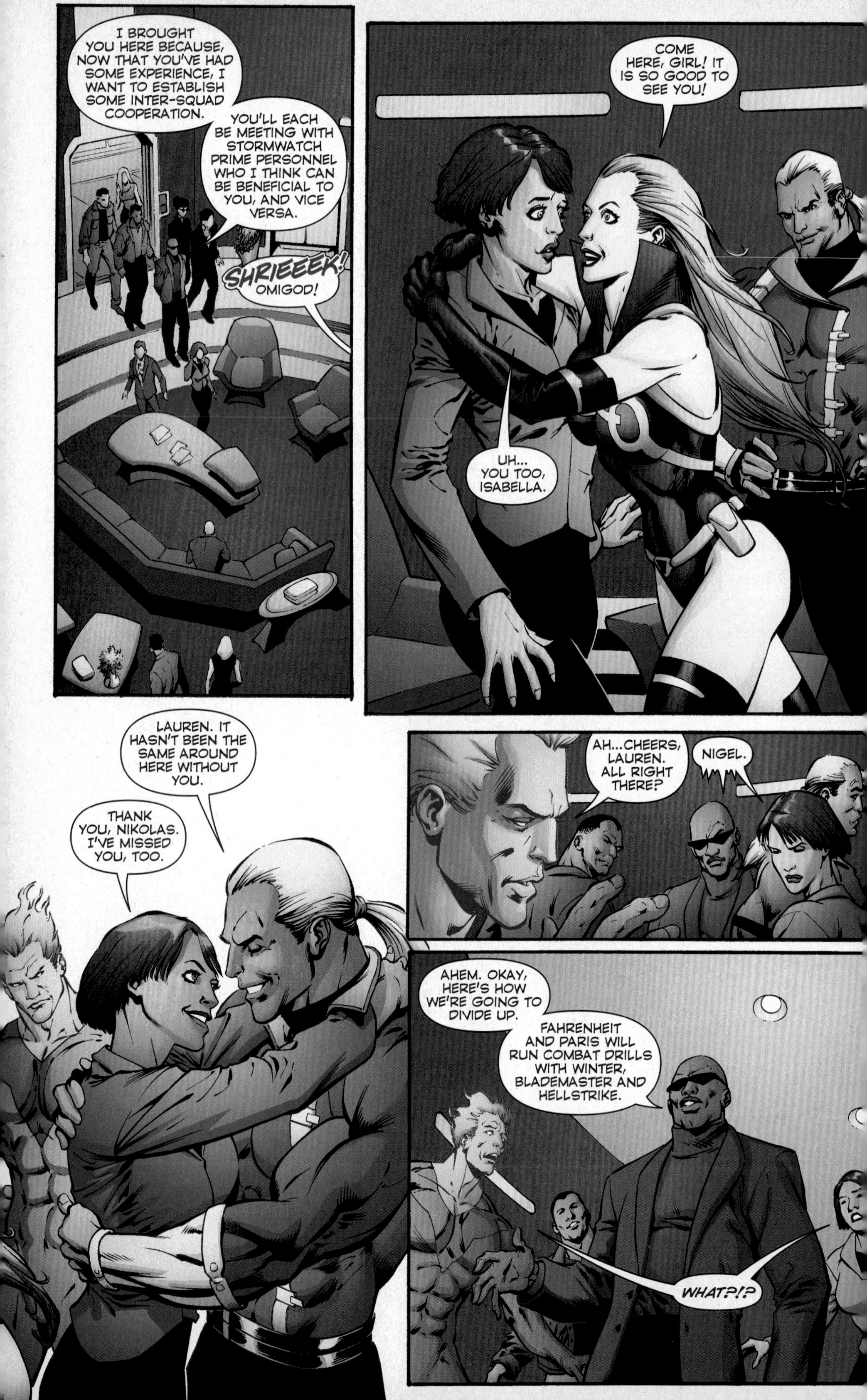

I BROUGHT YOU HERE BECAUSE, NOW THAT YOU'VE HAD SOME EXPERIENCE, I WANT TO ESTABLISH SOME INTER-SQUAD COOPERATION.
YOU'LL EACH BE MEETING WITH STORMWATCH PRIME PERSONNEL WHO I THINK CAN BE BENEFICIAL TO YOU, AND VICE VERSA.
SHRIEEEK!
OMIGOD!
COME HERE, GIRL! IT IS SO GOOD TO SEE YOU!
UH... YOU TOO, ISABELLA.
LAUREN. IT HASN'T BEEN THE SAME AROUND HERE WITHOUT YOU.
THANK YOU, NIKOLAS. I'VE MISSED YOU, TOO.
AH...CHEERS, LAUREN. ALL RIGHT THERE?
NIGEL.
AHEM. OKAY, HERE'S HOW WE'RE GOING TO DIVIDE UP.
FAHRENHEIT AND PARIS WILL RUN COMBAT DRILLS WITH WINTER, BLADEMASTER AND HELLSTRIKE.
WHAT?!?

PARIS AND BLADEMASTER CAN LEARN HAND-TO-HAND FROM EACH OTHER. YOU TWO ARE BOTH ENERGY CASTERS, AND WINTER CONTROLS ENERGY. STRATEGICALLY, IT MAKES SENSE.

IF YOU CAN'T PUT ASIDE PERSONAL ISSUES-- ESPECIALLY ONES A SIXTH-GRADER SHOULD HAVE THE MATURITY TO RESOLVE-- HAND IN YOUR RESIGNATIONS.

BETTY, I'D LIKE YOU TO MEET WITH DIVA. THERE ARE SOME...DETAILS SURROUNDING THE ACTIVATION OF HER POWERS YOU MIGHT BE ABLE TO SHED LIGHT ON.

DR. SHAW, OUR EXPERT ON POST-HUMAN AND ALIEN BIOLOGY, DR. MOLLY PERKINS, IS LOOKING FORWARD TO CONSULTING WITH YOU.

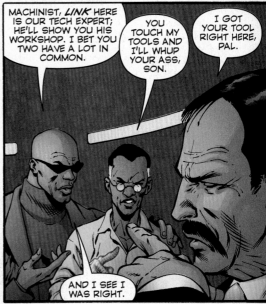

MACHINIST, LINK HERE IS OUR TECH EXPERT; HE'LL SHOW YOU HIS WORKSHOP. I BET YOU TWO HAVE A LOT IN COMMON.

YOU TOUCH MY TOOLS AND I'LL WHUP YOUR ASS, SON.

I GOT YOUR TOOL RIGHT HERE, PAL.

AND I SEE I WAS RIGHT.

GORGEOUS, THIS IS MY BROTHER MALCOLM, CODE-NAMED STRAFE. HE'LL BE ESCORTING YOU TO OUR WEATHERMAN, WHO'S ANXIOUS TO MEET YOU.

JOHN, YOU'RE WITH CHRISTINE AND ME. OKAY, EVERYONE...GO MAKE SOME NEW FRIENDS.

OR AT THE VERY LEAST, TRY NOT TO KILL EACH OTHER.

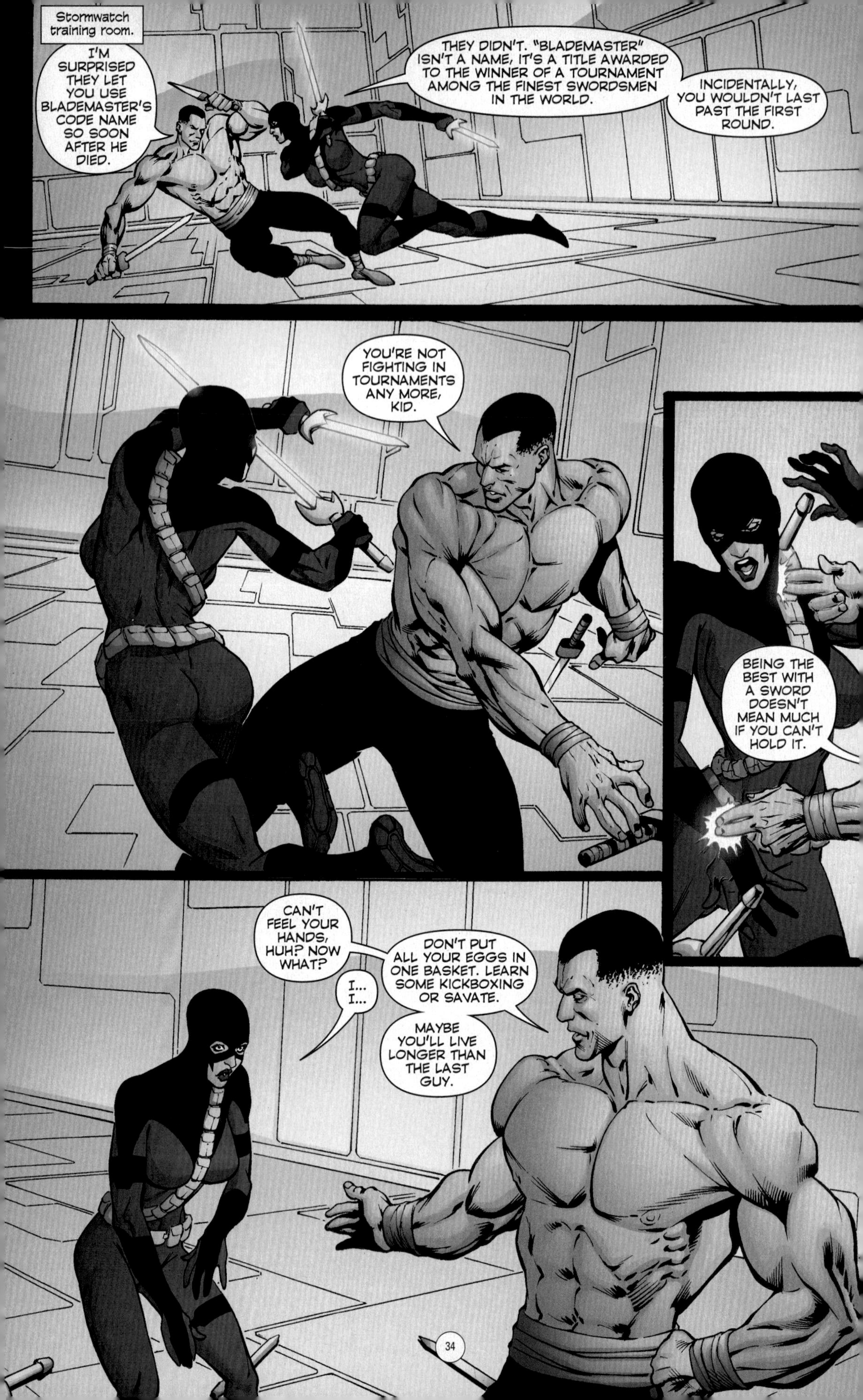
Stormwatch training room.
I'M SURPRISED THEY LET YOU USE BLADEMASTER'S CODE NAME SO SOON AFTER HE DIED.
THEY DIDN'T. "BLADEMASTER" ISN'T A NAME, IT'S A TITLE AWARDED TO THE WINNER OF A TOURNAMENT AMONG THE FINEST SWORDSMEN IN THE WORLD.
INCIDENTALLY, YOU WOULDN'T LAST PAST THE FIRST ROUND.
YOU'RE NOT FIGHTING IN TOURNAMENTS ANY MORE, KID.
BEING THE BEST WITH A SWORD DOESN'T MEAN MUCH IF YOU CAN'T HOLD IT.
CAN'T FEEL YOUR HANDS, HUH? NOW WHAT?
I... I...
DON'T PUT ALL YOUR EGGS IN ONE BASKET. LEARN SOME KICKBOXING OR SAVATE.
MAYBE YOU'LL LIVE LONGER THAN THE LAST GUY.

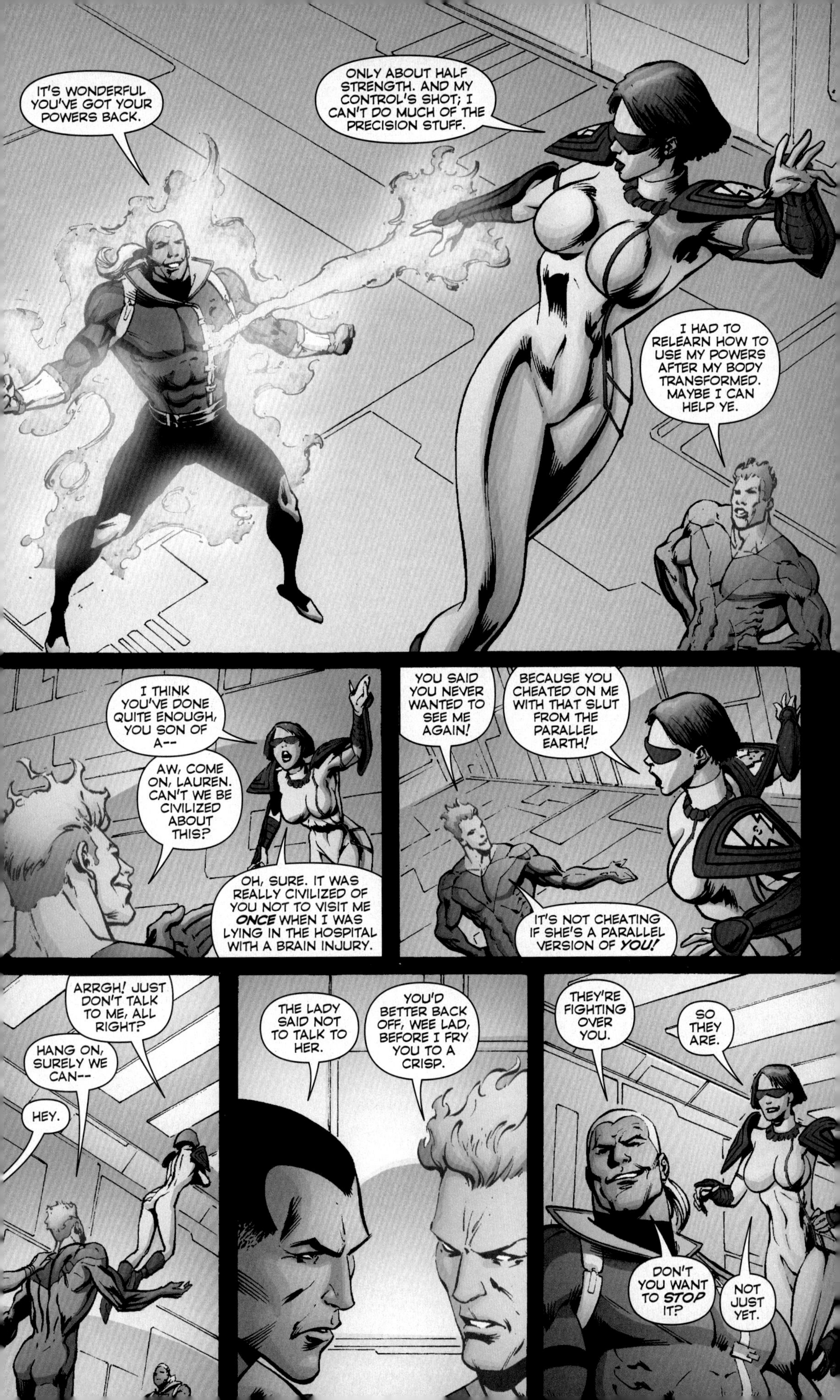

IT'S WONDERFUL YOU'VE GOT YOUR POWERS BACK.
ONLY ABOUT HALF STRENGTH. AND MY CONTROL'S SHOT; I CAN'T DO MUCH OF THE PRECISION STUFF.
I HAD TO RELEARN HOW TO USE MY POWERS AFTER MY BODY TRANSFORMED. MAYBE I CAN HELP YE.
I THINK YOU'VE DONE QUITE ENOUGH, YOU SON OF A--
AW, COME ON, LAUREN. CAN'T WE BE CIVILIZED ABOUT THIS?
OH, SURE. IT WAS REALLY CIVILIZED OF YOU NOT TO VISIT ME *ONCE* WHEN I WAS LYING IN THE HOSPITAL WITH A BRAIN INJURY.
YOU SAID YOU NEVER WANTED TO SEE ME AGAIN!
BECAUSE YOU CHEATED ON ME WITH THAT SLUT FROM THE PARALLEL EARTH!
IT'S NOT CHEATING IF SHE'S A PARALLEL VERSION OF *YOU!*
ARRGH! JUST DON'T TALK TO ME, ALL RIGHT?
HANG ON, SURELY WE CAN--
HEY.
THE LADY SAID NOT TO TALK TO HER.
YOU'D BETTER BACK OFF, WEE LAD, BEFORE I FRY YOU TO A CRISP.
THEY'RE FIGHTING OVER YOU.
SO THEY ARE.
DON'T YOU WANT TO *STOP* IT?
NOT JUST YET.

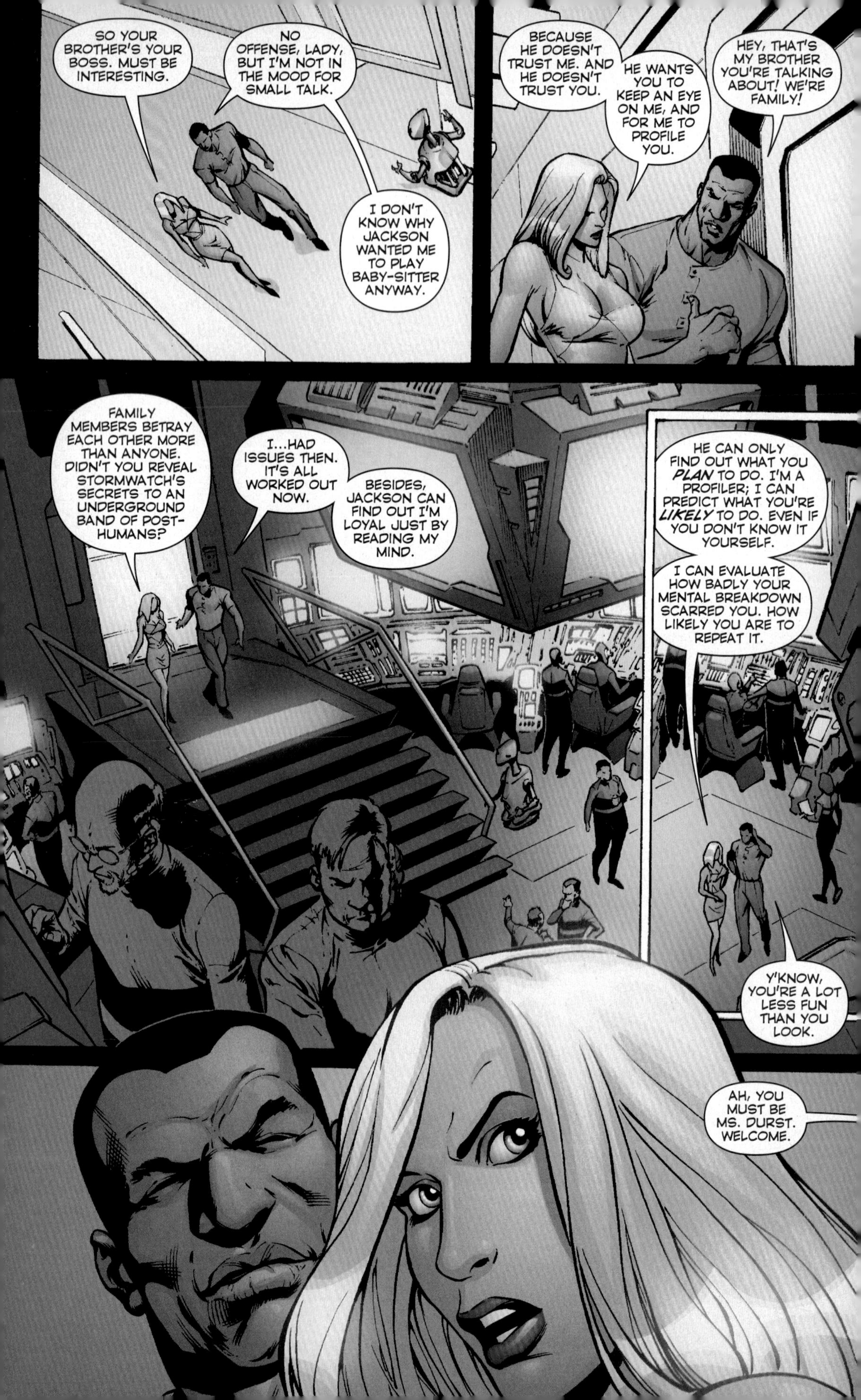
SO YOUR BROTHER'S YOUR BOSS. MUST BE INTERESTING.
NO OFFENSE, LADY, BUT I'M NOT IN THE MOOD FOR SMALL TALK.
I DON'T KNOW WHY JACKSON WANTED ME TO PLAY BABY-SITTER ANYWAY.
BECAUSE HE DOESN'T TRUST ME. AND HE DOESN'T TRUST YOU.
HE WANTS YOU TO KEEP AN EYE ON ME, AND FOR ME TO PROFILE YOU.
HEY, THAT'S MY BROTHER YOU'RE TALKING ABOUT! WE'RE FAMILY!
FAMILY MEMBERS BETRAY EACH OTHER MORE THAN ANYONE. DIDN'T YOU REVEAL STORMWATCH'S SECRETS TO AN UNDERGROUND BAND OF POST-HUMANS?
I...HAD ISSUES THEN. IT'S ALL WORKED OUT NOW.
BESIDES, JACKSON CAN FIND OUT I'M LOYAL JUST BY READING MY MIND.
HE CAN ONLY FIND OUT WHAT YOU *PLAN* TO DO. I'M A PROFILER; I CAN PREDICT WHAT YOU'RE *LIKELY* TO DO. EVEN IF YOU DON'T KNOW IT YOURSELF.
I CAN EVALUATE HOW BADLY YOUR MENTAL BREAKDOWN SCARRED YOU. HOW LIKELY YOU ARE TO REPEAT IT.
Y'KNOW, YOU'RE A LOT LESS FUN THAN YOU LOOK.
AH, YOU MUST BE MS. DURST. WELCOME.

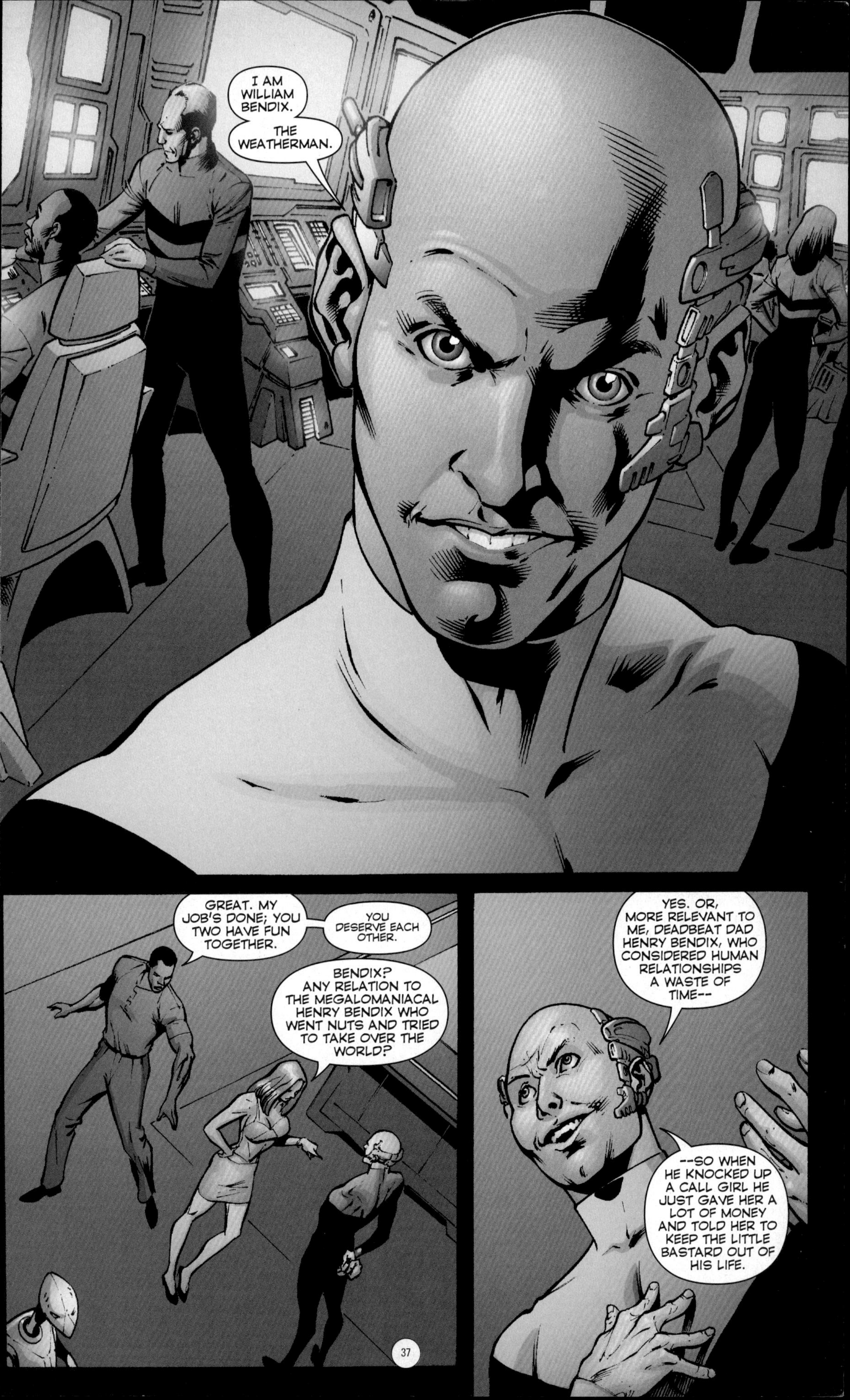
I AM WILLIAM BENDIX.
THE WEATHERMAN.
GREAT. MY JOB'S DONE; YOU TWO HAVE FUN TOGETHER.
YOU DESERVE EACH OTHER.
BENDIX? ANY RELATION TO THE MEGALOMANIACAL HENRY BENDIX WHO WENT NUTS AND TRIED TO TAKE OVER THE WORLD?
YES. OR, MORE RELEVANT TO ME, DEADBEAT DAD HENRY BENDIX, WHO CONSIDERED HUMAN RELATIONSHIPS A WASTE OF TIME--
--SO WHEN HE KNOCKED UP A CALL GIRL HE JUST GAVE HER A LOT OF MONEY AND TOLD HER TO KEEP THE LITTLE BASTARD OUT OF HIS LIFE.

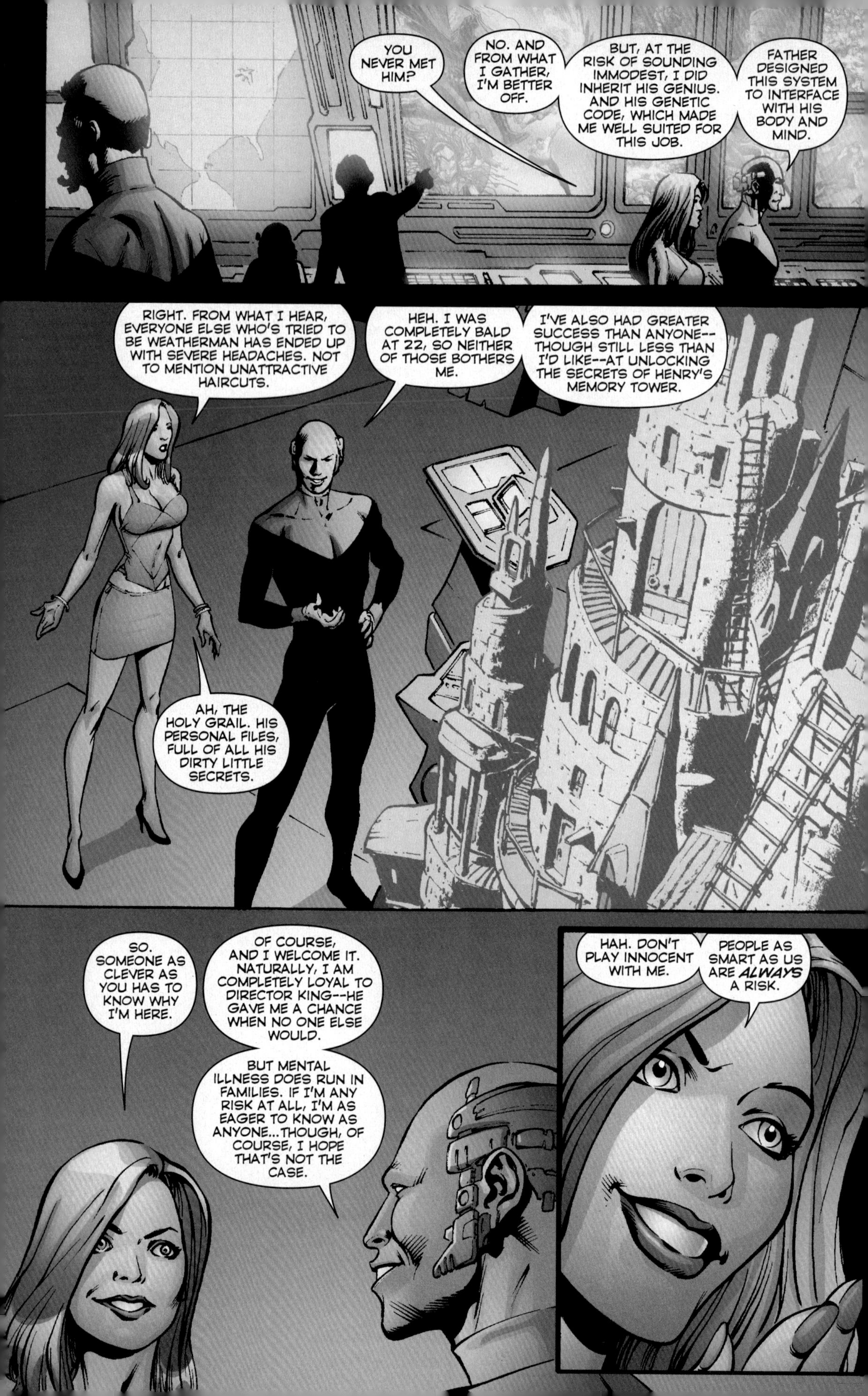
YOU NEVER MET HIM?
NO. AND FROM WHAT I GATHER, I'M BETTER OFF.
BUT, AT THE RISK OF SOUNDING IMMODEST, I DID INHERIT HIS GENIUS. AND HIS GENETIC CODE, WHICH MADE ME WELL SUITED FOR THIS JOB.
FATHER DESIGNED THIS SYSTEM TO INTERFACE WITH HIS BODY AND MIND.
RIGHT. FROM WHAT I HEAR, EVERYONE ELSE WHO'S TRIED TO BE WEATHERMAN HAS ENDED UP WITH SEVERE HEADACHES. NOT TO MENTION UNATTRACTIVE HAIRCUTS.
HEH. I WAS COMPLETELY BALD AT 22, SO NEITHER OF THOSE BOTHERS ME.
I'VE ALSO HAD GREATER SUCCESS THAN ANYONE--THOUGH STILL LESS THAN I'D LIKE--AT UNLOCKING THE SECRETS OF HENRY'S MEMORY TOWER.
AH, THE HOLY GRAIL. HIS PERSONAL FILES, FULL OF ALL HIS DIRTY LITTLE SECRETS.
SO. SOMEONE AS CLEVER AS YOU HAS TO KNOW WHY I'M HERE.
OF COURSE, AND I WELCOME IT. NATURALLY, I AM COMPLETELY LOYAL TO DIRECTOR KING--HE GAVE ME A CHANCE WHEN NO ONE ELSE WOULD.
BUT MENTAL ILLNESS DOES RUN IN FAMILIES. IF I'M ANY RISK AT ALL, I'M AS EAGER TO KNOW AS ANYONE...THOUGH, OF COURSE, I HOPE THAT'S NOT THE CASE.
HAH. DON'T PLAY INNOCENT WITH ME.
PEOPLE AS SMART AS US ARE *ALWAYS* A RISK.

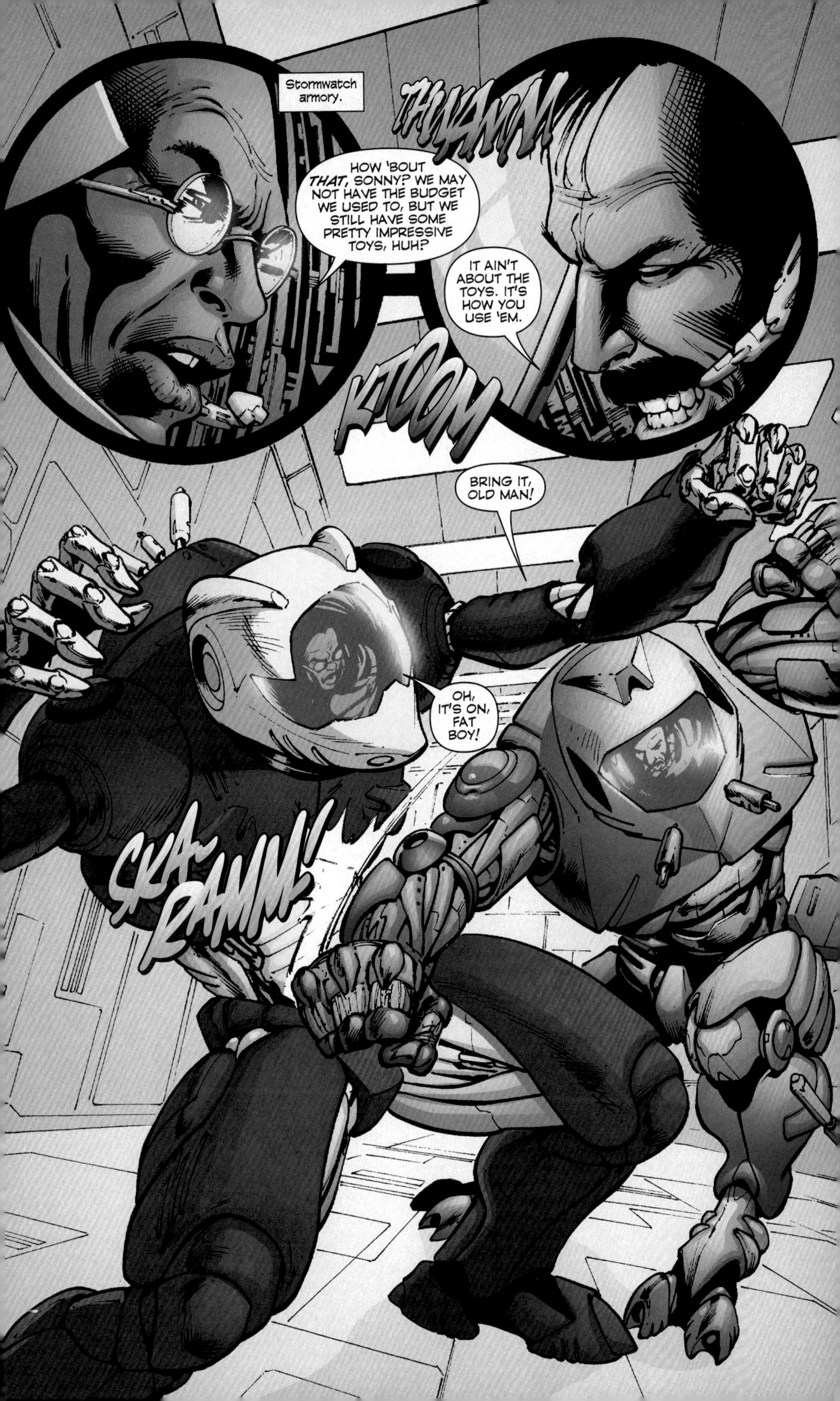
Stormwatch armory.
THWAMM!
HOW 'BOUT *THAT,* SONNY? WE MAY NOT HAVE THE BUDGET WE USED TO, BUT WE STILL HAVE SOME PRETTY IMPRESSIVE TOYS, HUH?
IT AIN'T ABOUT THE TOYS. IT'S HOW YOU USE 'EM.
KTOOM
BRING IT, OLD MAN!
OH, IT'S ON, FAT BOY!
SKA-RAMM!

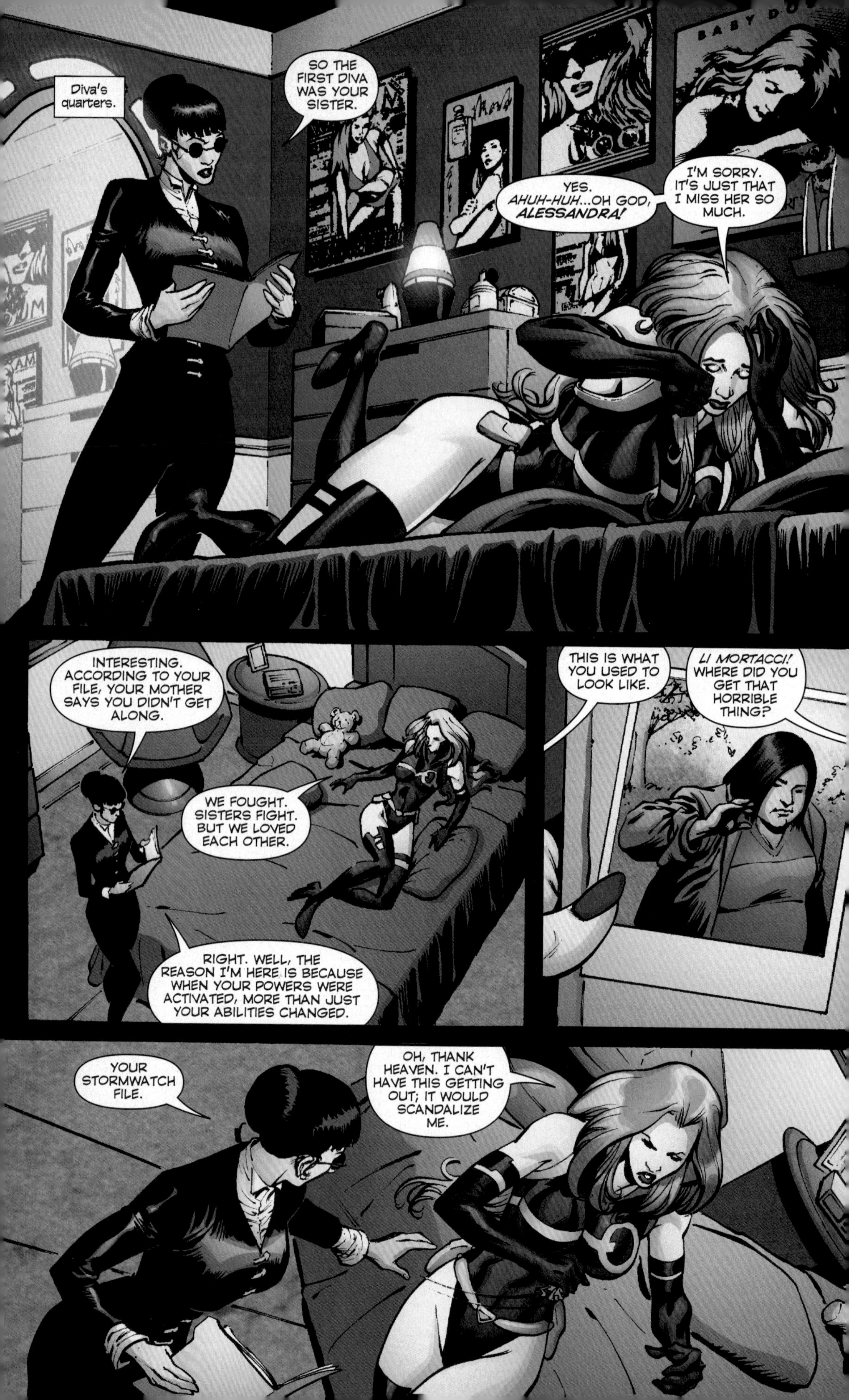
Diva's quarters.
SO THE FIRST DIVA WAS YOUR SISTER.
YES. AHUH-HUH...OH GOD, ALESSANDRA!
I'M SORRY. IT'S JUST THAT I MISS HER SO MUCH.
INTERESTING. ACCORDING TO YOUR FILE, YOUR MOTHER SAYS YOU DIDN'T GET ALONG.
WE FOUGHT. SISTERS FIGHT. BUT WE LOVED EACH OTHER.
RIGHT. WELL, THE REASON I'M HERE IS BECAUSE WHEN YOUR POWERS WERE ACTIVATED, MORE THAN JUST YOUR ABILITIES CHANGED.
THIS IS WHAT YOU USED TO LOOK LIKE.
LI MORTACCI! WHERE DID YOU GET THAT HORRIBLE THING?
YOUR STORMWATCH FILE.
OH, THANK HEAVEN. I CAN'T HAVE THIS GETTING OUT; IT WOULD SCANDALIZE ME.

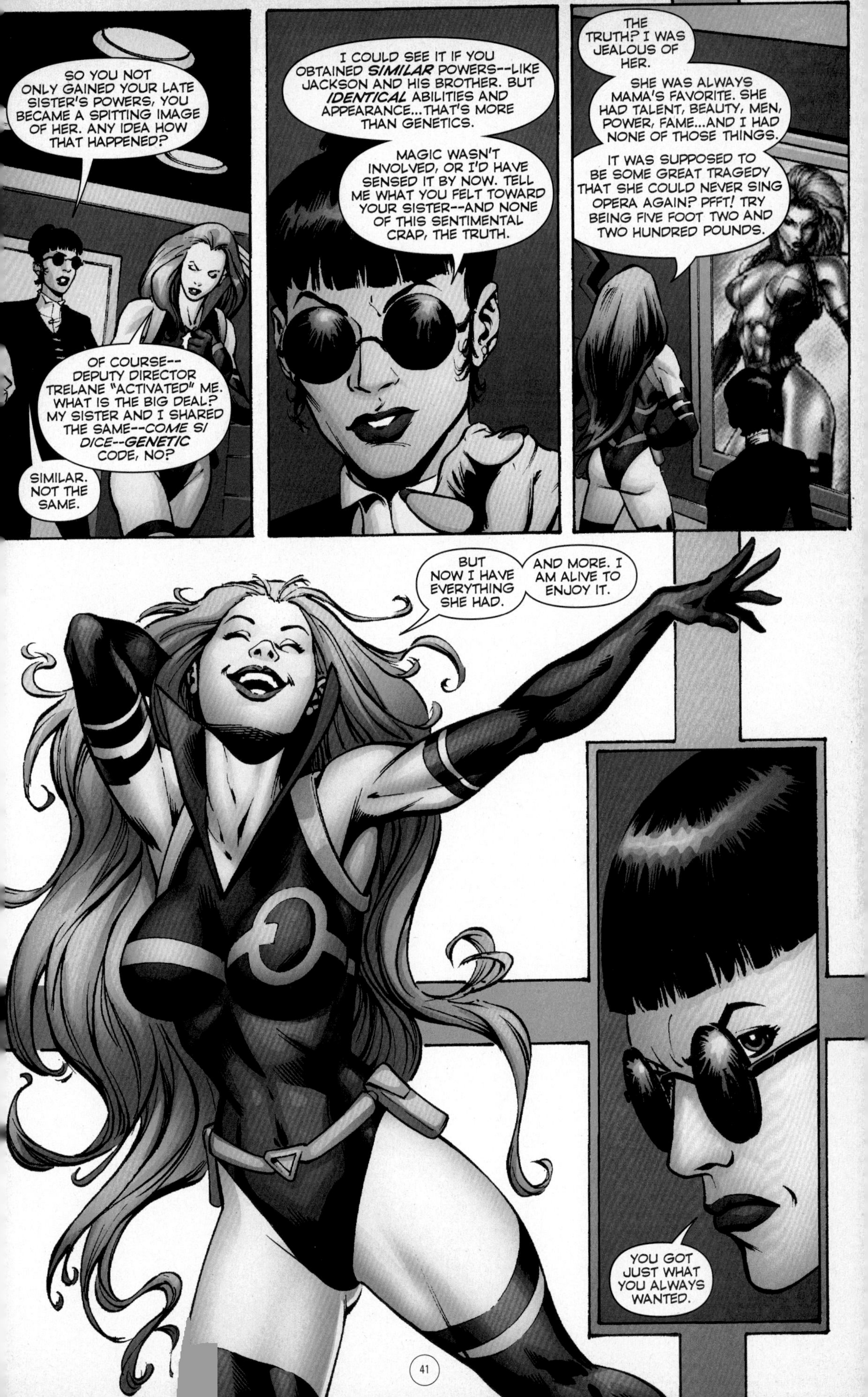
SO YOU NOT ONLY GAINED YOUR LATE SISTER'S POWERS, YOU BECAME A SPITTING IMAGE OF HER. ANY IDEA HOW THAT HAPPENED?
OF COURSE-- DEPUTY DIRECTOR TRELANE "ACTIVATED" ME. WHAT IS THE BIG DEAL? MY SISTER AND I SHARED THE SAME--COME SI DICE--GENETIC CODE, NO?
SIMILAR. NOT THE SAME.
I COULD SEE IT IF YOU OBTAINED SIMILAR POWERS--LIKE JACKSON AND HIS BROTHER. BUT IDENTICAL ABILITIES AND APPEARANCE...THAT'S MORE THAN GENETICS.
MAGIC WASN'T INVOLVED, OR I'D HAVE SENSED IT BY NOW. TELL ME WHAT YOU FELT TOWARD YOUR SISTER--AND NONE OF THIS SENTIMENTAL CRAP, THE TRUTH.
THE TRUTH? I WAS JEALOUS OF HER.
SHE WAS ALWAYS MAMA'S FAVORITE. SHE HAD TALENT, BEAUTY, MEN, POWER, FAME...AND I HAD NONE OF THOSE THINGS.
IT WAS SUPPOSED TO BE SOME GREAT TRAGEDY THAT SHE COULD NEVER SING OPERA AGAIN? PFFT! TRY BEING FIVE FOOT TWO AND TWO HUNDRED POUNDS.
BUT NOW I HAVE EVERYTHING SHE HAD.
AND MORE. I AM ALIVE TO ENJOY IT.
YOU GOT JUST WHAT YOU ALWAYS WANTED.

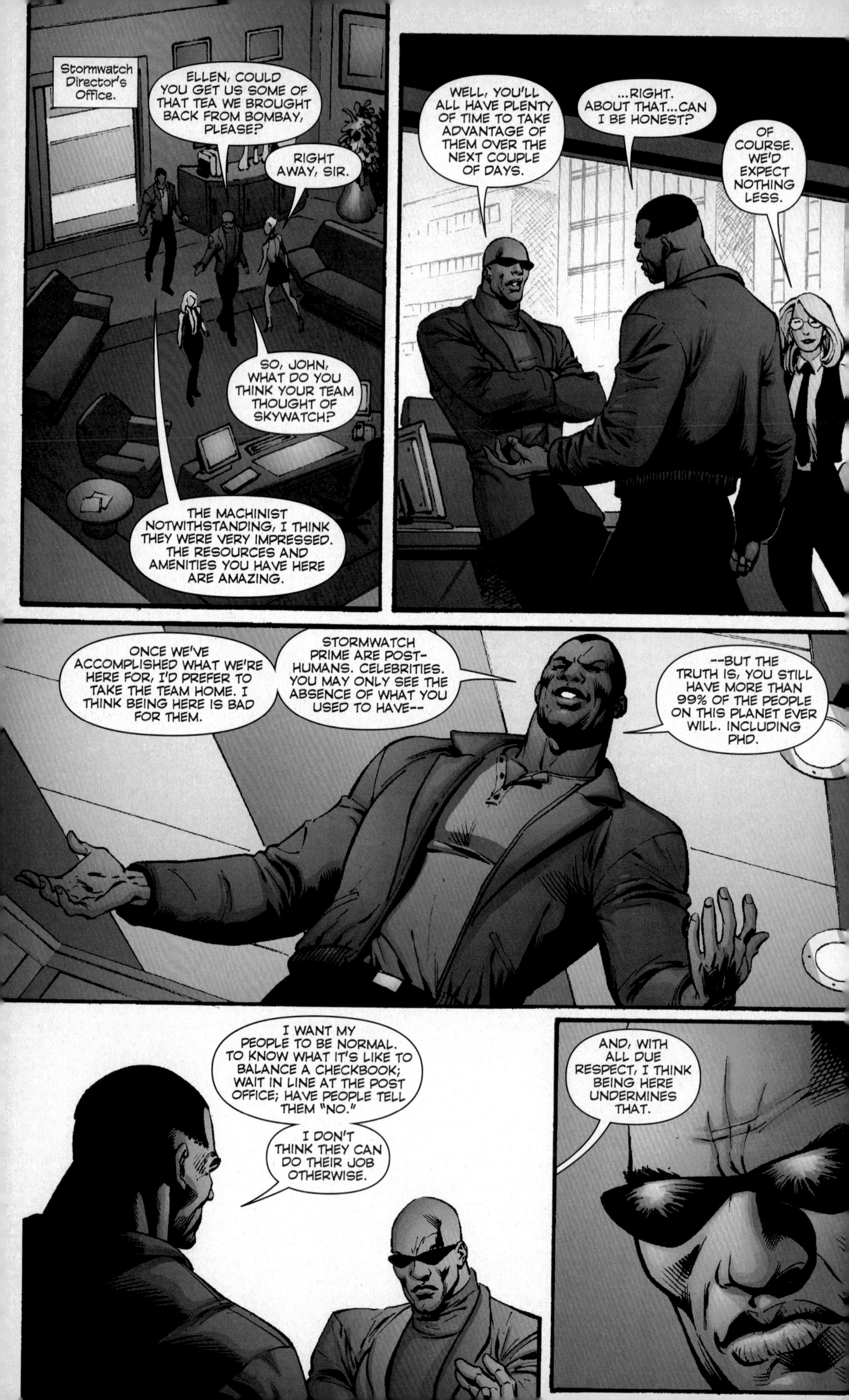
Stormwatch Director's Office.
ELLEN, COULD YOU GET US SOME OF THAT TEA WE BROUGHT BACK FROM BOMBAY, PLEASE?
RIGHT AWAY, SIR.
SO, JOHN, WHAT DO YOU THINK YOUR TEAM THOUGHT OF SKYWATCH?
THE MACHINIST NOTWITHSTANDING, I THINK THEY WERE VERY IMPRESSED. THE RESOURCES AND AMENITIES YOU HAVE HERE ARE AMAZING.
WELL, YOU'LL ALL HAVE PLENTY OF TIME TO TAKE ADVANTAGE OF THEM OVER THE NEXT COUPLE OF DAYS.
...RIGHT. ABOUT THAT...CAN I BE HONEST?
OF COURSE. WE'D EXPECT NOTHING LESS.
ONCE WE'VE ACCOMPLISHED WHAT WE'RE HERE FOR, I'D PREFER TO TAKE THE TEAM HOME. I THINK BEING HERE IS BAD FOR THEM.
STORMWATCH PRIME ARE POST-HUMANS. CELEBRITIES. YOU MAY ONLY SEE THE ABSENCE OF WHAT YOU USED TO HAVE--
--BUT THE TRUTH IS, YOU STILL HAVE MORE THAN 99% OF THE PEOPLE ON THIS PLANET EVER WILL. INCLUDING PHD.
I WANT MY PEOPLE TO BE NORMAL. TO KNOW WHAT IT'S LIKE TO BALANCE A CHECKBOOK; WAIT IN LINE AT THE POST OFFICE; HAVE PEOPLE TELL THEM "NO."
I DON'T THINK THEY CAN DO THEIR JOB OTHERWISE.
AND, WITH ALL DUE RESPECT, I THINK BEING HERE UNDERMINES THAT.

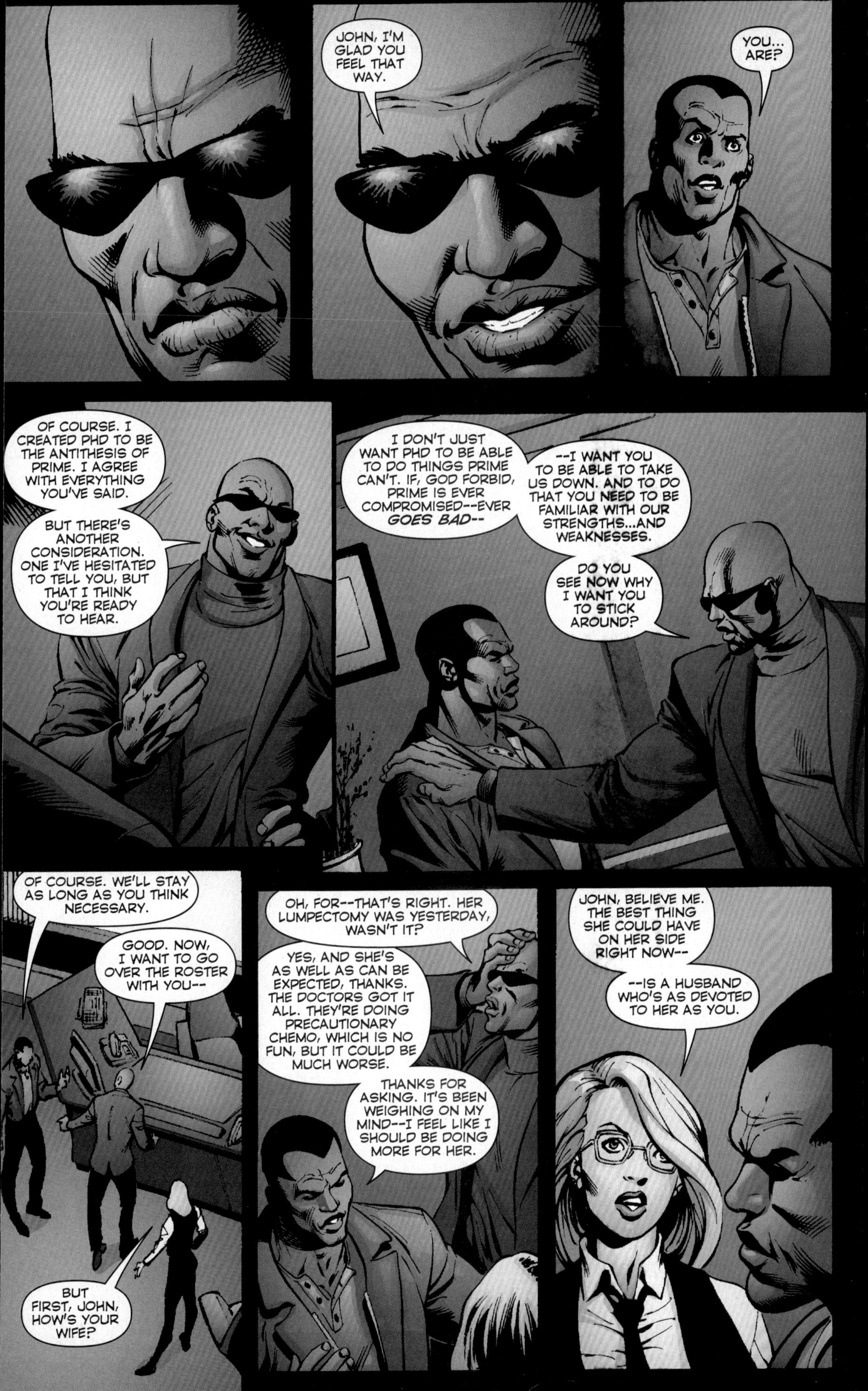
JOHN, I'M GLAD YOU FEEL THAT WAY.
YOU... ARE?
OF COURSE. I CREATED PHD TO BE THE ANTITHESIS OF PRIME. I AGREE WITH EVERYTHING YOU'VE SAID.
BUT THERE'S ANOTHER CONSIDERATION. ONE I'VE HESITATED TO TELL YOU, BUT THAT I THINK YOU'RE READY TO HEAR.
I DON'T JUST WANT PHD TO BE ABLE TO DO THINGS PRIME CAN'T. IF, GOD FORBID, PRIME IS EVER COMPROMISED--EVER *GOES BAD*--
--I WANT YOU TO BE ABLE TO TAKE US DOWN. AND TO DO THAT YOU NEED TO BE FAMILIAR WITH OUR STRENGTHS...AND WEAKNESSES.
DO YOU SEE NOW WHY I WANT YOU TO STICK AROUND?
OF COURSE. WE'LL STAY AS LONG AS YOU THINK NECESSARY.
GOOD. NOW, I WANT TO GO OVER THE ROSTER WITH YOU--
BUT FIRST, JOHN, HOW'S YOUR WIFE?
OH, FOR--THAT'S RIGHT. HER LUMPECTOMY WAS YESTERDAY, WASN'T IT?
YES, AND SHE'S AS WELL AS CAN BE EXPECTED, THANKS. THE DOCTORS GOT IT ALL. THEY'RE DOING PRECAUTIONARY CHEMO, WHICH IS NO FUN, BUT IT COULD BE MUCH WORSE.
THANKS FOR ASKING. IT'S BEEN WEIGHING ON MY MIND--I FEEL LIKE I SHOULD BE DOING MORE FOR HER.
JOHN, BELIEVE ME. THE BEST THING SHE COULD HAVE ON HER SIDE RIGHT NOW--
--IS A HUSBAND WHO'S AS DEVOTED TO HER AS YOU.

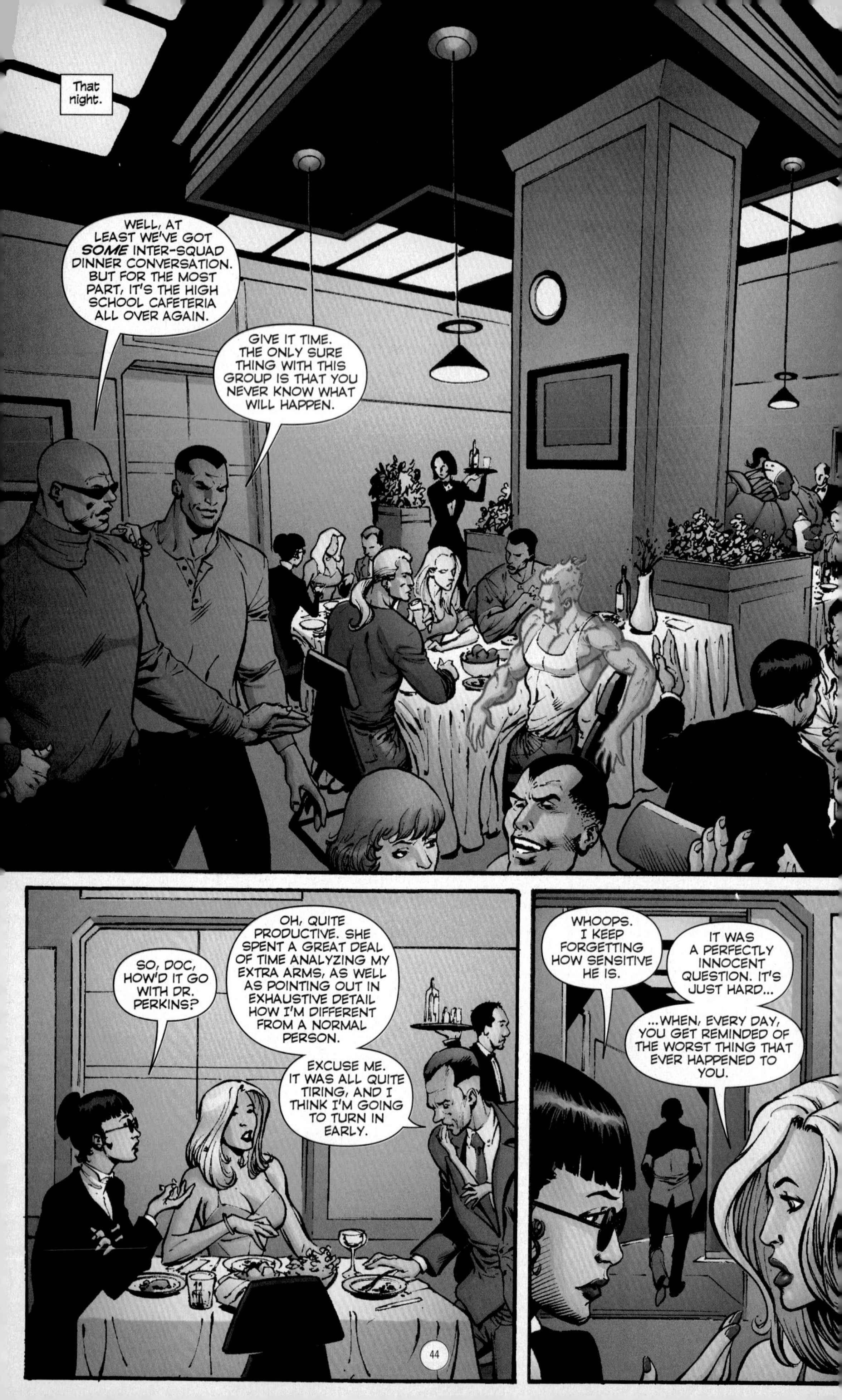
That night.
WELL, AT LEAST WE'VE GOT *SOME* INTER-SQUAD DINNER CONVERSATION. BUT FOR THE MOST PART, IT'S THE HIGH SCHOOL CAFETERIA ALL OVER AGAIN.
GIVE IT TIME. THE ONLY SURE THING WITH THIS GROUP IS THAT YOU NEVER KNOW WHAT WILL HAPPEN.
SO, DOC, HOW'D IT GO WITH DR. PERKINS?
OH, QUITE PRODUCTIVE. SHE SPENT A GREAT DEAL OF TIME ANALYZING MY EXTRA ARMS, AS WELL AS POINTING OUT IN EXHAUSTIVE DETAIL HOW I'M DIFFERENT FROM A NORMAL PERSON.
EXCUSE ME. IT WAS ALL QUITE TIRING, AND I THINK I'M GOING TO TURN IN EARLY.
WHOOPS. I KEEP FORGETTING HOW SENSITIVE HE IS.
IT WAS A PERFECTLY INNOCENT QUESTION. IT'S JUST HARD...
...WHEN, EVERY DAY, YOU GET REMINDED OF THE WORST THING THAT EVER HAPPENED TO YOU.

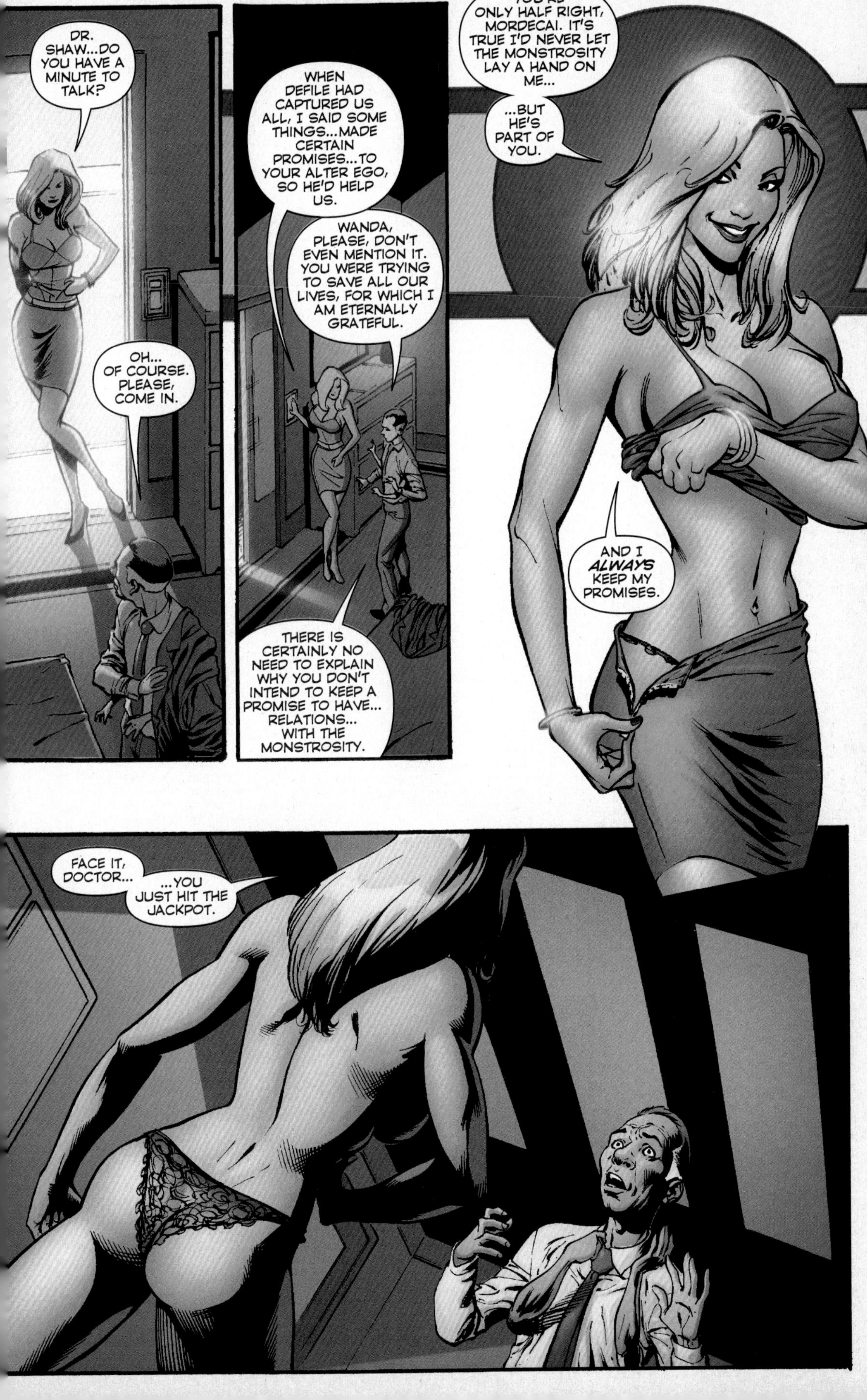
DR. SHAW...DO YOU HAVE A MINUTE TO TALK?
OH... OF COURSE. PLEASE, COME IN.
WHEN DEFILE HAD CAPTURED US ALL, I SAID SOME THINGS...MADE CERTAIN PROMISES...TO YOUR ALTER EGO, SO HE'D HELP US.
WANDA, PLEASE, DON'T EVEN MENTION IT. YOU WERE TRYING TO SAVE ALL OUR LIVES, FOR WHICH I AM ETERNALLY GRATEFUL.
THERE IS CERTAINLY NO NEED TO EXPLAIN WHY YOU DON'T INTEND TO KEEP A PROMISE TO HAVE... RELATIONS... WITH THE MONSTROSITY.
YOU'RE ONLY HALF RIGHT, MORDECAI. IT'S TRUE I'D NEVER LET THE MONSTROSITY LAY A HAND ON ME...
...BUT HE'S PART OF YOU.
AND I *ALWAYS* KEEP MY PROMISES.
FACE IT, DOCTOR...
...YOU JUST HIT THE JACKPOT.

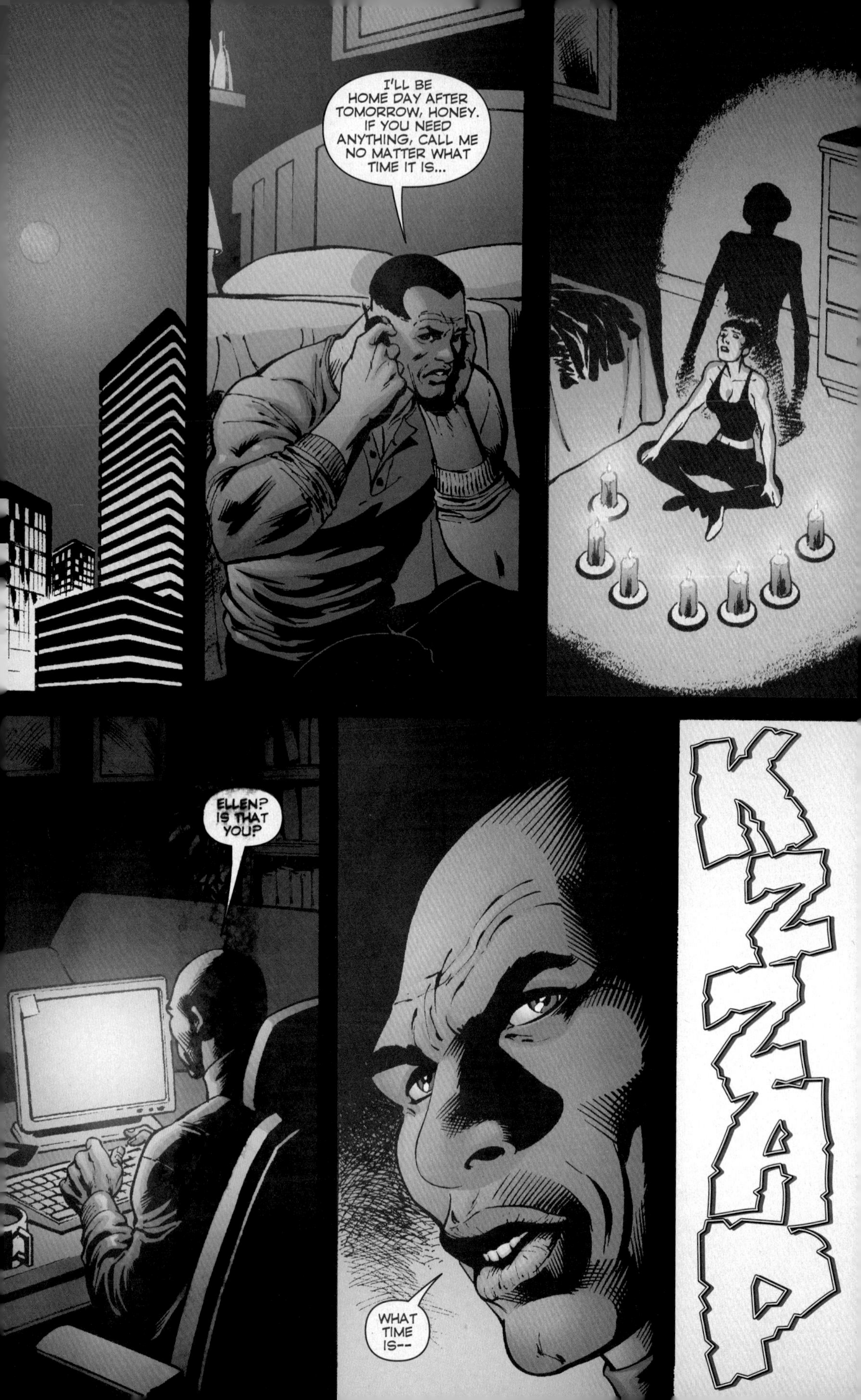
I'LL BE HOME DAY AFTER TOMORROW, HONEY. IF YOU NEED ANYTHING, CALL ME NO MATTER WHAT TIME IT IS...
ELLEN? IS THAT YOU?
WHAT TIME IS--
KNNAP

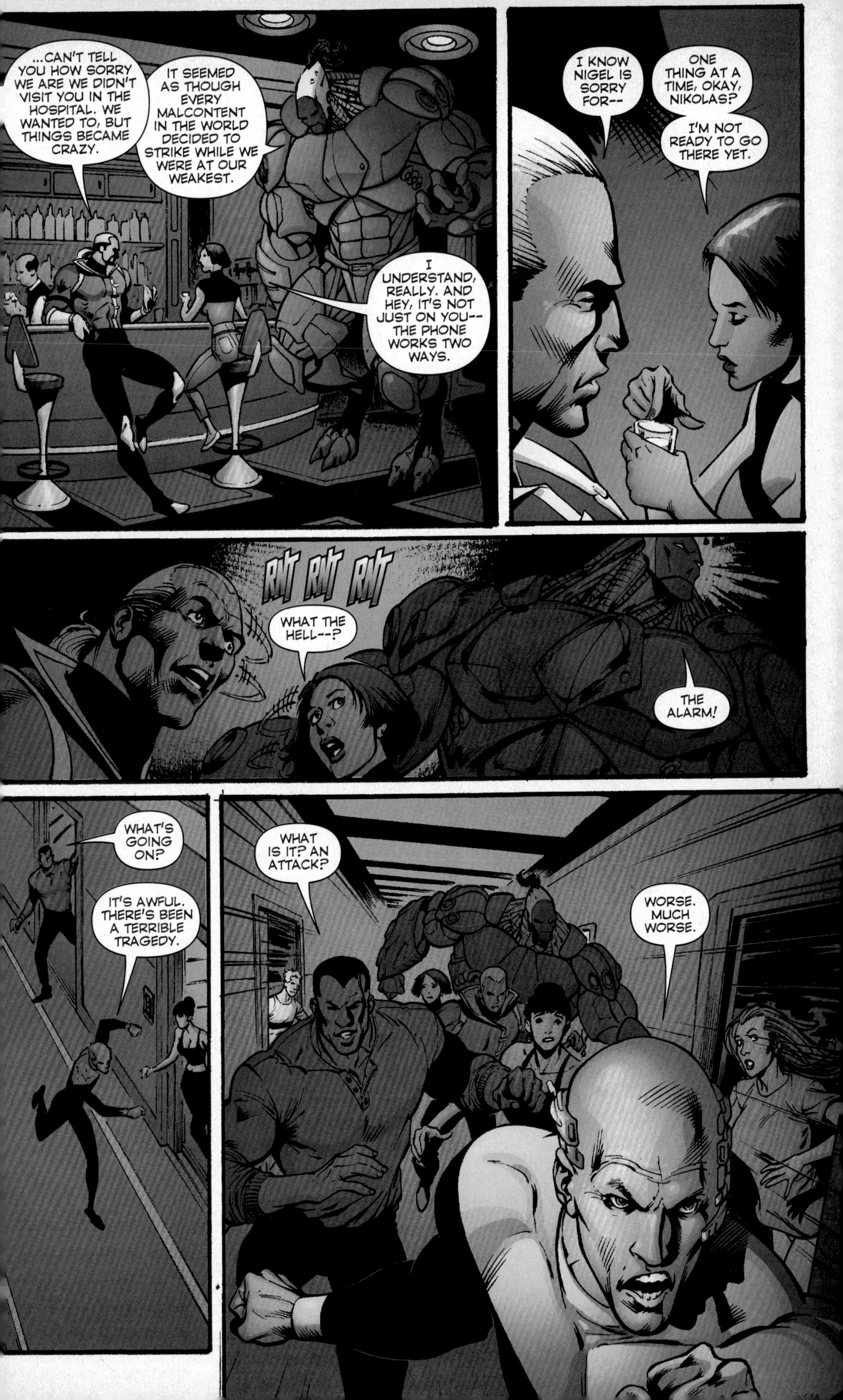
...CAN'T TELL YOU HOW SORRY WE ARE WE DIDN'T VISIT YOU IN THE HOSPITAL. WE WANTED TO, BUT THINGS BECAME CRAZY.
IT SEEMED AS THOUGH EVERY MALCONTENT IN THE WORLD DECIDED TO STRIKE WHILE WE WERE AT OUR WEAKEST.
I UNDERSTAND, REALLY. AND HEY, IT'S NOT JUST ON YOU-- THE PHONE WORKS TWO WAYS.
I KNOW NIGEL IS SORRY FOR--
ONE THING AT A TIME, OKAY, NIKOLAS?
I'M NOT READY TO GO THERE YET.
RNT RNT RNT
WHAT THE HELL--?
THE ALARM!
WHAT'S GOING ON?
IT'S AWFUL. THERE'S BEEN A TERRIBLE TRAGEDY.
WHAT IS IT? AN ATTACK?
WORSE. MUCH WORSE.

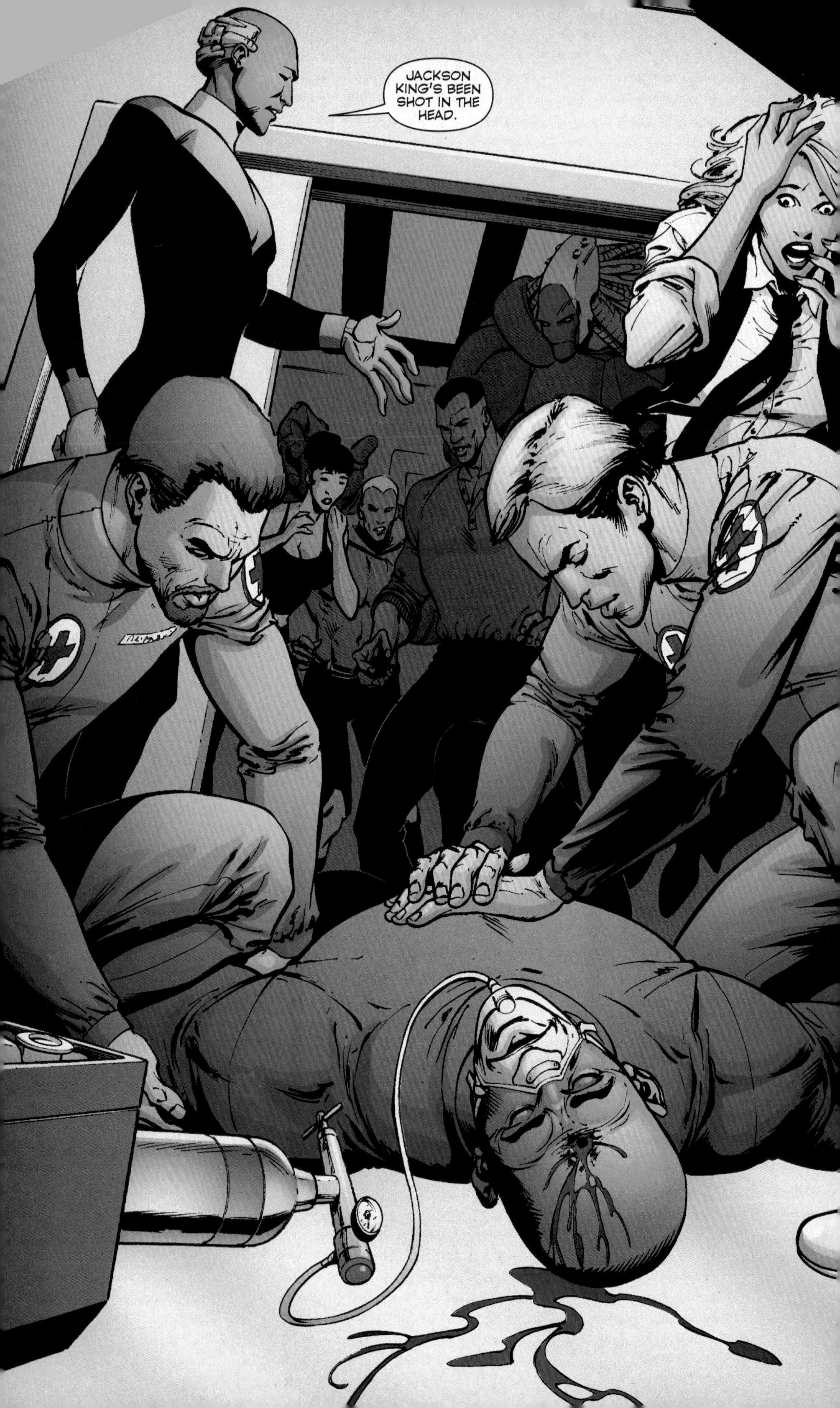
JACKSON KING'S BEEN SHOT IN THE HEAD.

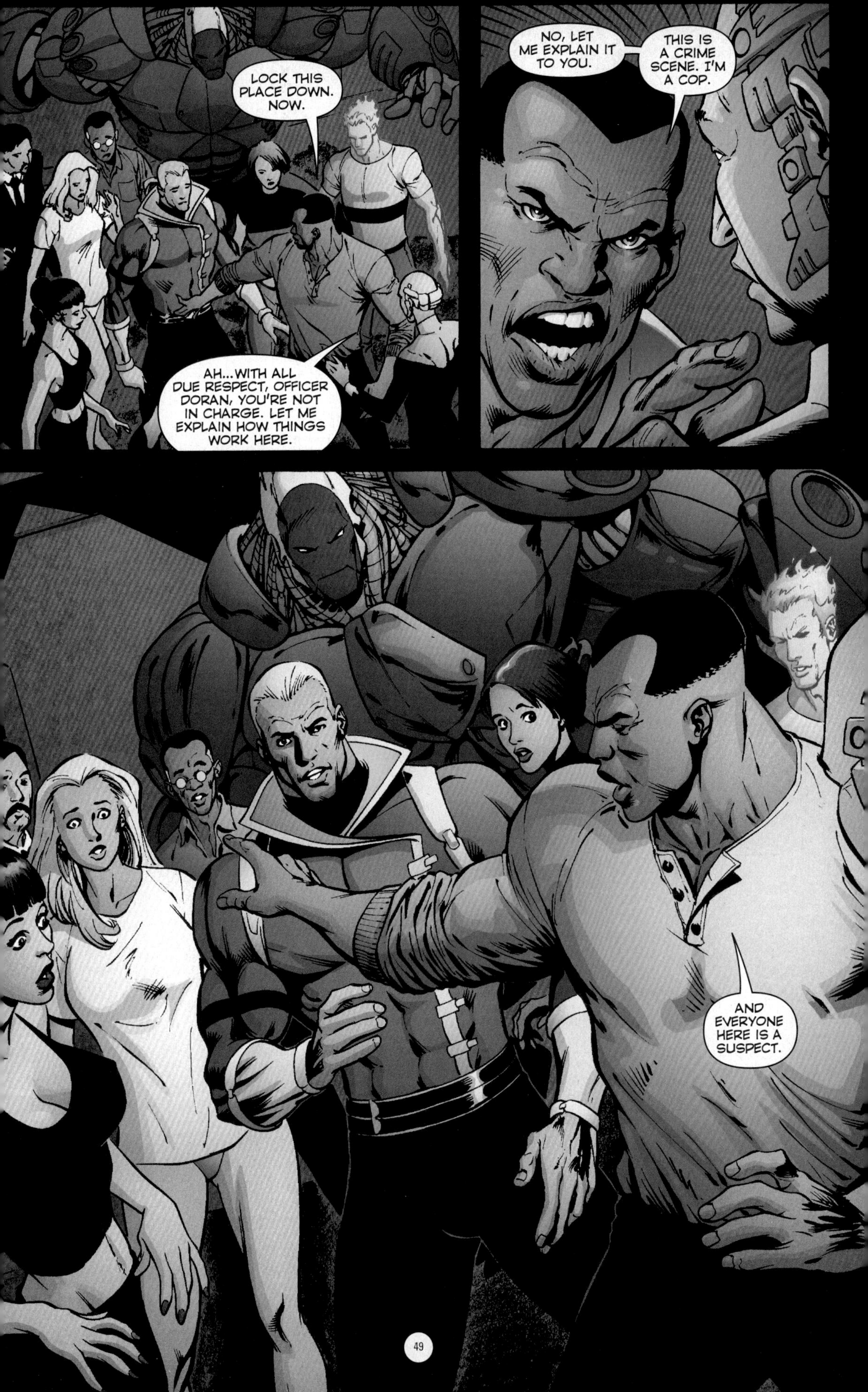
LOCK THIS PLACE DOWN. NOW.
AH...WITH ALL DUE RESPECT, OFFICER DORAN, YOU'RE NOT IN CHARGE. LET ME EXPLAIN HOW THINGS WORK HERE.
NO, LET ME EXPLAIN IT TO YOU.
THIS IS A CRIME SCENE. I'M A COP.
AND EVERYONE HERE IS A SUSPECT.

Chapter 3: Who Shot J.K.?

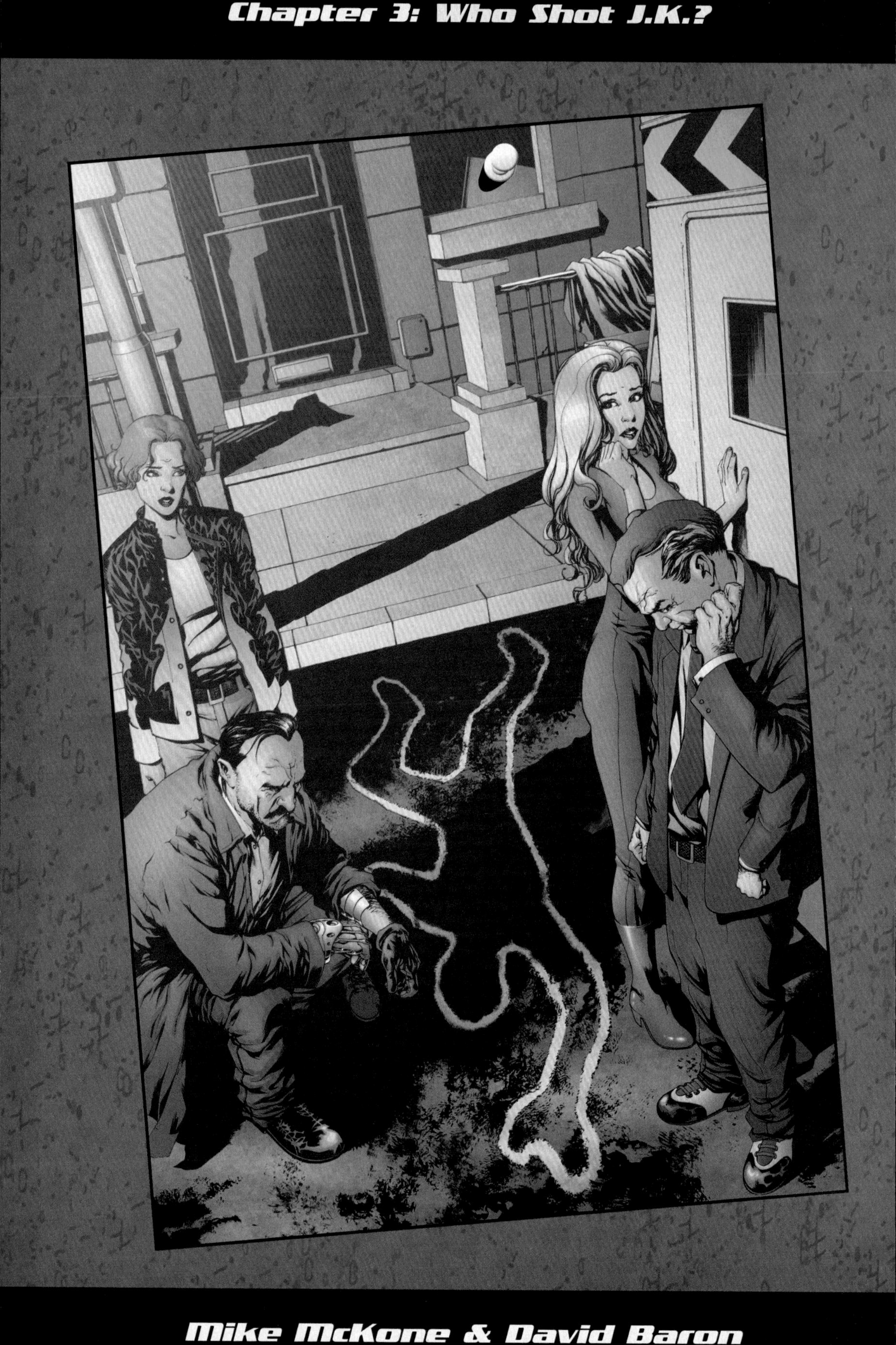

Mike McKone & David Baron

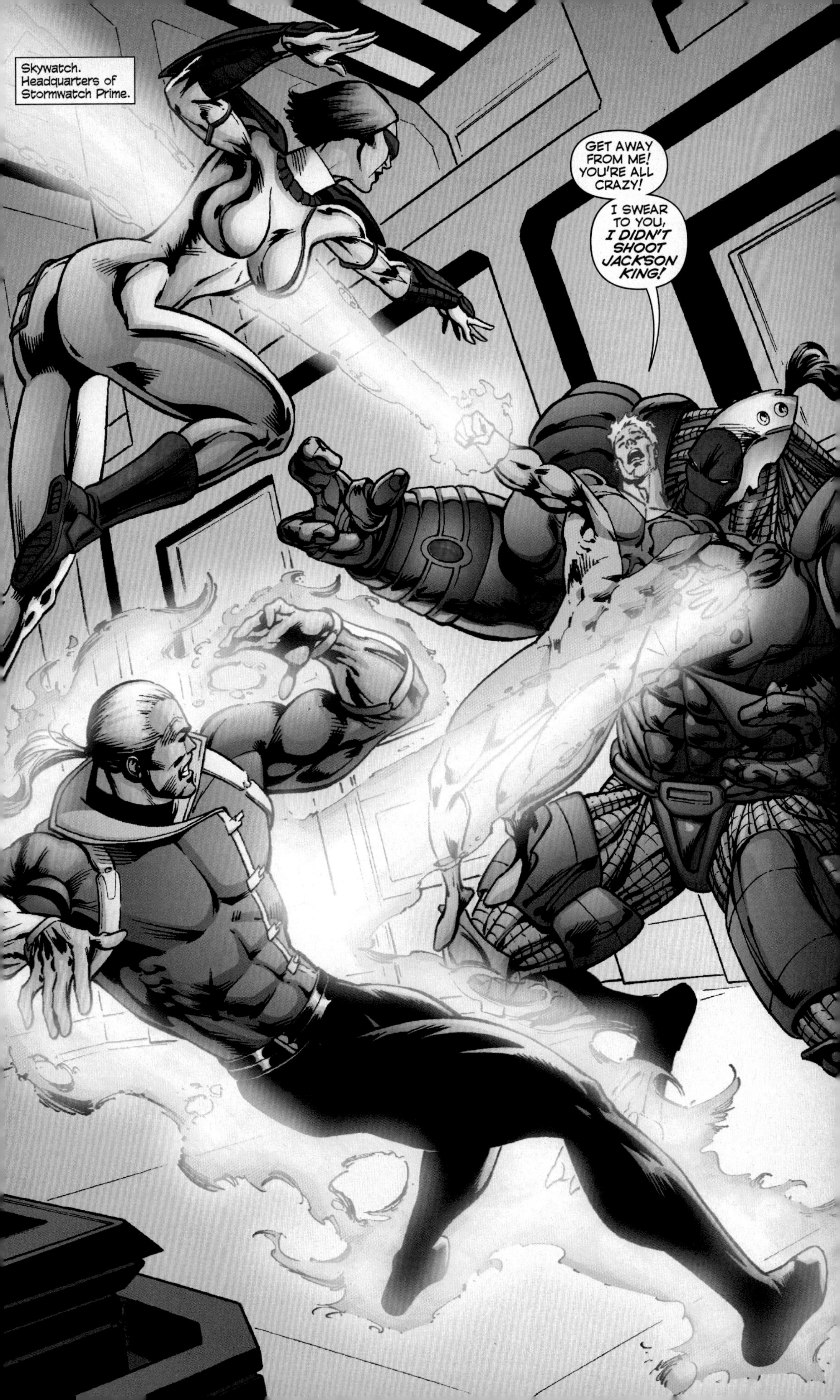
Skywatch. Headquarters of Stormwatch Prime.
GET AWAY FROM ME! YOU'RE ALL CRAZY!
I SWEAR TO YOU, I DIDN'T SHOOT JACKSON KING!

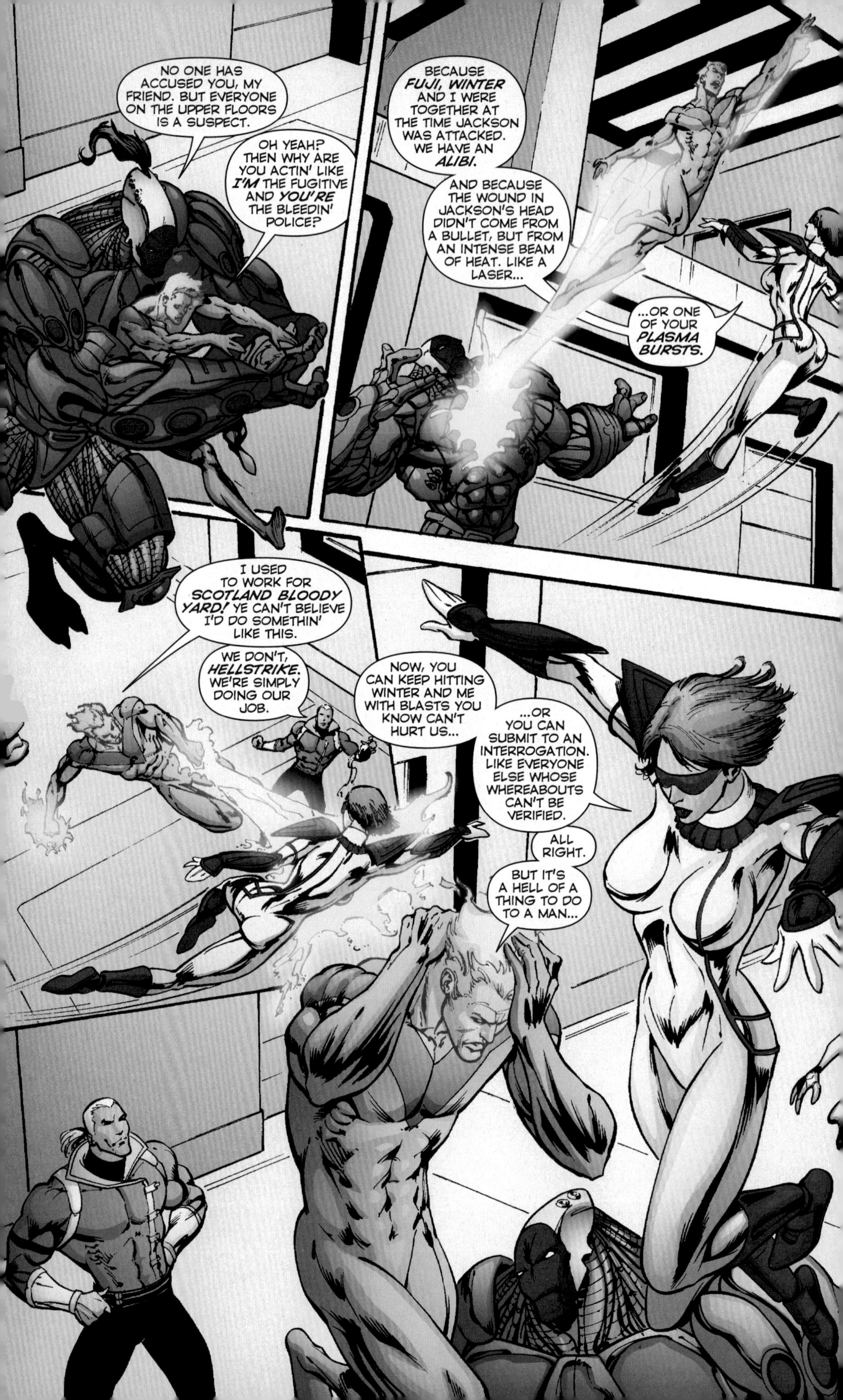

NO ONE HAS ACCUSED YOU, MY FRIEND. BUT EVERYONE ON THE UPPER FLOORS IS A SUSPECT.
OH YEAH? THEN WHY ARE YOU ACTIN' LIKE I'M THE FUGITIVE AND YOU'RE THE BLEEDIN' POLICE?
BECAUSE FUJI, WINTER AND I WERE TOGETHER AT THE TIME JACKSON WAS ATTACKED. WE HAVE AN ALIBI.
AND BECAUSE THE WOUND IN JACKSON'S HEAD DIDN'T COME FROM A BULLET, BUT FROM AN INTENSE BEAM OF HEAT. LIKE A LASER...
...OR ONE OF YOUR PLASMA BURSTS.
I USED TO WORK FOR SCOTLAND BLOODY YARD! YE CAN'T BELIEVE I'D DO SOMETHIN' LIKE THIS.
WE DON'T, HELLSTRIKE. WE'RE SIMPLY DOING OUR JOB.
NOW, YOU CAN KEEP HITTING WINTER AND ME WITH BLASTS YOU KNOW CAN'T HURT US...
...OR YOU CAN SUBMIT TO AN INTERROGATION. LIKE EVERYONE ELSE WHOSE WHEREABOUTS CAN'T BE VERIFIED.
ALL RIGHT.
BUT IT'S A HELL OF A THING TO DO TO A MAN...

"...ACCUSIN' HIM OF TRYIN' TO KILL A *FRIEND*."

I'VE KNOWN HIM SO LONG, JOHN. AND I'VE NEVER SEEN HIM LIKE THIS.

SO *HELPLESS*.

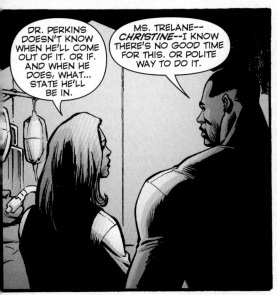

DR. PERKINS DOESN'T KNOW WHEN HE'LL COME OUT OF IT. OR IF. AND WHEN HE DOES, WHAT... STATE HE'LL BE IN.

MS. TRELANE-- *CHRISTINE*--I KNOW THERE'S NO GOOD TIME FOR THIS. OR POLITE WAY TO DO IT.

DON'T APOLOGIZE. I KNOW ENOUGH ABOUT POLICE PROCEDURE.

WHEN YOU'VE GOT A VICTIM, THE FIRST ONE YOU LOOK AT IS THE SPOUSE.

LET'S JUST GET IT OVER WITH SO I CAN COME BACK TO HIM, OKAY?

Skywatch conference room.

OKAY, PEOPLE, WE'VE GOT AN INVESTIGATION TO CONDUCT. GIVEN THAT THE TOP FIVE FLOORS OF THIS SKYSCRAPER ARE RESTRICTED TO *STORMWATCH PRIME* PERSONNEL...

...WE CAN RULE OUT MOST SUPPORT AND CLERICAL STAFF. THAT LEAVES THE MEMBERS OF STORMWATCH PRIME, THE FEW STAFFERS WITH ACCESS TO THE UPPER LEVELS...

...AND *US*.

53

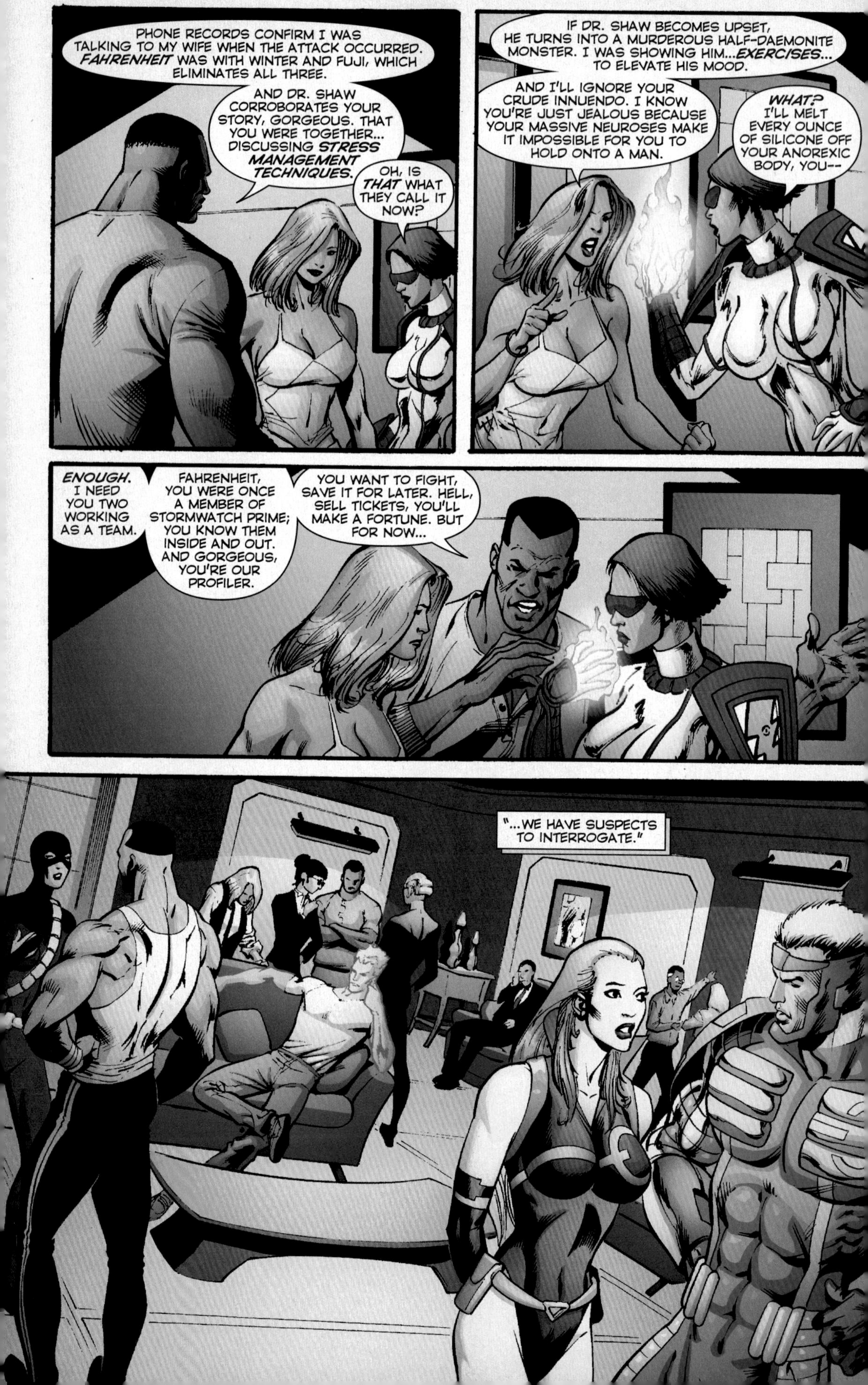
PHONE RECORDS CONFIRM I WAS TALKING TO MY WIFE WHEN THE ATTACK OCCURRED. FAHRENHEIT WAS WITH WINTER AND FUJI, WHICH ELIMINATES ALL THREE.
AND DR. SHAW CORROBORATES YOUR STORY, GORGEOUS. THAT YOU WERE TOGETHER... DISCUSSING STRESS MANAGEMENT TECHNIQUES.
OH, IS THAT WHAT THEY CALL IT NOW?
IF DR. SHAW BECOMES UPSET, HE TURNS INTO A MURDEROUS HALF-DAEMONITE MONSTER. I WAS SHOWING HIM...EXERCISES... TO ELEVATE HIS MOOD.
AND I'LL IGNORE YOUR CRUDE INNUENDO. I KNOW YOU'RE JUST JEALOUS BECAUSE YOUR MASSIVE NEUROSES MAKE IT IMPOSSIBLE FOR YOU TO HOLD ONTO A MAN.
WHAT? I'LL MELT EVERY OUNCE OF SILICONE OFF YOUR ANOREXIC BODY, YOU--
ENOUGH. I NEED YOU TWO WORKING AS A TEAM.
FAHRENHEIT, YOU WERE ONCE A MEMBER OF STORMWATCH PRIME; YOU KNOW THEM INSIDE AND OUT. AND GORGEOUS, YOU'RE OUR PROFILER.
YOU WANT TO FIGHT, SAVE IT FOR LATER. HELL, SELL TICKETS, YOU'LL MAKE A FORTUNE. BUT FOR NOW...
"...WE HAVE SUSPECTS TO INTERROGATE."

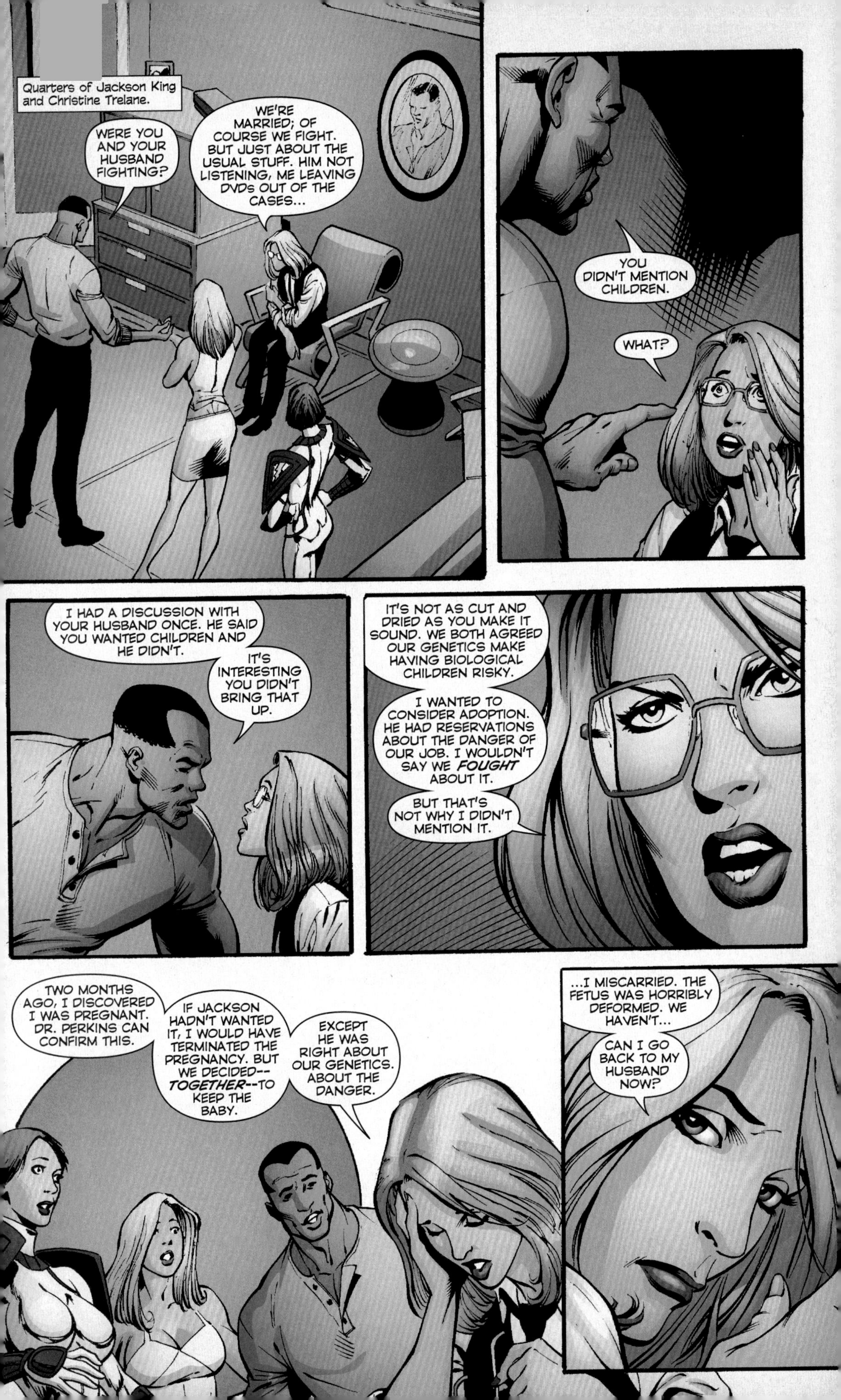

Quarters of Jackson King and Christine Trelane.
WERE YOU AND YOUR HUSBAND FIGHTING?
WE'RE MARRIED; OF COURSE WE FIGHT. BUT JUST ABOUT THE USUAL STUFF. HIM NOT LISTENING, ME LEAVING DVDs OUT OF THE CASES...
YOU DIDN'T MENTION CHILDREN.
WHAT?
I HAD A DISCUSSION WITH YOUR HUSBAND ONCE. HE SAID YOU WANTED CHILDREN AND HE DIDN'T.
IT'S INTERESTING YOU DIDN'T BRING THAT UP.
IT'S NOT AS CUT AND DRIED AS YOU MAKE IT SOUND. WE BOTH AGREED OUR GENETICS MAKE HAVING BIOLOGICAL CHILDREN RISKY.
I WANTED TO CONSIDER ADOPTION. HE HAD RESERVATIONS ABOUT THE DANGER OF OUR JOB. I WOULDN'T SAY WE *FOUGHT* ABOUT IT.
BUT THAT'S NOT WHY I DIDN'T MENTION IT.
TWO MONTHS AGO, I DISCOVERED I WAS PREGNANT. DR. PERKINS CAN CONFIRM THIS.
IF JACKSON HADN'T WANTED IT, I WOULD HAVE TERMINATED THE PREGNANCY. BUT WE DECIDED-- *TOGETHER*--TO KEEP THE BABY.
EXCEPT HE WAS RIGHT ABOUT OUR GENETICS. ABOUT THE DANGER.
...I MISCARRIED. THE FETUS WAS HORRIBLY DEFORMED. WE HAVEN'T...
CAN I GO BACK TO MY HUSBAND NOW?

WHAT'S YOUR TAKE ON CHRISTINE?

SHE'S GENUINELY GRIEVING FOR HIM. AND SHE SPOKE OF HIM IN THE PRESENT TENSE, MEANING SHE DOESN'T ALREADY THINK OF HIM AS GONE.

THE WAY SOMEONE WHO'D BEEN PLANNING TO KILL HIM WOULD. OKAY...BUT TO GET SO CLOSE, THE ATTACKER WOULD HAVE HAD TO BE SOMEONE JACKSON TRUSTED. SOMEONE LIKE--

WE KEEP COMING BACK TO ONE QUESTION, ELLEN: HOW DO YOU SNEAK UP ON SOMEONE WHO CAN READ MINDS?

DIRECTOR KING RESPECTED PEOPLE'S PRIVACY. HE DIDN'T INVADE THEIR THOUGHTS WITHOUT GOOD REASON.

EXCEPT I KNOW HE'D TRAINED HIMSELF TO BE ALERT TO HOSTILE INTENTIONS. A MENTAL EARLY WARNING SYSTEM, IF YOU WILL.

BUT IF THE THREAT CAME FROM HIS *PERSONAL ASSISTANT*, HE MIGHT QUESTION HIS SENSES LONG ENOUGH TO BE SHOT.

I HAVE NO REASON TO HURT HIM!

ON THE SURFACE, NO. BUT THE MAN HAS ENEMIES WITH TREMENDOUS POWER. THEY COULD BE BRIBING YOU, OR CONTROLLING YOU.

ORDINARILY, WE'D HAVE JACKSON PROBE YOUR MIND TO FIND OUT. BUT HE'S INCAPACITATED, SO WE'LL HAVE TO HAVE *MALCOLM* DO IT.

MR. KING'S *BROTHER?* HE DOESN'T HAVE THOSE KINDS OF MENTAL POWERS.

SURE HE DOES. THEY'RE JUST VERY RAW. YOU COULD END UP BRAIN DAMAGED, AMNESIAC, EVEN A *VEGETABLE.*

BUT THIS IS A NATIONAL SECURITY ISSUE, SO...

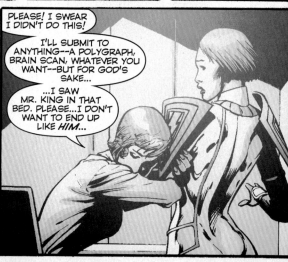

PLEASE! I SWEAR I DIDN'T DO THIS!

I'LL SUBMIT TO ANYTHING--A POLYGRAPH, BRAIN SCAN, WHATEVER YOU WANT--BUT FOR GOD'S SAKE...

...I SAW MR. KING IN THAT BED. PLEASE...I DON'T WANT TO END UP LIKE *HIM*...

SHE'S TELLING THE TRUTH. SHE HAS NO IDEA WE WERE BLUFFING ABOUT MALCOLM.

I CONCUR. AND SPEAKING OF THE PRODIGAL BROTHER...

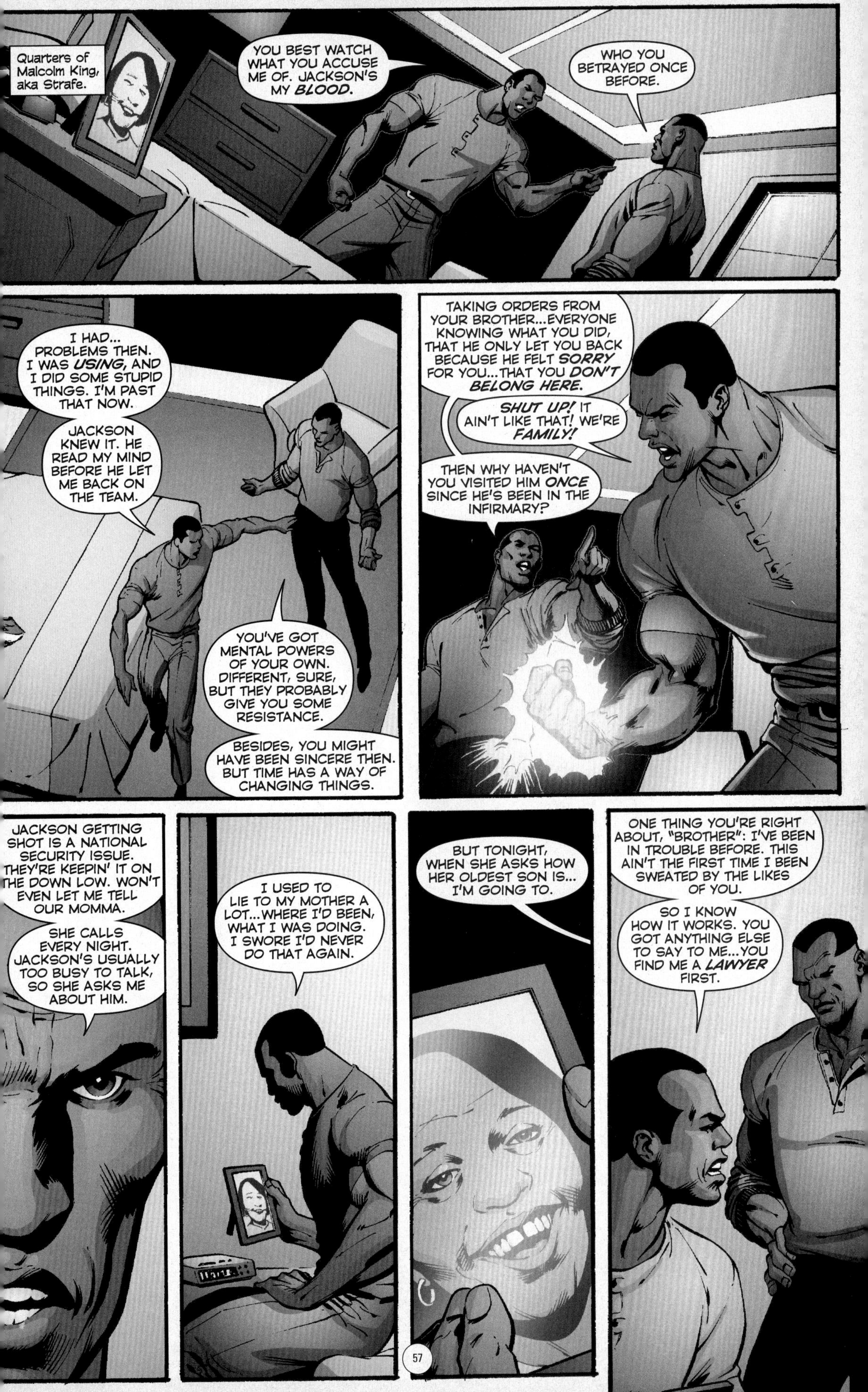
Quarters of Malcolm King, aka Strafe.
YOU BEST WATCH WHAT YOU ACCUSE ME OF. JACKSON'S MY *BLOOD.*
WHO YOU BETRAYED ONCE BEFORE.
I HAD... PROBLEMS THEN. I WAS *USING,* AND I DID SOME STUPID THINGS. I'M PAST THAT NOW.
JACKSON KNEW IT. HE READ MY MIND BEFORE HE LET ME BACK ON THE TEAM.
YOU'VE GOT MENTAL POWERS OF YOUR OWN. DIFFERENT, SURE, BUT THEY PROBABLY GIVE YOU SOME RESISTANCE.
BESIDES, YOU MIGHT HAVE BEEN SINCERE THEN. BUT TIME HAS A WAY OF CHANGING THINGS.
TAKING ORDERS FROM YOUR BROTHER...EVERYONE KNOWING WHAT YOU DID, THAT HE ONLY LET YOU BACK BECAUSE HE FELT *SORRY* FOR YOU...THAT YOU *DON'T BELONG HERE.*
SHUT UP! IT AIN'T LIKE THAT! WE'RE *FAMILY!*
THEN WHY HAVEN'T YOU VISITED HIM *ONCE* SINCE HE'S BEEN IN THE INFIRMARY?
JACKSON GETTING SHOT IS A NATIONAL SECURITY ISSUE. THEY'RE KEEPIN' IT ON THE DOWN LOW. WON'T EVEN LET ME TELL OUR MOMMA.
SHE CALLS EVERY NIGHT. JACKSON'S USUALLY TOO BUSY TO TALK, SO SHE ASKS ME ABOUT HIM.
I USED TO LIE TO MY MOTHER A LOT...WHERE I'D BEEN, WHAT I WAS DOING. I SWORE I'D NEVER DO THAT AGAIN.
BUT TONIGHT, WHEN SHE ASKS HOW HER OLDEST SON IS... I'M GOING TO.
ONE THING YOU'RE RIGHT ABOUT, "BROTHER": I'VE BEEN IN TROUBLE BEFORE. THIS AIN'T THE FIRST TIME I BEEN SWEATED BY THE LIKES OF YOU.
SO I KNOW HOW IT WORKS. YOU GOT ANYTHING ELSE TO SAY TO ME...YOU FIND ME A *LAWYER* FIRST.

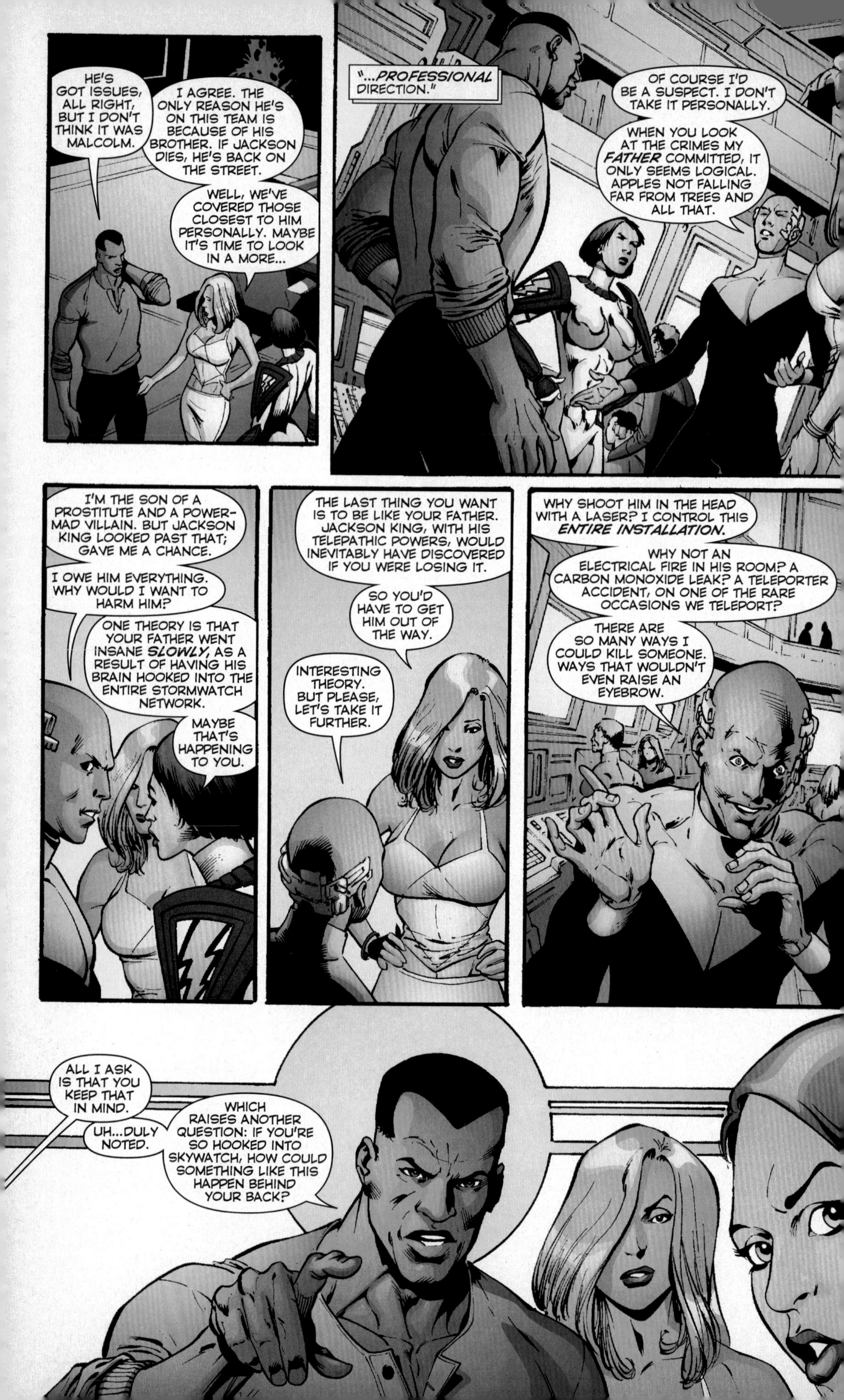
HE'S GOT ISSUES, ALL RIGHT, BUT I DON'T THINK IT WAS MALCOLM.
I AGREE. THE ONLY REASON HE'S ON THIS TEAM IS BECAUSE OF HIS BROTHER. IF JACKSON DIES, HE'S BACK ON THE STREET.
WELL, WE'VE COVERED THOSE CLOSEST TO HIM PERSONALLY. MAYBE IT'S TIME TO LOOK IN A MORE...
"...PROFESSIONAL DIRECTION."
OF COURSE I'D BE A SUSPECT. I DON'T TAKE IT PERSONALLY.
WHEN YOU LOOK AT THE CRIMES MY FATHER COMMITTED, IT ONLY SEEMS LOGICAL. APPLES NOT FALLING FAR FROM TREES AND ALL THAT.
I'M THE SON OF A PROSTITUTE AND A POWER-MAD VILLAIN. BUT JACKSON KING LOOKED PAST THAT; GAVE ME A CHANCE.
I OWE HIM EVERYTHING. WHY WOULD I WANT TO HARM HIM?
ONE THEORY IS THAT YOUR FATHER WENT INSANE SLOWLY, AS A RESULT OF HAVING HIS BRAIN HOOKED INTO THE ENTIRE STORMWATCH NETWORK.
MAYBE THAT'S HAPPENING TO YOU.
THE LAST THING YOU WANT IS TO BE LIKE YOUR FATHER. JACKSON KING, WITH HIS TELEPATHIC POWERS, WOULD INEVITABLY HAVE DISCOVERED IF YOU WERE LOSING IT.
SO YOU'D HAVE TO GET HIM OUT OF THE WAY.
INTERESTING THEORY. BUT PLEASE, LET'S TAKE IT FURTHER.
WHY SHOOT HIM IN THE HEAD WITH A LASER? I CONTROL THIS ENTIRE INSTALLATION.
WHY NOT AN ELECTRICAL FIRE IN HIS ROOM? A CARBON MONOXIDE LEAK? A TELEPORTER ACCIDENT, ON ONE OF THE RARE OCCASIONS WE TELEPORT?
THERE ARE SO MANY WAYS I COULD KILL SOMEONE. WAYS THAT WOULDN'T EVEN RAISE AN EYEBROW.
ALL I ASK IS THAT YOU KEEP THAT IN MIND.
UH...DULY NOTED.
WHICH RAISES ANOTHER QUESTION: IF YOU'RE SO HOOKED INTO SKYWATCH, HOW COULD SOMETHING LIKE THIS HAPPEN BEHIND YOUR BACK?

I'M NOT OMNISCIENT. THAT WAY LIES MADNESS, AS MY FATHER PROVED.

OUR SECURITY SYSTEMS ARE AUTOMATED. UPPER FLOORS ARE FOR THE HIGHEST LEVEL PERSONNEL, SO WE TAKE PRIVACY INTO ACCOUNT--NO CAMERAS IN THE ROOMS.

WE HAD A MONITORING PROGRAM BASED ON BIO-SIGNATURES, BUT THAT WAS RECENTLY COMPROMISED BY AN INTRUDER, SO WE'RE RE-TOOLING THE ENTIRE NETWORK.

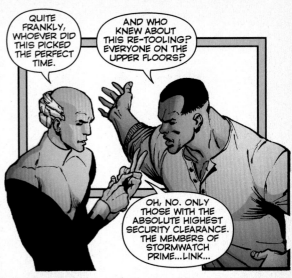

QUITE FRANKLY, WHOEVER DID THIS PICKED THE PERFECT TIME.

AND WHO KNEW ABOUT THIS RE-TOOLING? EVERYONE ON THE UPPER FLOORS?

OH, NO. ONLY THOSE WITH THE ABSOLUTE HIGHEST SECURITY CLEARANCE. THE MEMBERS OF STORMWATCH PRIME...LINK...

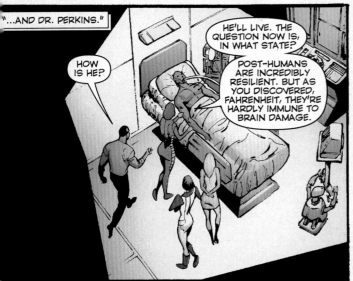

"...AND DR. PERKINS."

HOW IS HE?

HE'LL LIVE. THE QUESTION NOW IS, IN WHAT STATE?

POST-HUMANS ARE INCREDIBLY RESILIENT. BUT AS YOU DISCOVERED, FAHRENHEIT, THEY'RE HARDLY IMMUNE TO BRAIN DAMAGE.

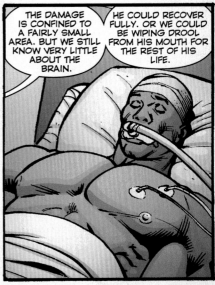

THE DAMAGE IS CONFINED TO A FAIRLY SMALL AREA. BUT WE STILL KNOW VERY LITTLE ABOUT THE BRAIN.

HE COULD RECOVER FULLY. OR WE COULD BE WIPING DROOL FROM HIS MOUTH FOR THE REST OF HIS LIFE.

I...EXCUSE ME. I CAN'T... EXCUSE ME.

I'LL BE FRANK, DR. PERKINS. YOU HAVE NO MOTIVE TO HURT JACKSON KING. WHAT YOU DO HAVE IS ACCESS TO *LASER CAUTERIZERS* THAT WOULD CAUSE A WOUND LIKE HIS.

IN A FACILITY LIKE THIS, LASER PROJECTORS ARE A DIME A DOZEN. THE MAINTENANCE CREW HAS THEM, FOR HEAVEN'S SAKE. GETTING ONE WOULD BE EASY.

WHAT WOULD BE HARD IS GETTING ONTO THE UPPER FLOORS. MOST SUPPORT STAFF IS MADE UP OF ROBOTS. ONLY A FEW PEOPLE HAVE ACCESS.

AND YOU'RE ONE OF THE FEW.

JACKSON AND I SURVIVED THE ALIEN ATTACK THAT DESTROYED THE PREVIOUS SKYWATCH. SO MANY DEAD...IT FELT LIKE *OUR FAULT* STORMWATCH DISBANDED.

SEEING IT REBUILT WAS A DREAM COME TRUE. WITHOUT JACKSON, THAT DREAM COULD DIE. I CAN'T IMAGINE ANYONE WHO WAS WITH THE TEAM BACK THEN DOING THIS.

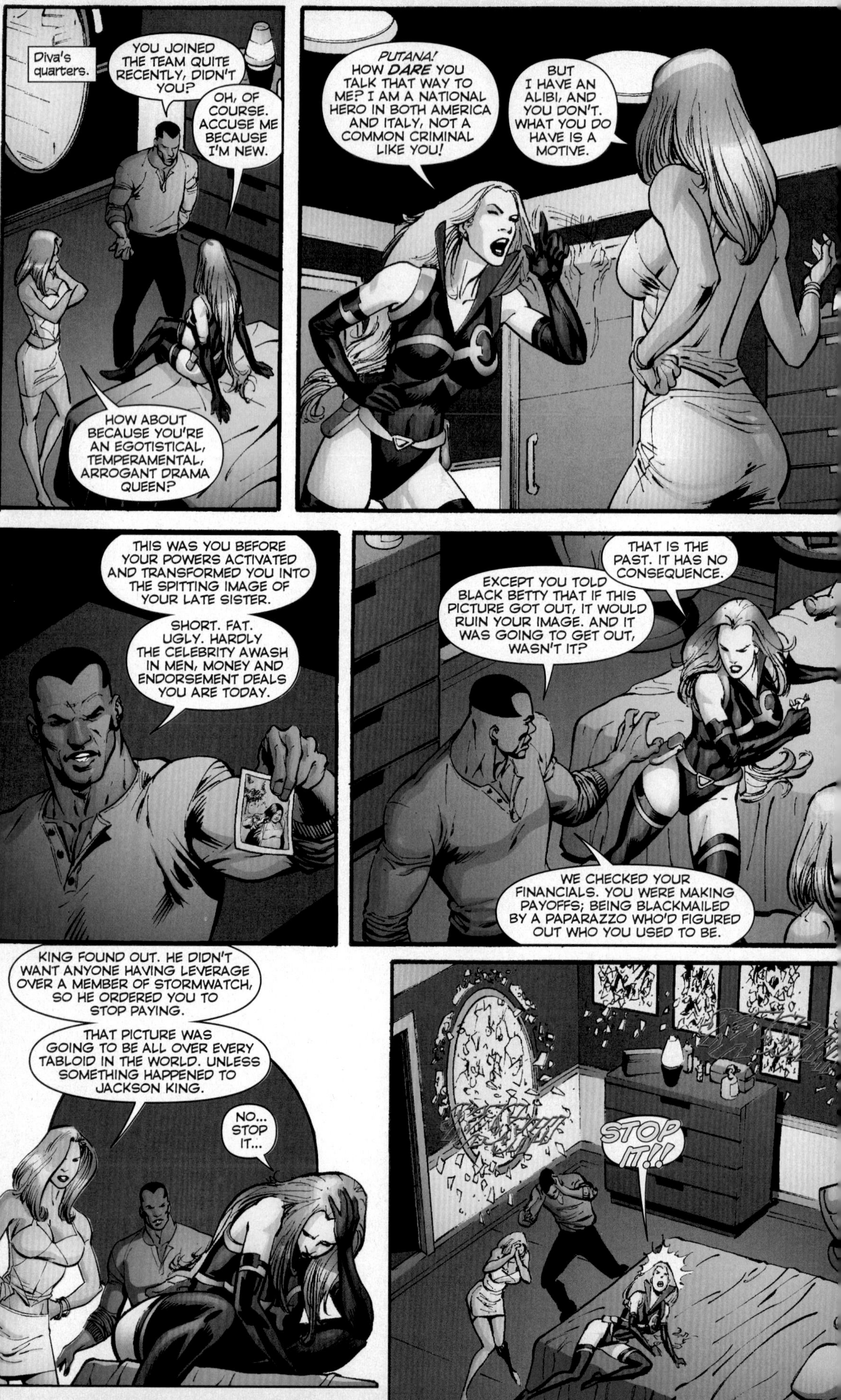
Diva's quarters.
YOU JOINED THE TEAM QUITE RECENTLY, DIDN'T YOU?
OH, OF COURSE. ACCUSE ME BECAUSE I'M NEW.
HOW ABOUT BECAUSE YOU'RE AN EGOTISTICAL, TEMPERAMENTAL, ARROGANT DRAMA QUEEN?
PUTANA! HOW DARE YOU TALK THAT WAY TO ME? I AM A NATIONAL HERO IN BOTH AMERICA AND ITALY, NOT A COMMON CRIMINAL LIKE YOU!
BUT I HAVE AN ALIBI, AND YOU DON'T. WHAT YOU DO HAVE IS A MOTIVE.
THIS WAS YOU BEFORE YOUR POWERS ACTIVATED AND TRANSFORMED YOU INTO THE SPITTING IMAGE OF YOUR LATE SISTER.
SHORT. FAT. UGLY. HARDLY THE CELEBRITY AWASH IN MEN, MONEY AND ENDORSEMENT DEALS YOU ARE TODAY.
THAT IS THE PAST. IT HAS NO CONSEQUENCE.
EXCEPT YOU TOLD BLACK BETTY THAT IF THIS PICTURE GOT OUT, IT WOULD RUIN YOUR IMAGE. AND IT WAS GOING TO GET OUT, WASN'T IT?
WE CHECKED YOUR FINANCIALS. YOU WERE MAKING PAYOFFS; BEING BLACKMAILED BY A PAPARAZZO WHO'D FIGURED OUT WHO YOU USED TO BE.
KING FOUND OUT. HE DIDN'T WANT ANYONE HAVING LEVERAGE OVER A MEMBER OF STORMWATCH, SO HE ORDERED YOU TO STOP PAYING.
THAT PICTURE WAS GOING TO BE ALL OVER EVERY TABLOID IN THE WORLD. UNLESS SOMETHING HAPPENED TO JACKSON KING.
NO... STOP IT...
STOP IT!!

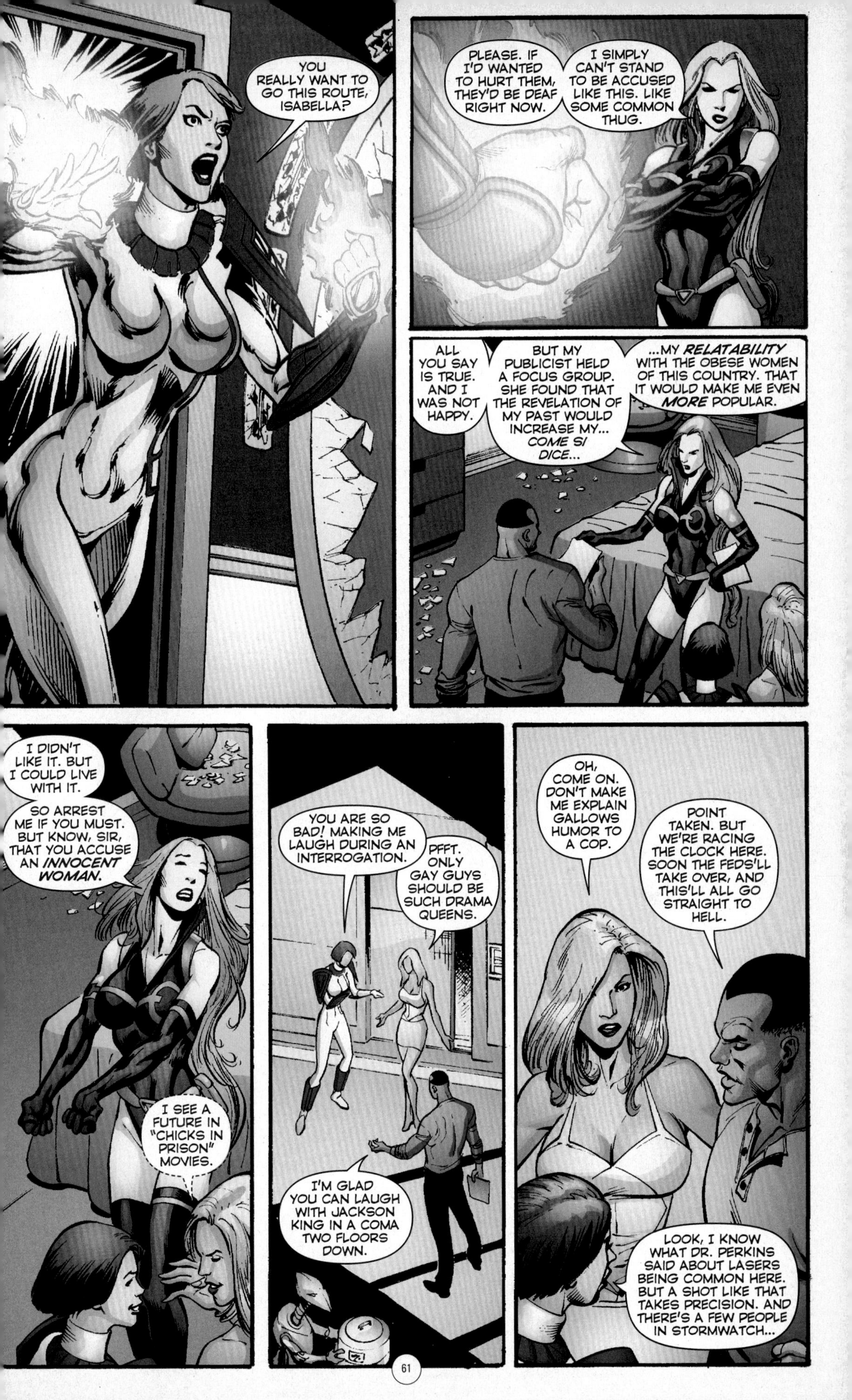
YOU REALLY WANT TO GO THIS ROUTE, ISABELLA?
PLEASE. IF I'D WANTED TO HURT THEM, THEY'D BE DEAF RIGHT NOW.
I SIMPLY CAN'T STAND TO BE ACCUSED LIKE THIS. LIKE SOME COMMON THUG.
ALL YOU SAY IS TRUE. AND I WAS NOT HAPPY.
BUT MY PUBLICIST HELD A FOCUS GROUP. SHE FOUND THAT THE REVELATION OF MY PAST WOULD INCREASE MY... *COME SI DICE...*
...MY ***RELATABILITY*** WITH THE OBESE WOMEN OF THIS COUNTRY. THAT IT WOULD MAKE ME EVEN ***MORE*** POPULAR.
I DIDN'T LIKE IT. BUT I COULD LIVE WITH IT.
SO ARREST ME IF YOU MUST. BUT KNOW, SIR, THAT YOU ACCUSE AN ***INNOCENT WOMAN.***
I SEE A FUTURE IN "CHICKS IN PRISON" MOVIES.
YOU ARE SO BAD! MAKING ME LAUGH DURING AN INTERROGATION.
PFFT. ONLY GAY GUYS SHOULD BE SUCH DRAMA QUEENS.
I'M GLAD YOU CAN LAUGH WITH JACKSON KING IN A COMA TWO FLOORS DOWN.
OH, COME ON. DON'T MAKE ME EXPLAIN GALLOWS HUMOR TO A COP.
POINT TAKEN. BUT WE'RE RACING THE CLOCK HERE. SOON THE FEDS'LL TAKE OVER, AND THIS'LL ALL GO STRAIGHT TO HELL.
LOOK, I KNOW WHAT DR. PERKINS SAID ABOUT LASERS BEING COMMON HERE. BUT A SHOT LIKE THAT TAKES PRECISION. AND THERE'S A FEW PEOPLE IN STORMWATCH...

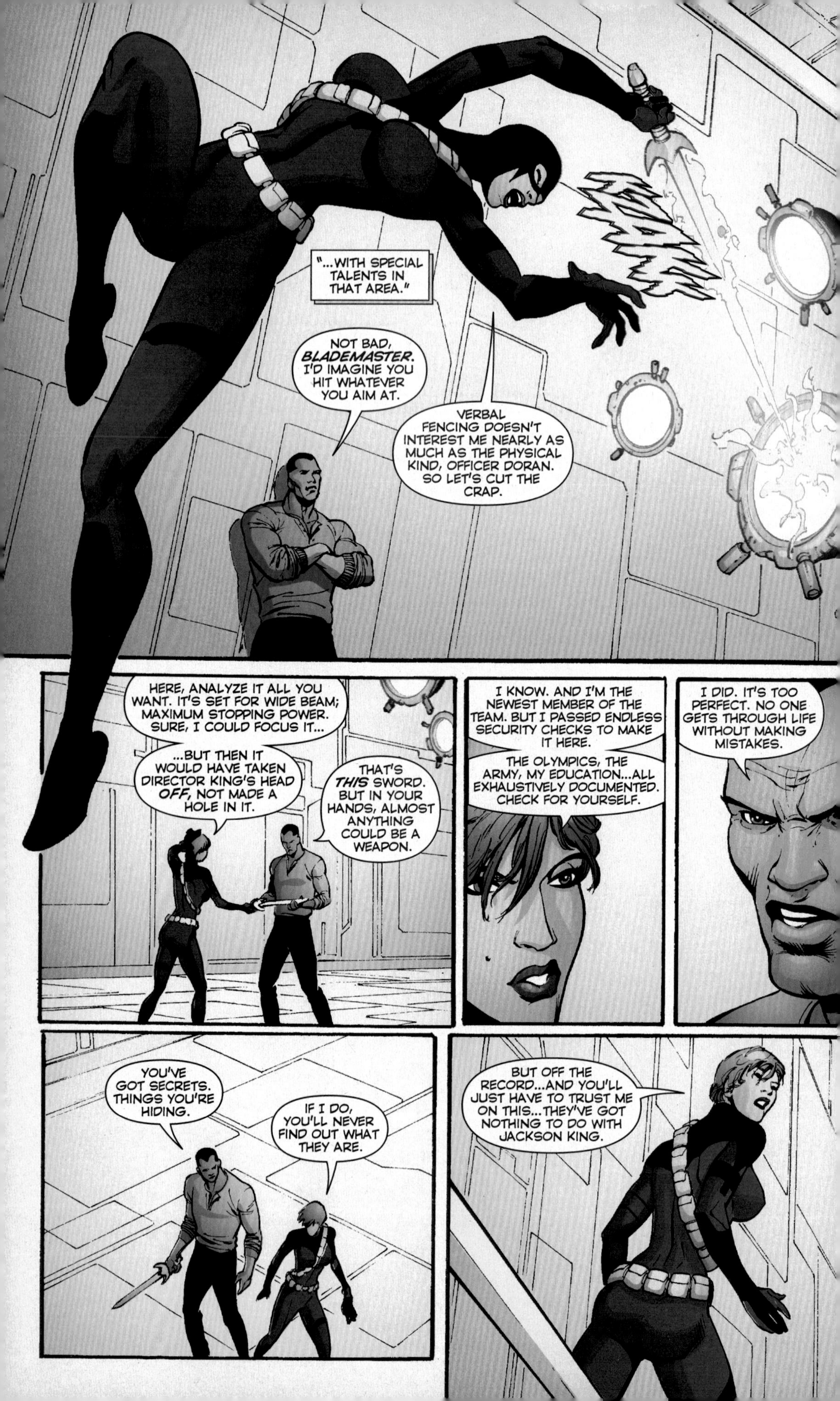

"...WITH SPECIAL TALENTS IN THAT AREA."
NOT BAD, BLADEMASTER. I'D IMAGINE YOU HIT WHATEVER YOU AIM AT.
VERBAL FENCING DOESN'T INTEREST ME NEARLY AS MUCH AS THE PHYSICAL KIND, OFFICER DORAN. SO LET'S CUT THE CRAP.
HERE, ANALYZE IT ALL YOU WANT. IT'S SET FOR WIDE BEAM; MAXIMUM STOPPING POWER. SURE, I COULD FOCUS IT...
...BUT THEN IT WOULD HAVE TAKEN DIRECTOR KING'S HEAD OFF, NOT MADE A HOLE IN IT.
THAT'S THIS SWORD. BUT IN YOUR HANDS, ALMOST ANYTHING COULD BE A WEAPON.
I KNOW. AND I'M THE NEWEST MEMBER OF THE TEAM. BUT I PASSED ENDLESS SECURITY CHECKS TO MAKE IT HERE.
THE OLYMPICS, THE ARMY, MY EDUCATION...ALL EXHAUSTIVELY DOCUMENTED. CHECK FOR YOURSELF.
I DID. IT'S TOO PERFECT. NO ONE GETS THROUGH LIFE WITHOUT MAKING MISTAKES.
YOU'VE GOT SECRETS. THINGS YOU'RE HIDING.
IF I DO, YOU'LL NEVER FIND OUT WHAT THEY ARE.
BUT OFF THE RECORD...AND YOU'LL JUST HAVE TO TRUST ME ON THIS...THEY'VE GOT NOTHING TO DO WITH JACKSON KING.

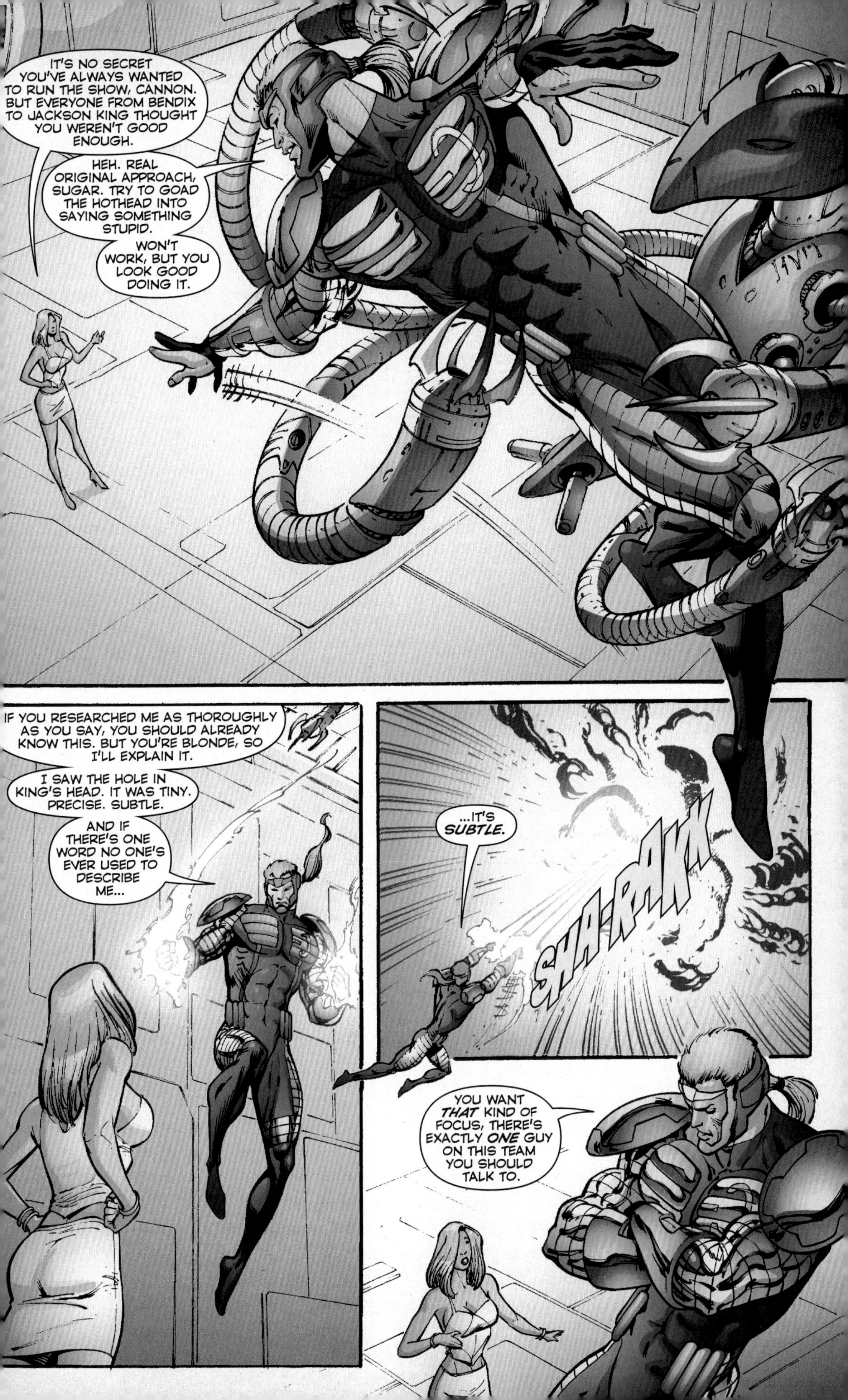

IT'S NO SECRET YOU'VE ALWAYS WANTED TO RUN THE SHOW, CANNON. BUT EVERYONE FROM BENDIX TO JACKSON KING THOUGHT YOU WEREN'T GOOD ENOUGH.
HEH. REAL ORIGINAL APPROACH, SUGAR. TRY TO GOAD THE HOTHEAD INTO SAYING SOMETHING STUPID.
WON'T WORK, BUT YOU LOOK GOOD DOING IT.
IF YOU RESEARCHED ME AS THOROUGHLY AS YOU SAY, YOU SHOULD ALREADY KNOW THIS. BUT YOU'RE BLONDE, SO I'LL EXPLAIN IT.
I SAW THE HOLE IN KING'S HEAD. IT WAS TINY. PRECISE. SUBTLE.
AND IF THERE'S ONE WORD NO ONE'S EVER USED TO DESCRIBE ME...
...IT'S *SUBTLE*.
SHA-RAKK
YOU WANT *THAT* KIND OF FOCUS, THERE'S EXACTLY *ONE* GUY ON THIS TEAM YOU SHOULD TALK TO.

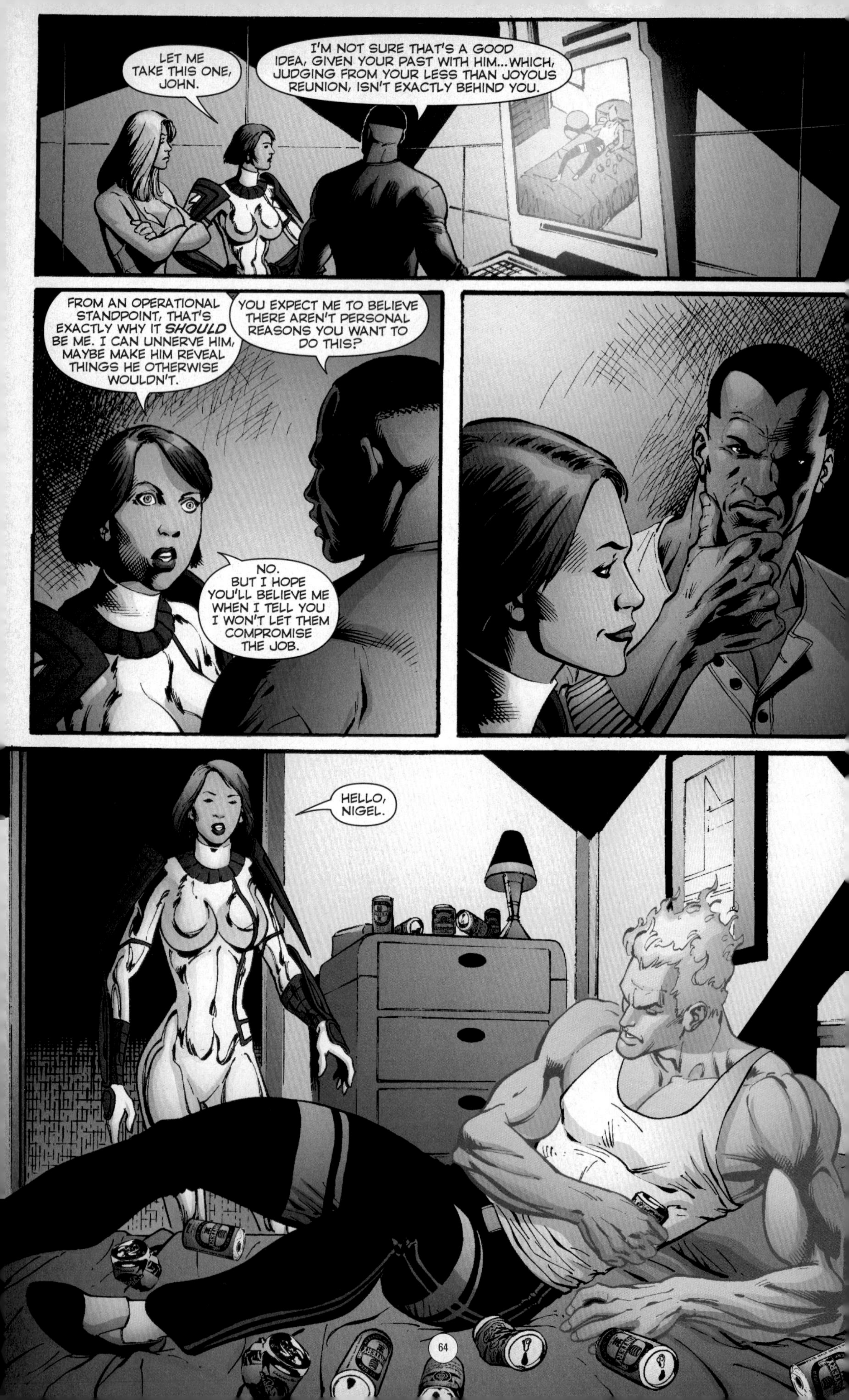
LET ME TAKE THIS ONE, JOHN.
I'M NOT SURE THAT'S A GOOD IDEA, GIVEN YOUR PAST WITH HIM...WHICH, JUDGING FROM YOUR LESS THAN JOYOUS REUNION, ISN'T EXACTLY BEHIND YOU.
FROM AN OPERATIONAL STANDPOINT, THAT'S EXACTLY WHY IT *SHOULD* BE ME. I CAN UNNERVE HIM, MAYBE MAKE HIM REVEAL THINGS HE OTHERWISE WOULDN'T.
YOU EXPECT ME TO BELIEVE THERE AREN'T PERSONAL REASONS YOU WANT TO DO THIS?
NO. BUT I HOPE YOU'LL BELIEVE ME WHEN I TELL YOU I WON'T LET THEM COMPROMISE THE JOB.
HELLO, NIGEL.

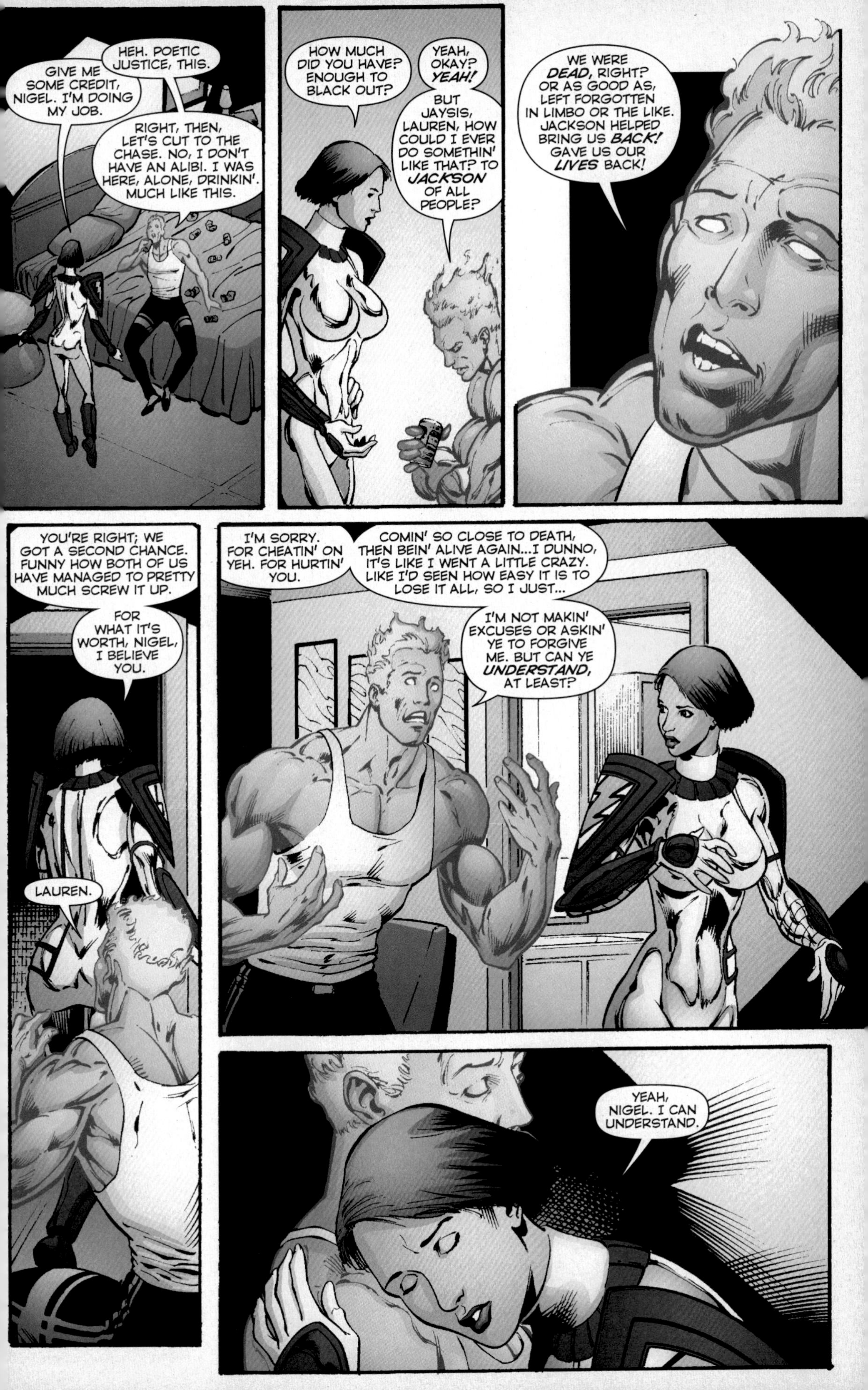

GIVE ME SOME CREDIT, NIGEL. I'M DOING MY JOB.
HEH. POETIC JUSTICE, THIS.
RIGHT, THEN, LET'S CUT TO THE CHASE. NO, I DON'T HAVE AN ALIBI. I WAS HERE, ALONE, DRINKIN'. MUCH LIKE THIS.
HOW MUCH DID YOU HAVE? ENOUGH TO BLACK OUT?
YEAH, OKAY? YEAH!
BUT JAYSIS, LAUREN, HOW COULD I EVER DO SOMETHIN' LIKE THAT? TO JACKSON OF ALL PEOPLE?
WE WERE DEAD, RIGHT? OR AS GOOD AS, LEFT FORGOTTEN IN LIMBO OR THE LIKE. JACKSON HELPED BRING US BACK! GAVE US OUR LIVES BACK!
YOU'RE RIGHT; WE GOT A SECOND CHANCE. FUNNY HOW BOTH OF US HAVE MANAGED TO PRETTY MUCH SCREW IT UP.
FOR WHAT IT'S WORTH, NIGEL, I BELIEVE YOU.
LAUREN.
I'M SORRY. FOR CHEATIN' ON YEH. FOR HURTIN' YOU.
COMIN' SO CLOSE TO DEATH, THEN BEIN' ALIVE AGAIN...I DUNNO, IT'S LIKE I WENT A LITTLE CRAZY. LIKE I'D SEEN HOW EASY IT IS TO LOSE IT ALL, SO I JUST...
I'M NOT MAKIN' EXCUSES OR ASKIN' YE TO FORGIVE ME. BUT CAN YE UNDERSTAND, AT LEAST?
YEAH, NIGEL. I CAN UNDERSTAND.

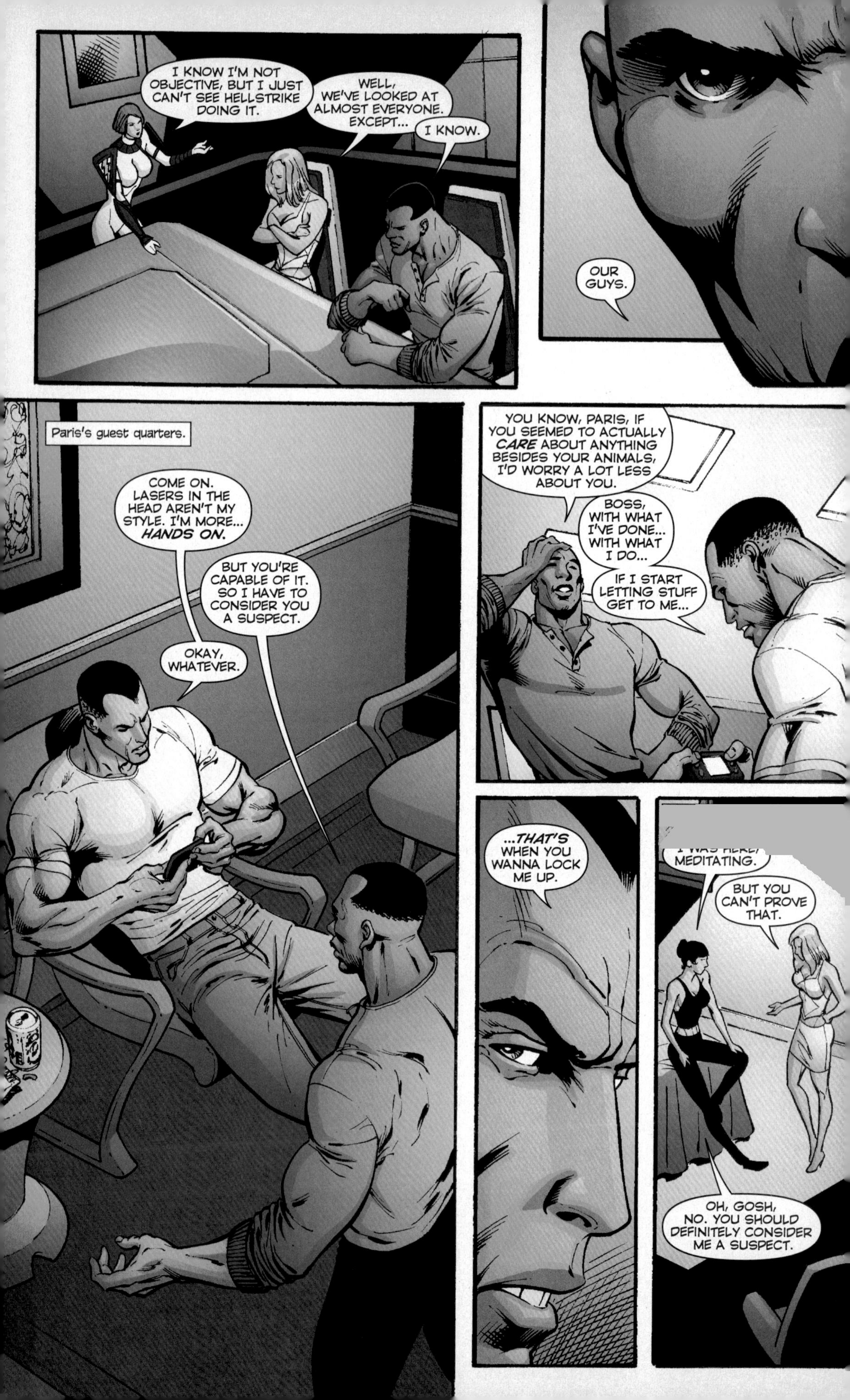
I KNOW I'M NOT OBJECTIVE, BUT I JUST CAN'T SEE HELLSTRIKE DOING IT.
WELL, WE'VE LOOKED AT ALMOST EVERYONE. EXCEPT...
I KNOW.
OUR GUYS.
Paris's guest quarters.
COME ON. LASERS IN THE HEAD AREN'T MY STYLE. I'M MORE... HANDS ON.
BUT YOU'RE CAPABLE OF IT. SO I HAVE TO CONSIDER YOU A SUSPECT.
OKAY, WHATEVER.
YOU KNOW, PARIS, IF YOU SEEMED TO ACTUALLY CARE ABOUT ANYTHING BESIDES YOUR ANIMALS, I'D WORRY A LOT LESS ABOUT YOU.
BOSS, WITH WHAT I'VE DONE... WITH WHAT I DO...
IF I START LETTING STUFF GET TO ME...
...THAT'S WHEN YOU WANNA LOCK ME UP.
MEDITATING.
BUT YOU CAN'T PROVE THAT.
OH, GOSH, NO. YOU SHOULD DEFINITELY CONSIDER ME A SUSPECT.

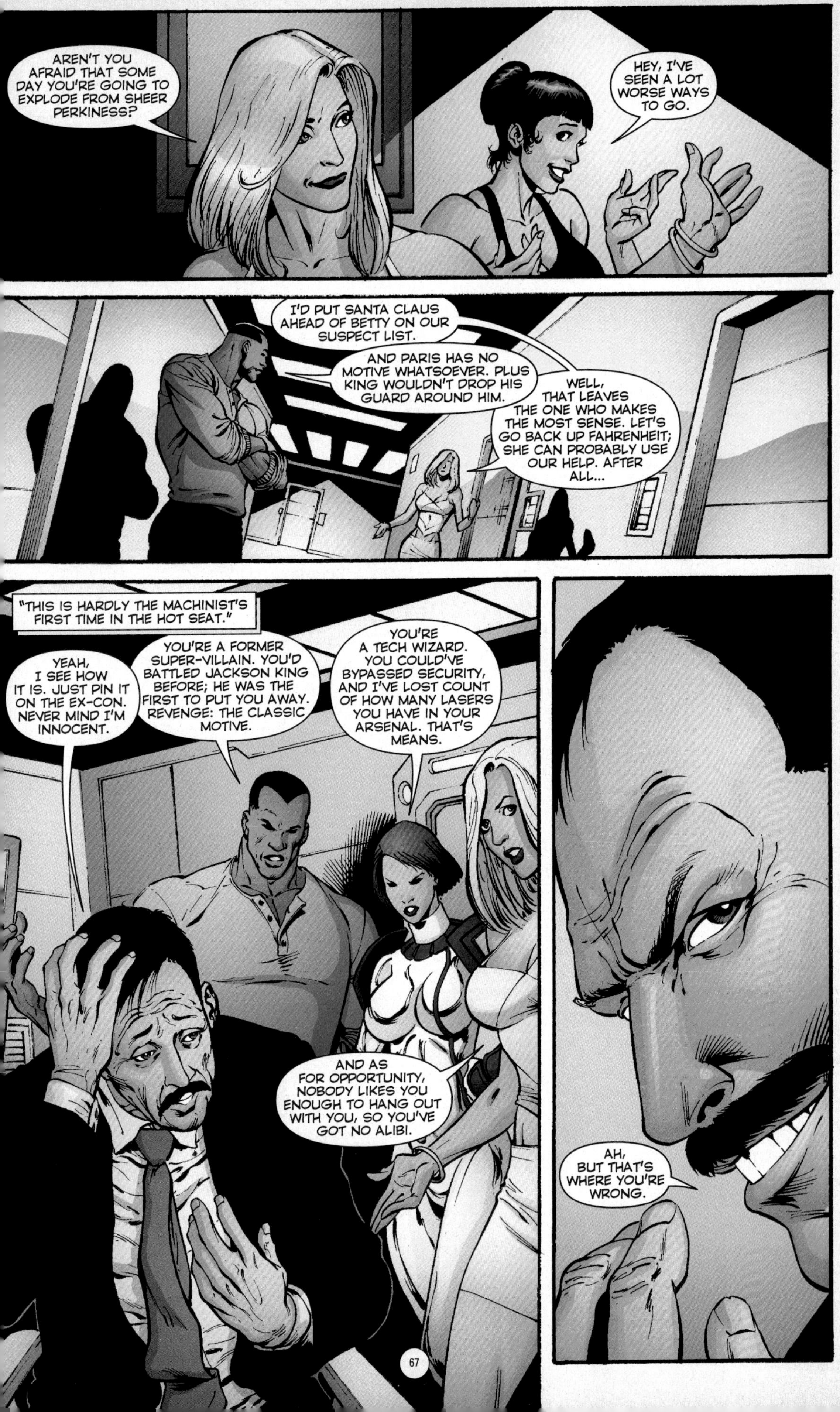

AREN'T YOU AFRAID THAT SOME DAY YOU'RE GOING TO EXPLODE FROM SHEER PERKINESS?
HEY, I'VE SEEN A LOT WORSE WAYS TO GO.
I'D PUT SANTA CLAUS AHEAD OF BETTY ON OUR SUSPECT LIST.
AND PARIS HAS NO MOTIVE WHATSOEVER. PLUS KING WOULDN'T DROP HIS GUARD AROUND HIM.
WELL, THAT LEAVES THE ONE WHO MAKES THE MOST SENSE. LET'S GO BACK UP FAHRENHEIT; SHE CAN PROBABLY USE OUR HELP. AFTER ALL...
"THIS IS HARDLY THE MACHINIST'S FIRST TIME IN THE HOT SEAT."
YOU'RE A FORMER SUPER-VILLAIN. YOU'D BATTLED JACKSON KING BEFORE; HE WAS THE FIRST TO PUT YOU AWAY. REVENGE: THE CLASSIC MOTIVE.
YOU'RE A TECH WIZARD. YOU COULD'VE BYPASSED SECURITY, AND I'VE LOST COUNT OF HOW MANY LASERS YOU HAVE IN YOUR ARSENAL. THAT'S MEANS.
AND AS FOR OPPORTUNITY, NOBODY LIKES YOU ENOUGH TO HANG OUT WITH YOU, SO YOU'VE GOT NO ALIBI.
YEAH, I SEE HOW IT IS. JUST PIN IT ON THE EX-CON. NEVER MIND I'M INNOCENT.
AH, BUT THAT'S WHERE YOU'RE WRONG.

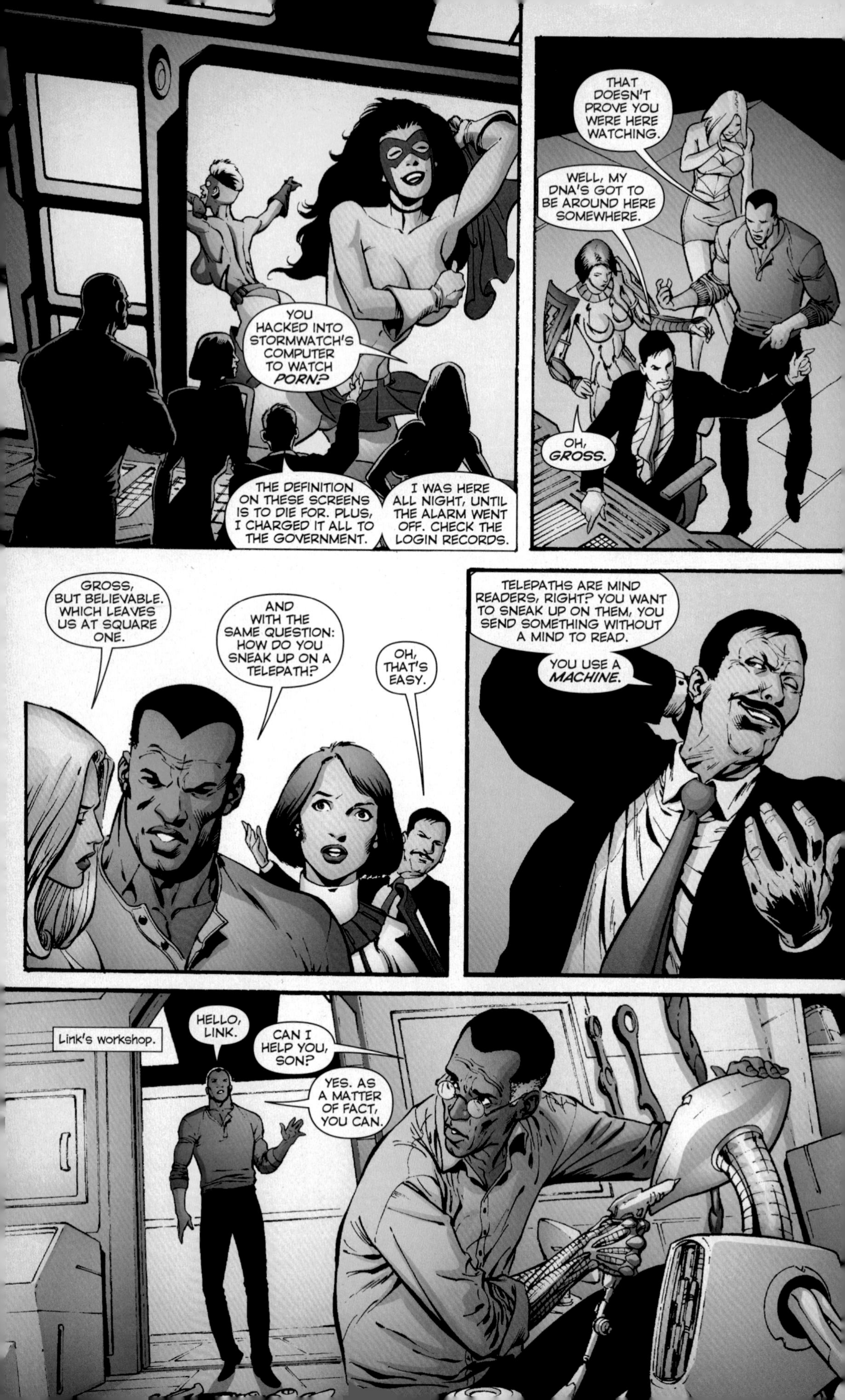
YOU HACKED INTO STORMWATCH'S COMPUTER TO WATCH PORN?
THE DEFINITION ON THESE SCREENS IS TO DIE FOR. PLUS, I CHARGED IT ALL TO THE GOVERNMENT.
I WAS HERE ALL NIGHT, UNTIL THE ALARM WENT OFF. CHECK THE LOGIN RECORDS.
THAT DOESN'T PROVE YOU WERE HERE WATCHING.
WELL, MY DNA'S GOT TO BE AROUND HERE SOMEWHERE.
OH, GROSS.
GROSS, BUT BELIEVABLE. WHICH LEAVES US AT SQUARE ONE.
AND WITH THE SAME QUESTION: HOW DO YOU SNEAK UP ON A TELEPATH?
OH, THAT'S EASY.
TELEPATHS ARE MIND READERS, RIGHT? YOU WANT TO SNEAK UP ON THEM, YOU SEND SOMETHING WITHOUT A MIND TO READ.
YOU USE A MACHINE.
Link's workshop.
HELLO, LINK.
CAN I HELP YOU, SON?
YES. AS A MATTER OF FACT, YOU CAN.

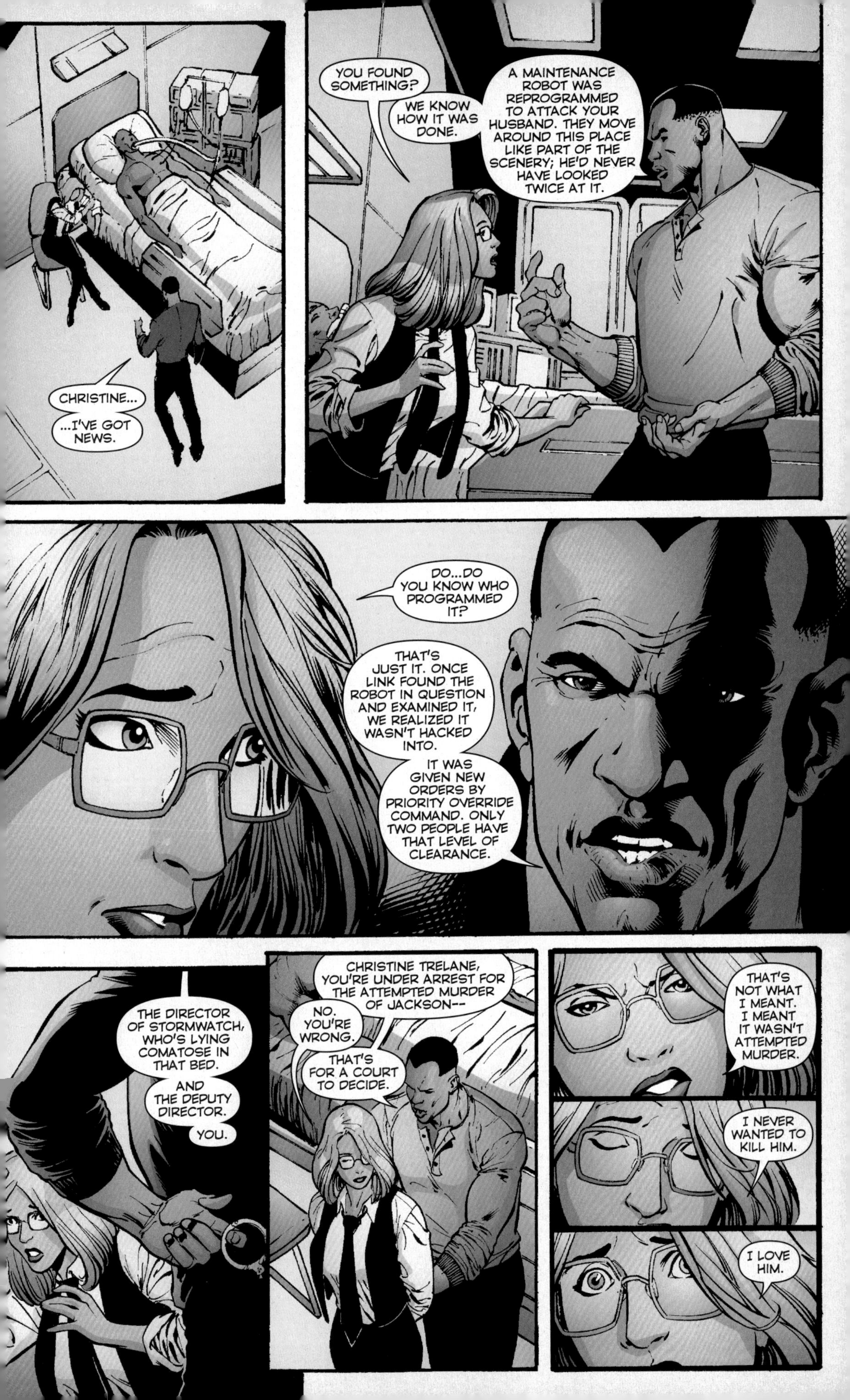

CHRISTINE...
...I'VE GOT NEWS.
YOU FOUND SOMETHING?
WE KNOW HOW IT WAS DONE.
A MAINTENANCE ROBOT WAS REPROGRAMMED TO ATTACK YOUR HUSBAND. THEY MOVE AROUND THIS PLACE LIKE PART OF THE SCENERY; HE'D NEVER HAVE LOOKED TWICE AT IT.
DO...DO YOU KNOW WHO PROGRAMMED IT?
THAT'S JUST IT. ONCE LINK FOUND THE ROBOT IN QUESTION AND EXAMINED IT, WE REALIZED IT WASN'T HACKED INTO.
IT WAS GIVEN NEW ORDERS BY PRIORITY OVERRIDE COMMAND. ONLY TWO PEOPLE HAVE THAT LEVEL OF CLEARANCE.
THE DIRECTOR OF STORMWATCH, WHO'S LYING COMATOSE IN THAT BED.
AND THE DEPUTY DIRECTOR.
YOU.
CHRISTINE TRELANE, YOU'RE UNDER ARREST FOR THE ATTEMPTED MURDER OF JACKSON--
NO. YOU'RE WRONG.
THAT'S FOR A COURT TO DECIDE.
THAT'S NOT WHAT I MEANT. I MEANT IT WASN'T ATTEMPTED MURDER.
I NEVER WANTED TO KILL HIM.
I LOVE HIM.

AND HE LOVES ME.

BUT HE LOVES STORMWATCH MORE.

I TOLD THE TRUTH. WE DECIDED TO KEEP THE BABY. BUT WHEN I LOST IT...

...HE WAS *RELIEVED.* I COULD SEE IT, PLAIN AS DAY.

"YEARS AGO, WE PUNCHED A HOLE THROUGH THE BLEED, INTO AN ALTERNATE UNIVERSE. JUST ENOUGH TO SEE IT.

"I SAW MYSELF. WITH KIDS. A FAMILY.

"I LOOKED *HAPPY.*

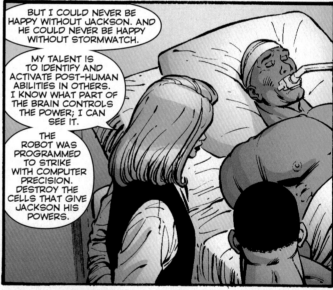

BUT I COULD NEVER BE HAPPY WITHOUT JACKSON. AND HE COULD NEVER BE HAPPY WITHOUT STORMWATCH.

MY TALENT IS TO IDENTIFY AND ACTIVATE POST-HUMAN ABILITIES IN OTHERS. I KNOW WHAT PART OF THE BRAIN CONTROLS THE POWER; I CAN SEE IT.

THE ROBOT WAS PROGRAMMED TO STRIKE WITH COMPUTER PRECISION. DESTROY THE CELLS THAT GIVE JACKSON HIS POWERS.

MAYBE THEN HE'D CUT BACK. TAKE A DESK JOB.

HAVE TIME FOR ME. FOR A FAMILY.

THAT'S WHAT I WANTED. BUT NOW...I JUST WANT HIM TO WAKE UP.

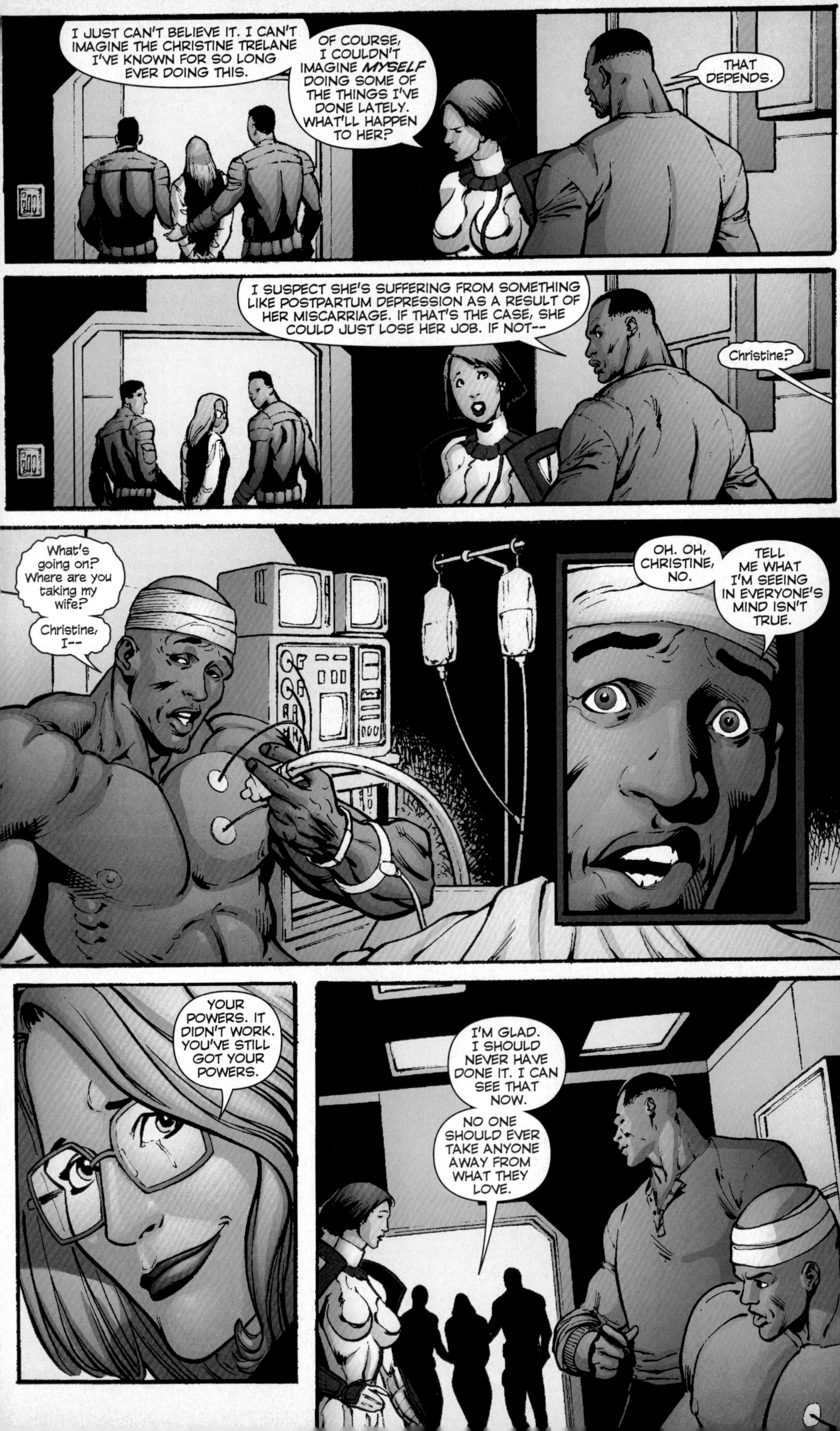
I JUST CAN'T BELIEVE IT. I CAN'T IMAGINE THE CHRISTINE TRELANE I'VE KNOWN FOR SO LONG EVER DOING THIS.
OF COURSE, I COULDN'T IMAGINE MYSELF DOING SOME OF THE THINGS I'VE DONE LATELY. WHAT'LL HAPPEN TO HER?
THAT DEPENDS.
I SUSPECT SHE'S SUFFERING FROM SOMETHING LIKE POSTPARTUM DEPRESSION AS A RESULT OF HER MISCARRIAGE. IF THAT'S THE CASE, SHE COULD JUST LOSE HER JOB. IF NOT--
Christine?
What's going on? Where are you taking my wife?
Christine, I--
OH. OH, CHRISTINE, NO.
TELL ME WHAT I'M SEEING IN EVERYONE'S MIND ISN'T TRUE.
YOUR POWERS. IT DIDN'T WORK. YOU'VE STILL GOT YOUR POWERS.
I'M GLAD. I SHOULD NEVER HAVE DONE IT. I CAN SEE THAT NOW.
NO ONE SHOULD EVER TAKE ANYONE AWAY FROM WHAT THEY LOVE.

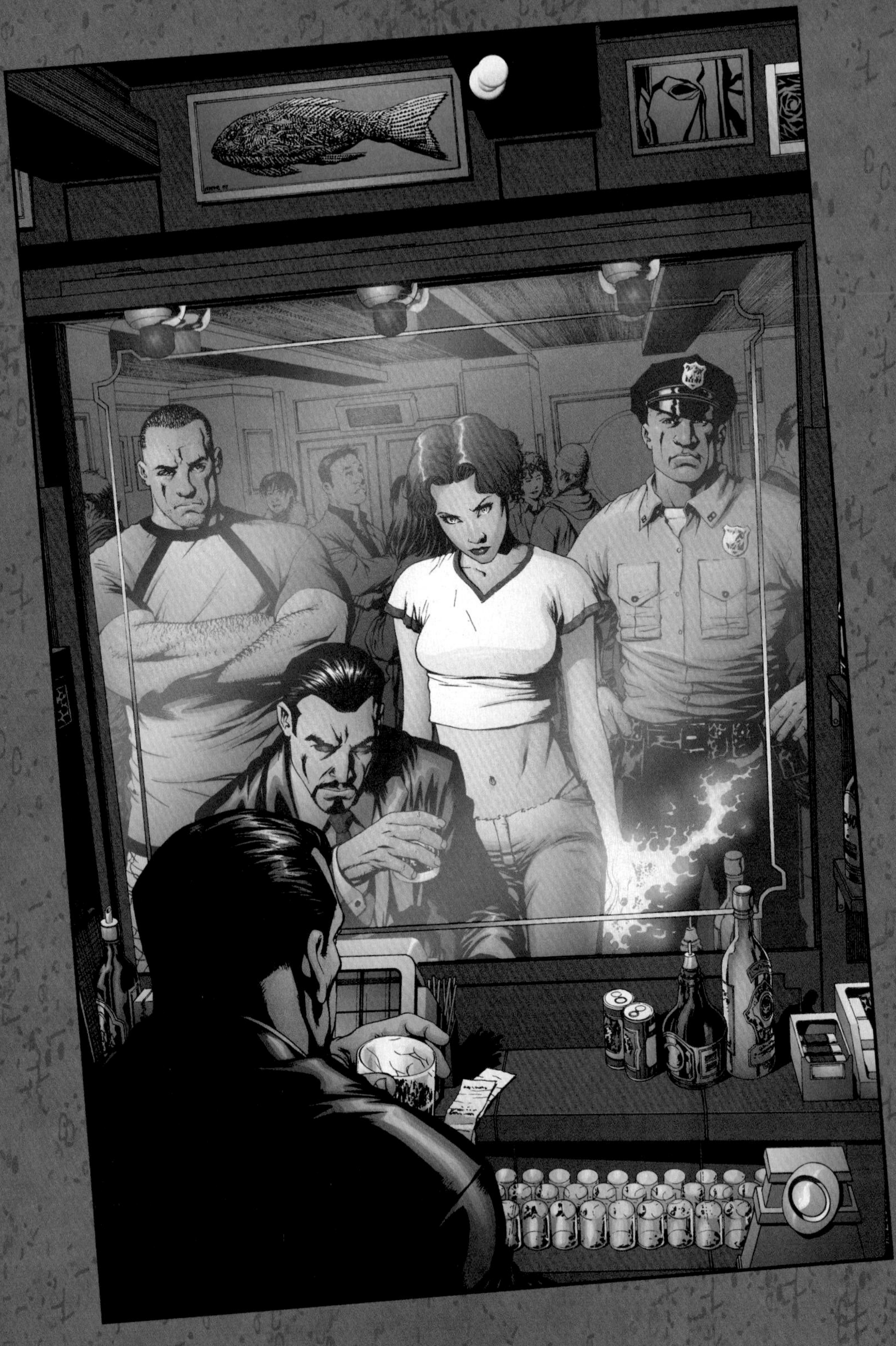

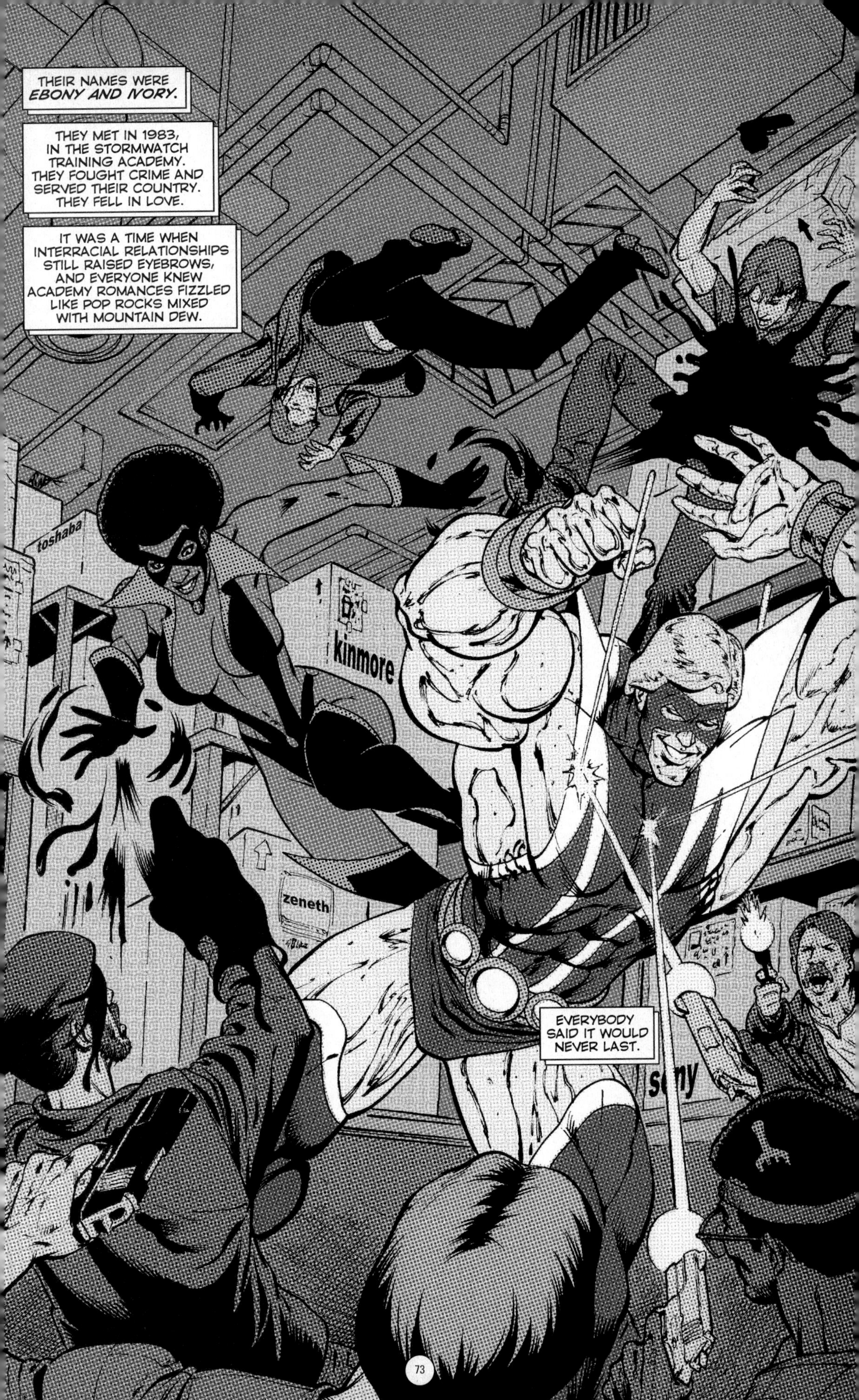

THEIR NAMES WERE EBONY AND IVORY.
THEY MET IN 1983, IN THE STORMWATCH TRAINING ACADEMY. THEY FOUGHT CRIME AND SERVED THEIR COUNTRY. THEY FELL IN LOVE.
IT WAS A TIME WHEN INTERRACIAL RELATIONSHIPS STILL RAISED EYEBROWS, AND EVERYONE KNEW ACADEMY ROMANCES FIZZLED LIKE POP ROCKS MIXED WITH MOUNTAIN DEW.
toshaba
kinmore
zeneth
EVERYBODY SAID IT WOULD NEVER LAST.
sony

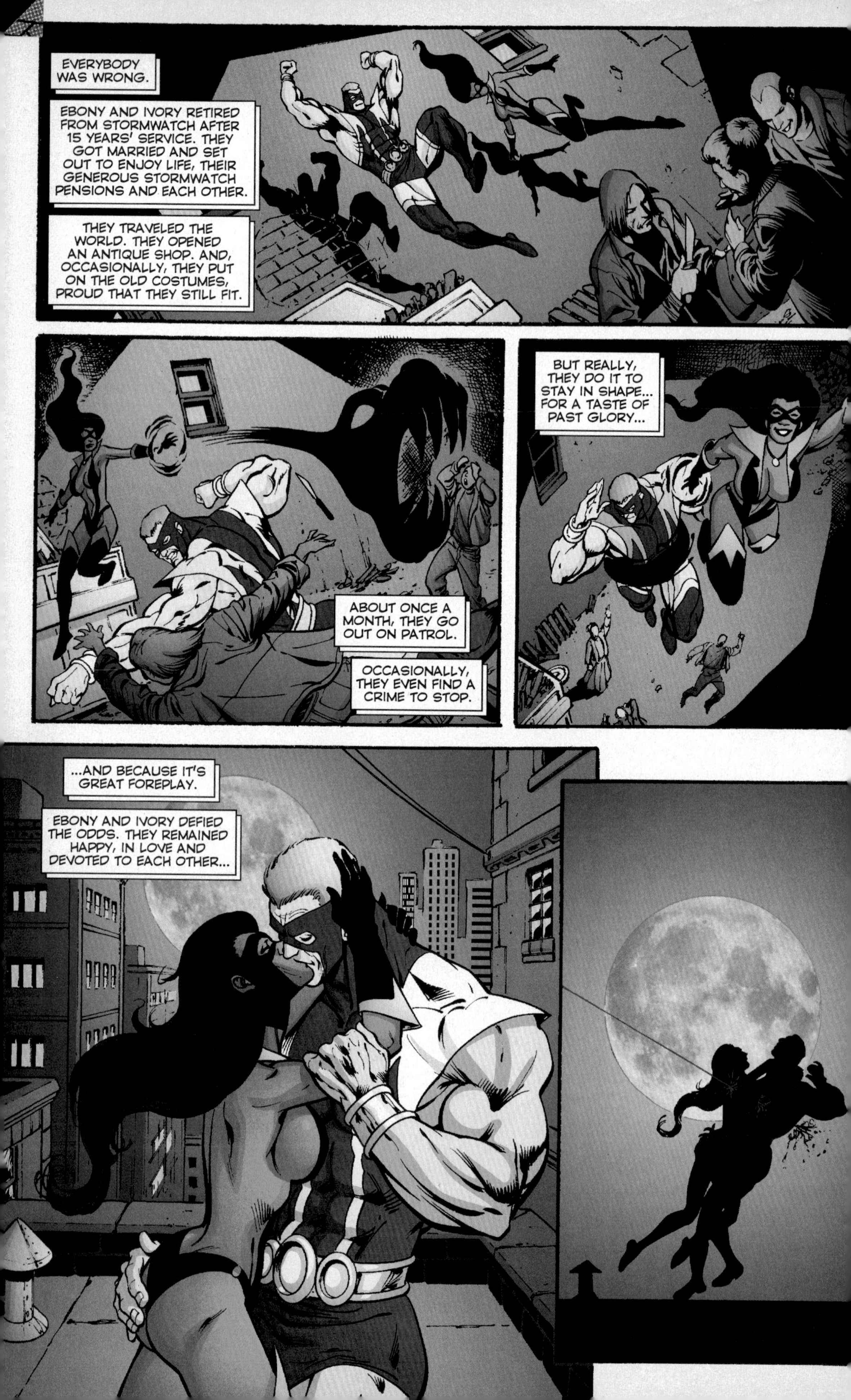
EVERYBODY WAS WRONG.
EBONY AND IVORY RETIRED FROM STORMWATCH AFTER 15 YEARS' SERVICE. THEY GOT MARRIED AND SET OUT TO ENJOY LIFE, THEIR GENEROUS STORMWATCH PENSIONS AND EACH OTHER.
THEY TRAVELED THE WORLD. THEY OPENED AN ANTIQUE SHOP. AND, OCCASIONALLY, THEY PUT ON THE OLD COSTUMES, PROUD THAT THEY STILL FIT.
ABOUT ONCE A MONTH, THEY GO OUT ON PATROL.
OCCASIONALLY, THEY EVEN FIND A CRIME TO STOP.
BUT REALLY, THEY DO IT TO STAY IN SHAPE... FOR A TASTE OF PAST GLORY...
...AND BECAUSE IT'S GREAT FOREPLAY.
EBONY AND IVORY DEFIED THE ODDS. THEY REMAINED HAPPY, IN LOVE AND DEVOTED TO EACH OTHER...

HOW'D THEY DIE?

I KNEW THEM. STORMWATCH '83 TO '98, MOSTLY IN THE RESERVES.

THAT'S WHY WE CALLED YOU INSTEAD OF HOMICIDE. NOW THAT THE I.D.'S CONFIRMED, THIS IS PHD'S CASE.

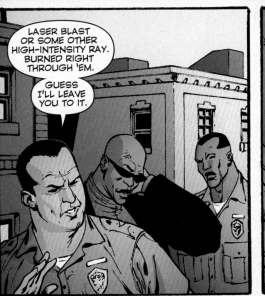

LASER BLAST OR SOME OTHER HIGH-INTENSITY RAY. BURNED RIGHT THROUGH 'EM.

GUESS I'LL LEAVE YOU TO IT.

YOU OKAY, JACKSON? I MEAN, SHOULD YOU BE BACK ON THE JOB THIS SOON AFTER--

BEING BACK IS EXACTLY WHAT I NEED.

I GET THAT. BUT IF THE CASE HITS TOO CLOSE TO HOME...

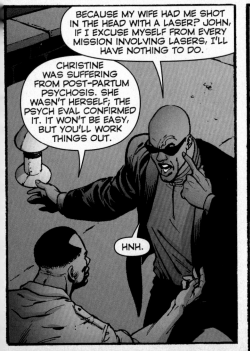

BECAUSE MY WIFE HAD ME SHOT IN THE HEAD WITH A LASER? JOHN, IF I EXCUSE MYSELF FROM EVERY MISSION INVOLVING LASERS, I'LL HAVE NOTHING TO DO.

CHRISTINE WAS SUFFERING FROM POST-PARTUM PSYCHOSIS. SHE WASN'T HERSELF; THE PSYCH EVAL CONFIRMED IT. IT WON'T BE EASY, BUT YOU'LL WORK THINGS OUT.

HNH.

THESE TWO HAD THE MOST PERFECT MARRIAGE I EVER SAW. IF THEY CAN END UP LIKE THIS...

...ALL IT TAKES IS A SECOND. ONE SECOND FOR YOUR WHOLE FOUNDATION TO CRUMBLE UNDER YOU.

THEY WERE GOOD PEOPLE, JOHN. SOLVE THIS ONE FAST.

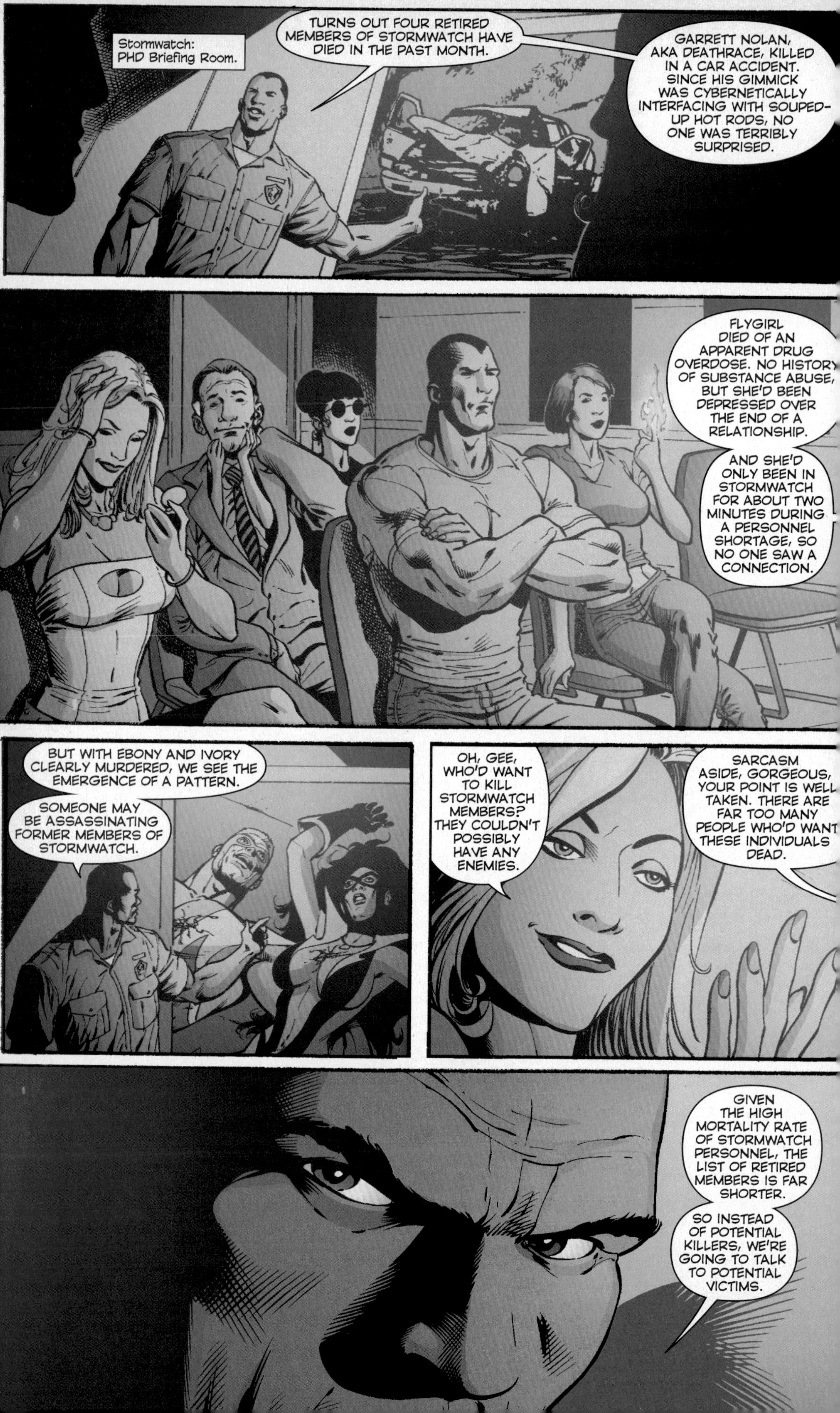
Stormwatch: PHD Briefing Room.
TURNS OUT FOUR RETIRED MEMBERS OF STORMWATCH HAVE DIED IN THE PAST MONTH.
GARRETT NOLAN, AKA DEATHRACE, KILLED IN A CAR ACCIDENT. SINCE HIS GIMMICK WAS CYBERNETICALLY INTERFACING WITH SOUPED-UP HOT RODS, NO ONE WAS TERRIBLY SURPRISED.
FLYGIRL DIED OF AN APPARENT DRUG OVERDOSE. NO HISTORY OF SUBSTANCE ABUSE, BUT SHE'D BEEN DEPRESSED OVER THE END OF A RELATIONSHIP.
AND SHE'D ONLY BEEN IN STORMWATCH FOR ABOUT TWO MINUTES DURING A PERSONNEL SHORTAGE, SO NO ONE SAW A CONNECTION.
BUT WITH EBONY AND IVORY CLEARLY MURDERED, WE SEE THE EMERGENCE OF A PATTERN.
SOMEONE MAY BE ASSASSINATING FORMER MEMBERS OF STORMWATCH.
OH, GEE, WHO'D WANT TO KILL STORMWATCH MEMBERS? THEY COULDN'T POSSIBLY HAVE ANY ENEMIES.
SARCASM ASIDE, GORGEOUS, YOUR POINT IS WELL TAKEN. THERE ARE FAR TOO MANY PEOPLE WHO'D WANT THESE INDIVIDUALS DEAD.
GIVEN THE HIGH MORTALITY RATE OF STORMWATCH PERSONNEL, THE LIST OF RETIRED MEMBERS IS FAR SHORTER.
SO INSTEAD OF POTENTIAL KILLERS, WE'RE GOING TO TALK TO POTENTIAL VICTIMS.

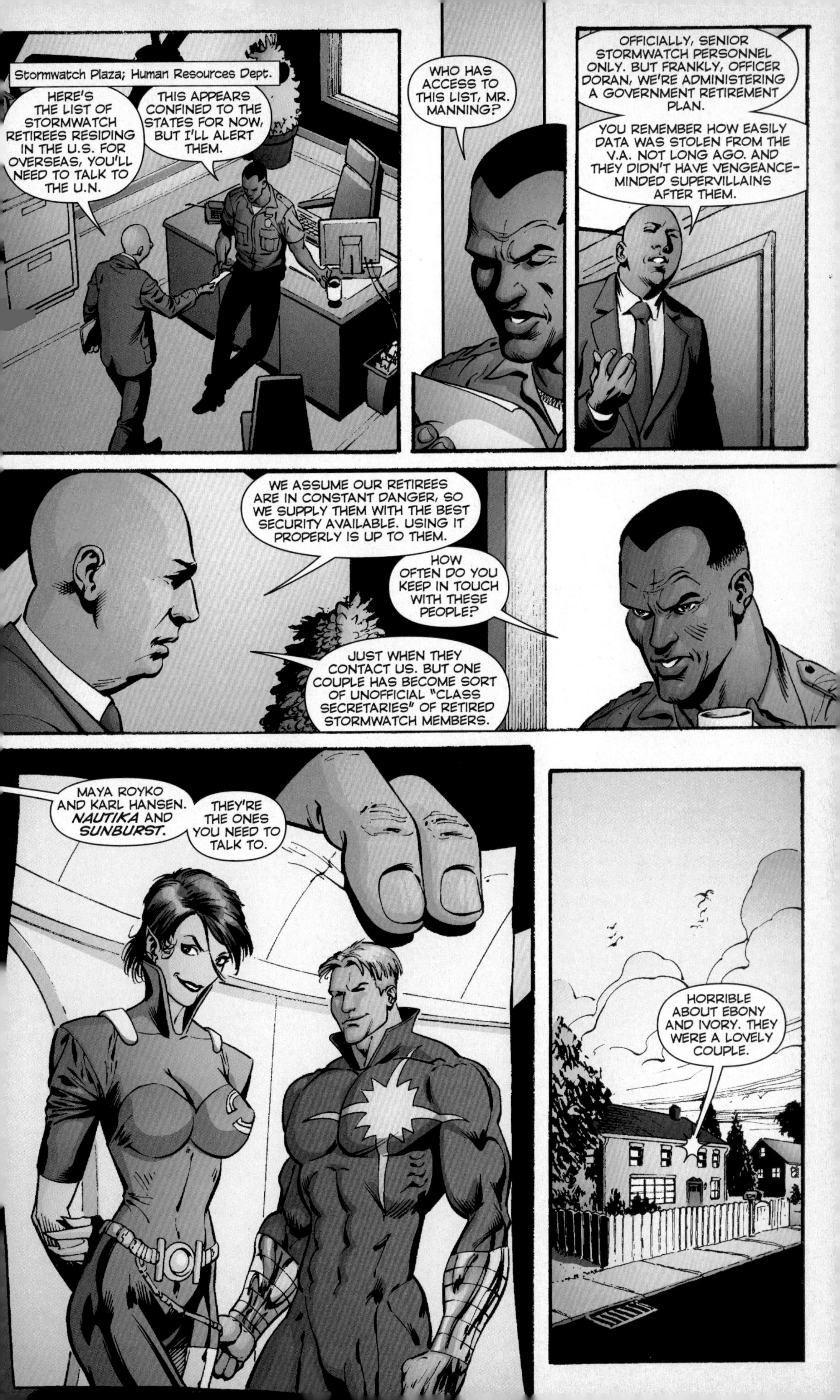
Stormwatch Plaza; Human Resources Dept.
HERE'S THE LIST OF STORMWATCH RETIREES RESIDING IN THE U.S. FOR OVERSEAS, YOU'LL NEED TO TALK TO THE U.N.
THIS APPEARS CONFINED TO THE STATES FOR NOW, BUT I'LL ALERT THEM.
WHO HAS ACCESS TO THIS LIST, MR. MANNING?
OFFICIALLY, SENIOR STORMWATCH PERSONNEL ONLY. BUT FRANKLY, OFFICER DORAN, WE'RE ADMINISTERING A GOVERNMENT RETIREMENT PLAN.
YOU REMEMBER HOW EASILY DATA WAS STOLEN FROM THE V.A. NOT LONG AGO. AND THEY DIDN'T HAVE VENGEANCE-MINDED SUPERVILLAINS AFTER THEM.
WE ASSUME OUR RETIREES ARE IN CONSTANT DANGER, SO WE SUPPLY THEM WITH THE BEST SECURITY AVAILABLE. USING IT PROPERLY IS UP TO THEM.
HOW OFTEN DO YOU KEEP IN TOUCH WITH THESE PEOPLE?
JUST WHEN THEY CONTACT US. BUT ONE COUPLE HAS BECOME SORT OF UNOFFICIAL "CLASS SECRETARIES" OF RETIRED STORMWATCH MEMBERS.
MAYA ROYKO AND KARL HANSEN. *NAUTIKA* AND *SUNBURST*.
THEY'RE THE ONES YOU NEED TO TALK TO.
HORRIBLE ABOUT EBONY AND IVORY. THEY WERE A LOVELY COUPLE.

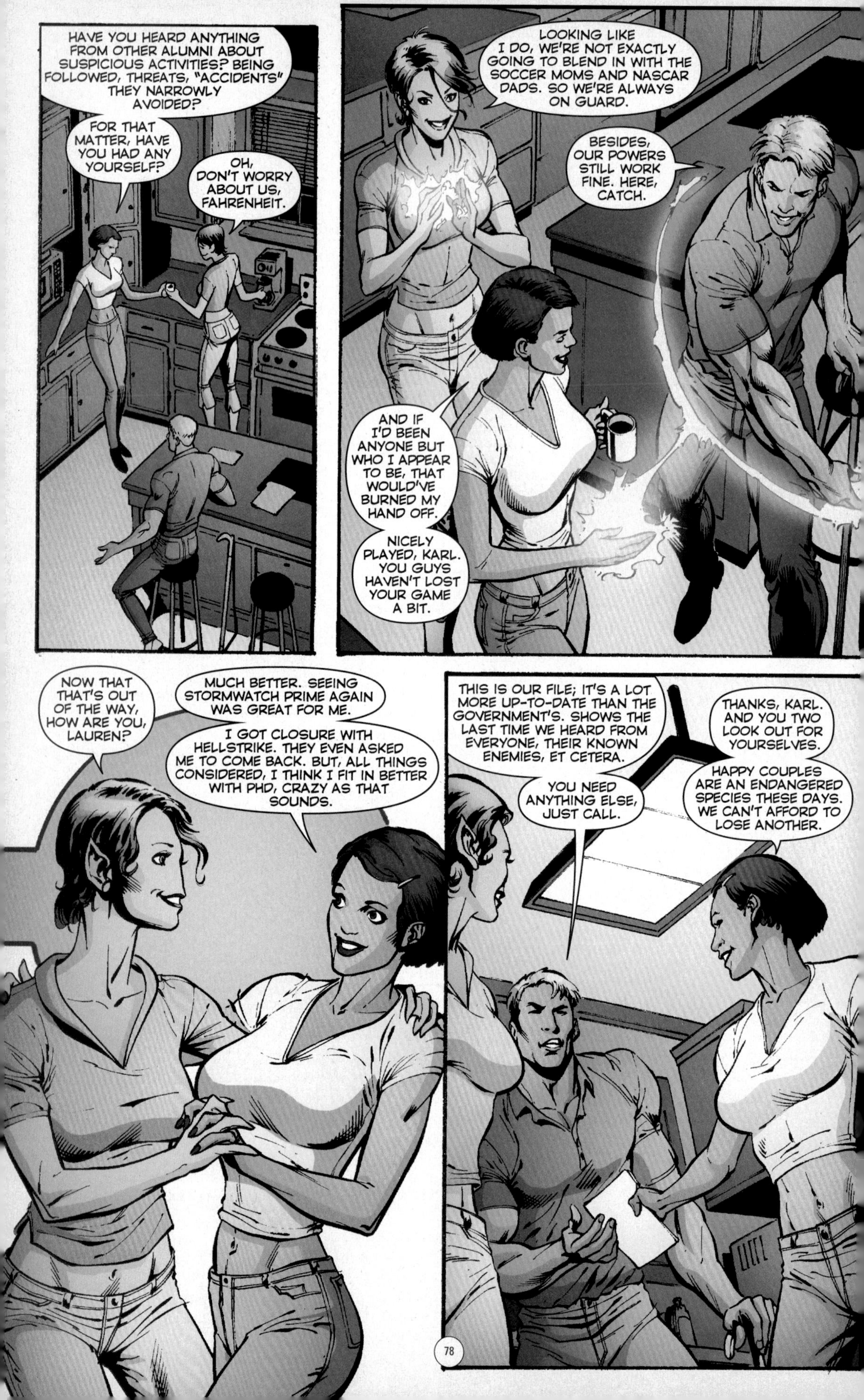
HAVE YOU HEARD ANYTHING FROM OTHER ALUMNI ABOUT SUSPICIOUS ACTIVITIES? BEING FOLLOWED, THREATS, "ACCIDENTS" THEY NARROWLY AVOIDED?
FOR THAT MATTER, HAVE YOU HAD ANY YOURSELF?
OH, DON'T WORRY ABOUT US, FAHRENHEIT.
LOOKING LIKE I DO, WE'RE NOT EXACTLY GOING TO BLEND IN WITH THE SOCCER MOMS AND NASCAR DADS. SO WE'RE ALWAYS ON GUARD.
BESIDES, OUR POWERS STILL WORK FINE. HERE, CATCH.
AND IF I'D BEEN ANYONE BUT WHO I APPEAR TO BE, THAT WOULD'VE BURNED MY HAND OFF.
NICELY PLAYED, KARL. YOU GUYS HAVEN'T LOST YOUR GAME A BIT.
NOW THAT THAT'S OUT OF THE WAY, HOW ARE YOU, LAUREN?
MUCH BETTER. SEEING STORMWATCH PRIME AGAIN WAS GREAT FOR ME.
I GOT CLOSURE WITH HELLSTRIKE. THEY EVEN ASKED ME TO COME BACK. BUT, ALL THINGS CONSIDERED, I THINK I FIT IN BETTER WITH PHD, CRAZY AS THAT SOUNDS.
THIS IS OUR FILE; IT'S A LOT MORE UP-TO-DATE THAN THE GOVERNMENT'S. SHOWS THE LAST TIME WE HEARD FROM EVERYONE, THEIR KNOWN ENEMIES, ET CETERA.
YOU NEED ANYTHING ELSE, JUST CALL.
THANKS, KARL. AND YOU TWO LOOK OUT FOR YOURSELVES.
HAPPY COUPLES ARE AN ENDANGERED SPECIES THESE DAYS. WE CAN'T AFFORD TO LOSE ANOTHER.

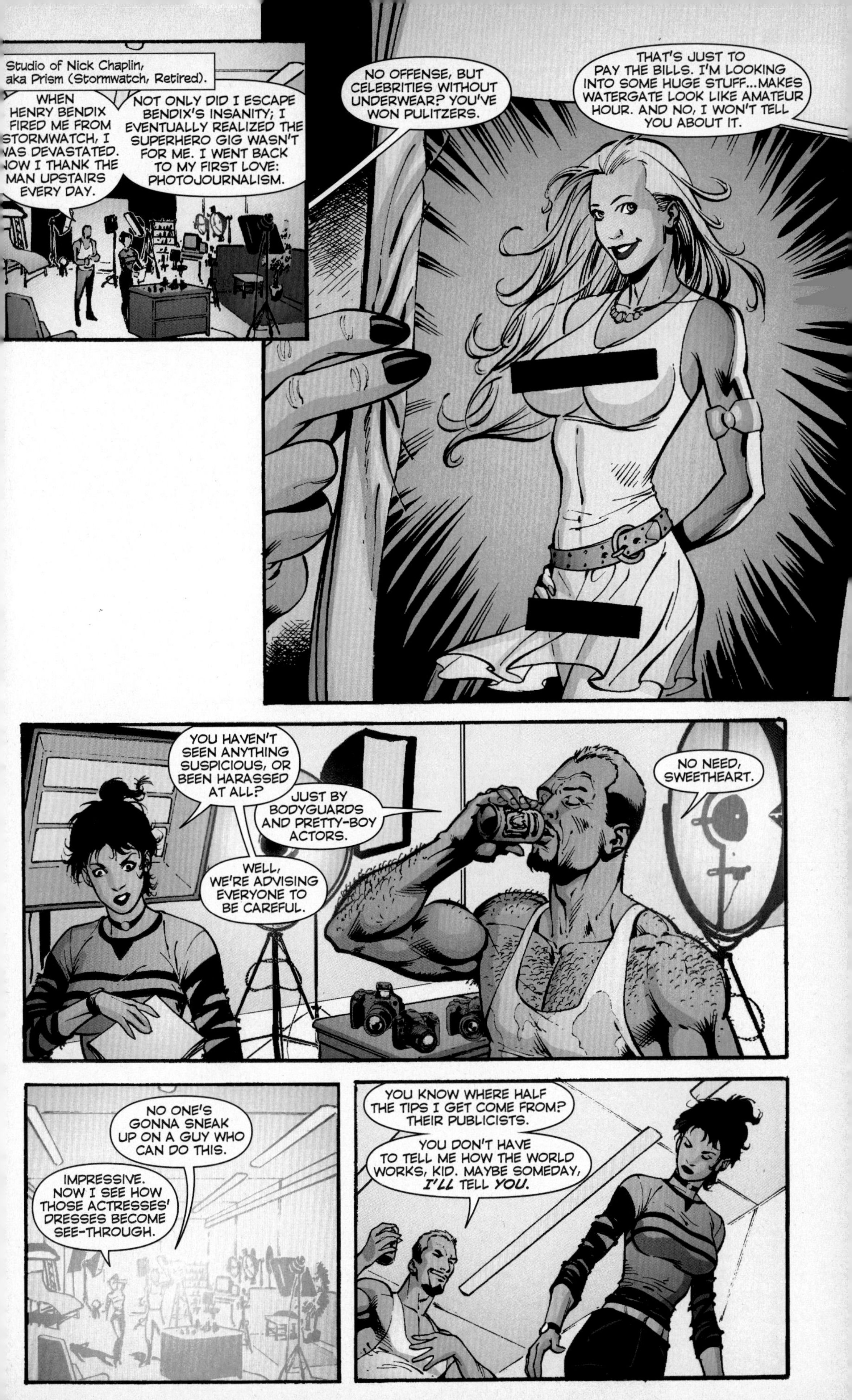
Studio of Nick Chaplin, aka Prism (Stormwatch, Retired).
WHEN HENRY BENDIX FIRED ME FROM STORMWATCH, I WAS DEVASTATED. NOW I THANK THE MAN UPSTAIRS EVERY DAY.
NOT ONLY DID I ESCAPE BENDIX'S INSANITY; I EVENTUALLY REALIZED THE SUPERHERO GIG WASN'T FOR ME. I WENT BACK TO MY FIRST LOVE: PHOTOJOURNALISM.
NO OFFENSE, BUT CELEBRITIES WITHOUT UNDERWEAR? YOU'VE WON PULITZERS.
THAT'S JUST TO PAY THE BILLS. I'M LOOKING INTO SOME HUGE STUFF...MAKES WATERGATE LOOK LIKE AMATEUR HOUR. AND NO, I WON'T TELL YOU ABOUT IT.
YOU HAVEN'T SEEN ANYTHING SUSPICIOUS, OR BEEN HARASSED AT ALL?
JUST BY BODYGUARDS AND PRETTY-BOY ACTORS.
WELL, WE'RE ADVISING EVERYONE TO BE CAREFUL.
NO NEED, SWEETHEART.
NO ONE'S GONNA SNEAK UP ON A GUY WHO CAN DO THIS.
IMPRESSIVE. NOW I SEE HOW THOSE ACTRESSES' DRESSES BECOME SEE-THROUGH.
YOU KNOW WHERE HALF THE TIPS I GET COME FROM? THEIR PUBLICISTS.
YOU DON'T HAVE TO TELL ME HOW THE WORLD WORKS, KID. MAYBE SOMEDAY, *I'LL* TELL *YOU*.

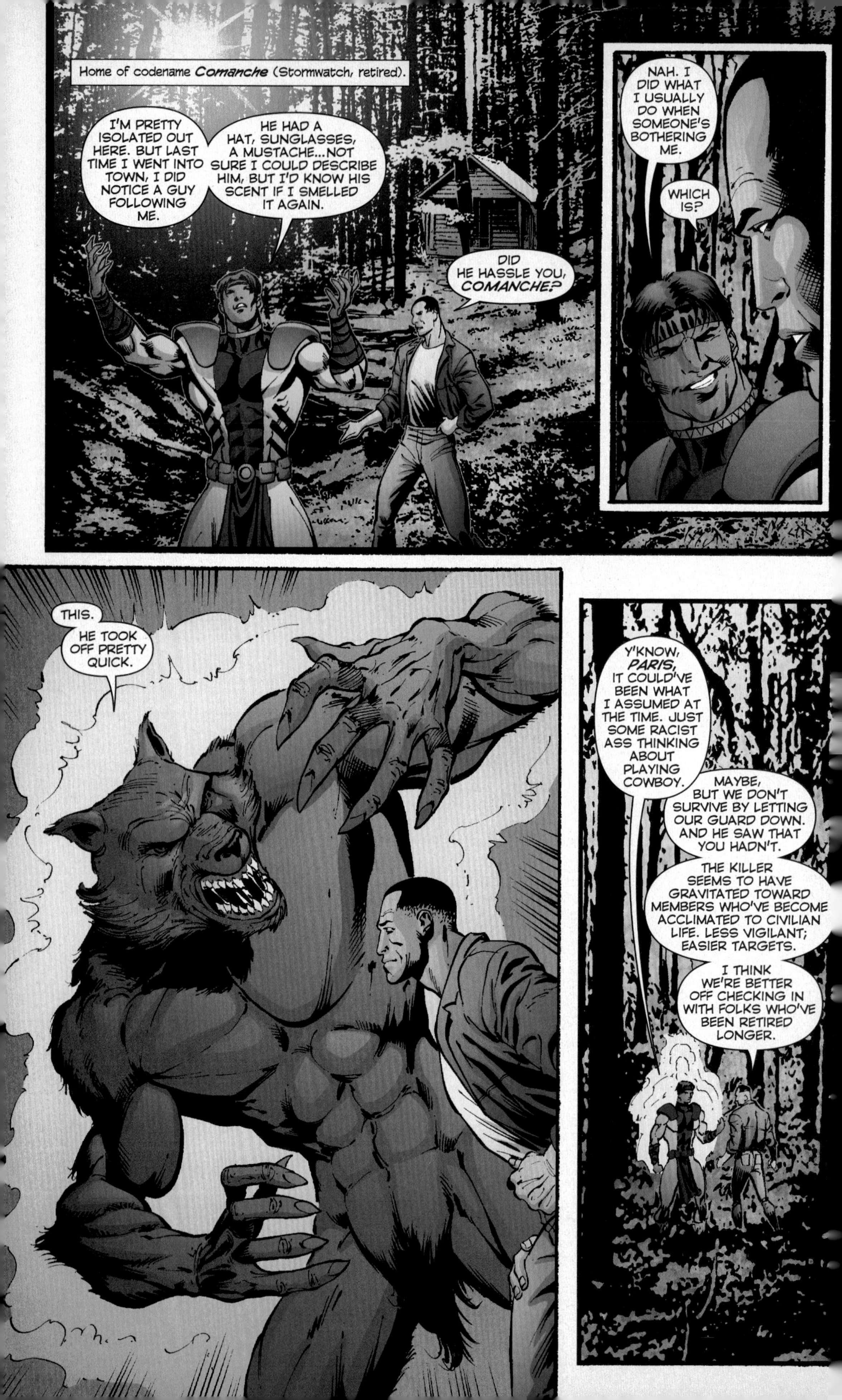
Home of codename *Comanche* (Stormwatch, retired).
I'M PRETTY ISOLATED OUT HERE. BUT LAST TIME I WENT INTO TOWN, I DID NOTICE A GUY FOLLOWING ME.
HE HAD A HAT, SUNGLASSES, A MUSTACHE...NOT SURE I COULD DESCRIBE HIM, BUT I'D KNOW HIS SCENT IF I SMELLED IT AGAIN.
DID HE HASSLE YOU, *COMANCHE?*
NAH. I DID WHAT I USUALLY DO WHEN SOMEONE'S BOTHERING ME.
WHICH IS?
THIS.
HE TOOK OFF PRETTY QUICK.
Y'KNOW, *PARIS*, IT COULD'VE BEEN WHAT I ASSUMED AT THE TIME. JUST SOME RACIST ASS THINKING ABOUT PLAYING COWBOY.
MAYBE, BUT WE DON'T SURVIVE BY LETTING OUR GUARD DOWN. AND HE SAW THAT YOU HADN'T.
THE KILLER SEEMS TO HAVE GRAVITATED TOWARD MEMBERS WHO'VE BECOME ACCLIMATED TO CIVILIAN LIFE. LESS VIGILANT; EASIER TARGETS.
I THINK WE'RE BETTER OFF CHECKING IN WITH FOLKS WHO'VE BEEN RETIRED LONGER.

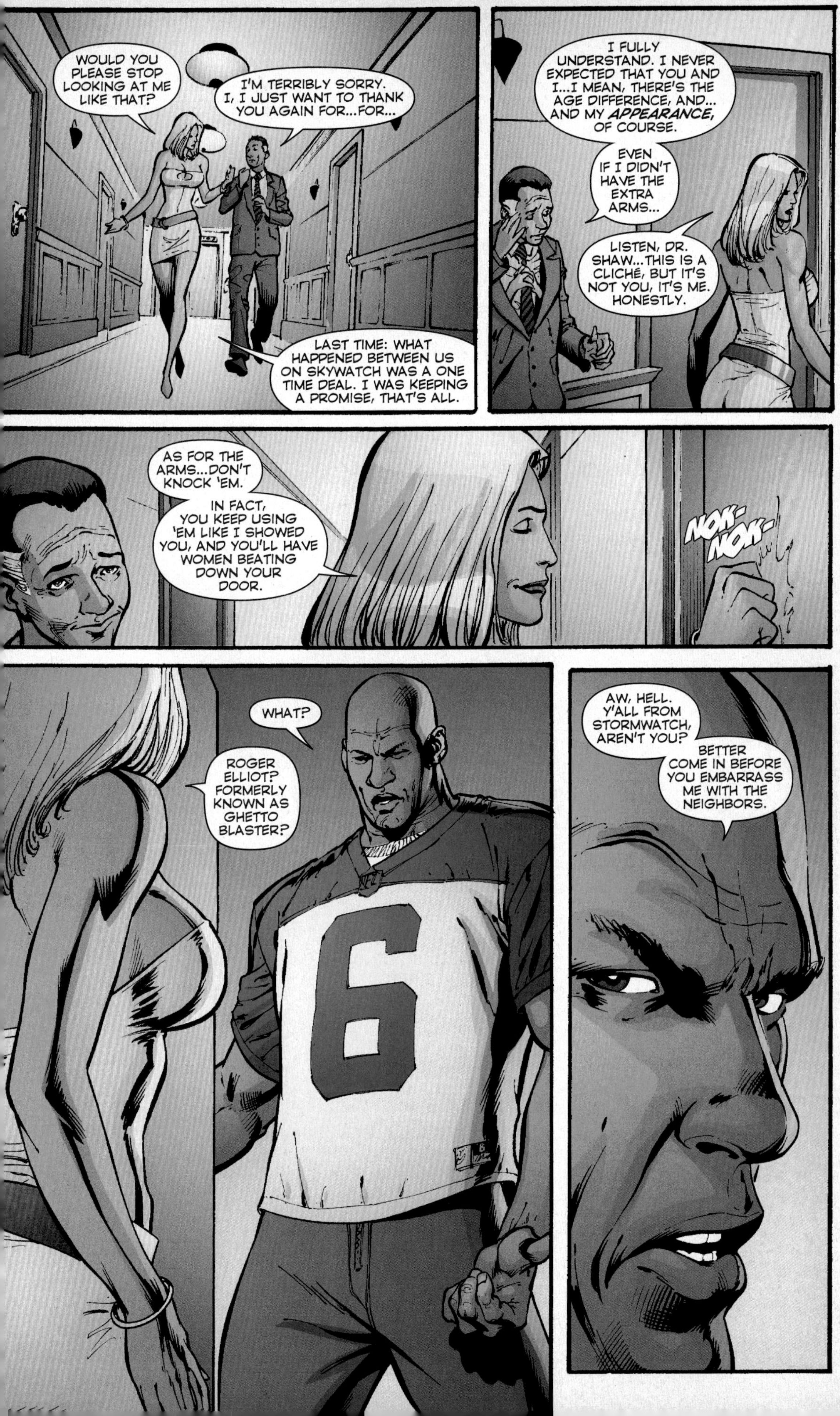
WOULD YOU PLEASE STOP LOOKING AT ME LIKE THAT?
I'M TERRIBLY SORRY. I, I JUST WANT TO THANK YOU AGAIN FOR...FOR...
LAST TIME: WHAT HAPPENED BETWEEN US ON SKYWATCH WAS A ONE TIME DEAL. I WAS KEEPING A PROMISE, THAT'S ALL.
I FULLY UNDERSTAND. I NEVER EXPECTED THAT YOU AND I...I MEAN, THERE'S THE AGE DIFFERENCE, AND... AND MY *APPEARANCE,* OF COURSE.
EVEN IF I DIDN'T HAVE THE EXTRA ARMS...
LISTEN, DR. SHAW...THIS IS A CLICHÉ, BUT IT'S NOT YOU, IT'S ME. HONESTLY.
AS FOR THE ARMS...DON'T KNOCK 'EM.
IN FACT, YOU KEEP USING 'EM LIKE I SHOWED YOU, AND YOU'LL HAVE WOMEN BEATING DOWN YOUR DOOR.
NOK-NOK-
WHAT?
ROGER ELLIOT? FORMERLY KNOWN AS GHETTO BLASTER?
AW, HELL. Y'ALL FROM STORMWATCH, AREN'T YOU?
BETTER COME IN BEFORE YOU EMBARRASS ME WITH THE NEIGHBORS.

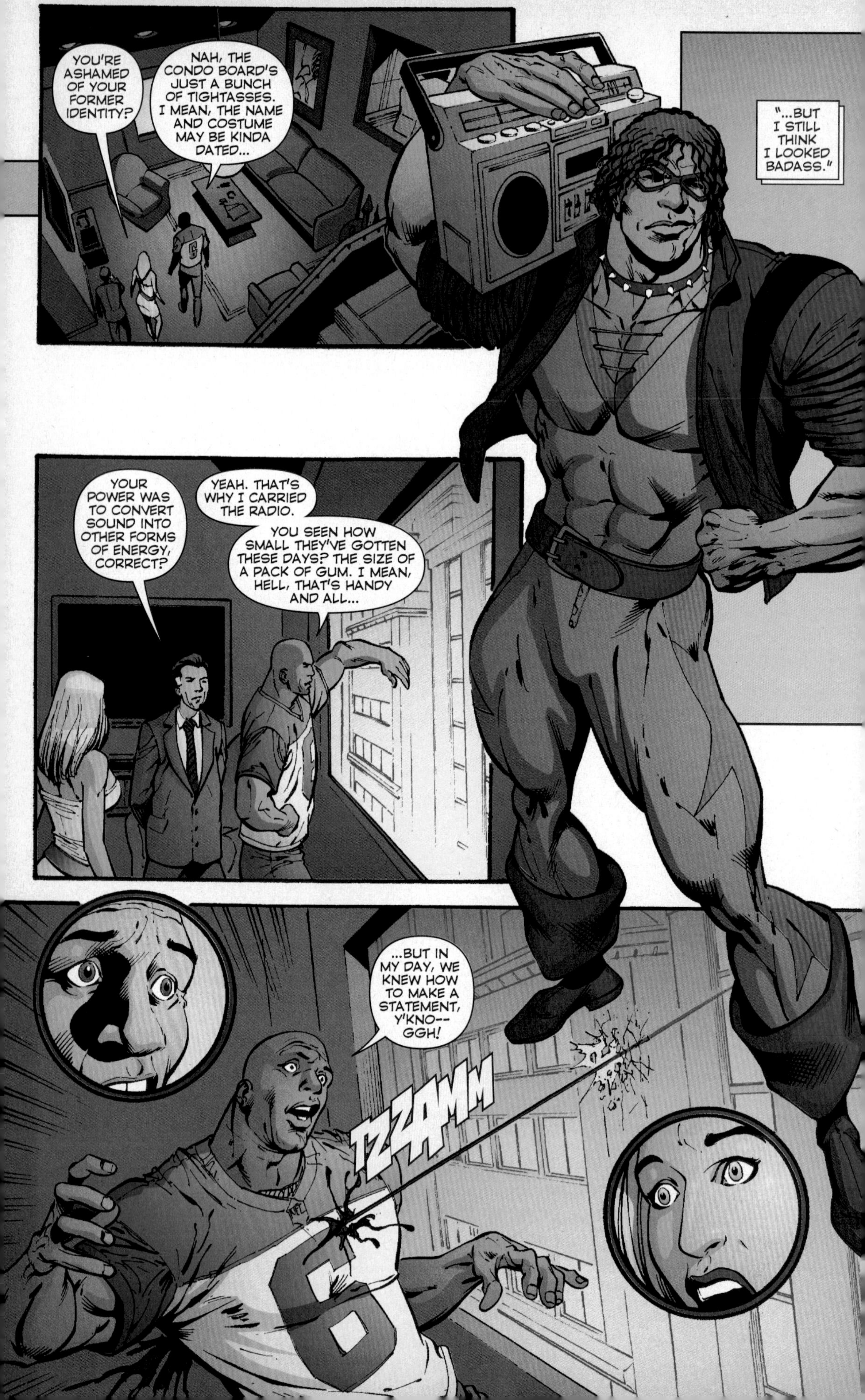
YOU'RE ASHAMED OF YOUR FORMER IDENTITY?
NAH, THE CONDO BOARD'S JUST A BUNCH OF TIGHTASSES. I MEAN, THE NAME AND COSTUME MAY BE KINDA DATED...
"...BUT I STILL THINK I LOOKED BADASS."
YOUR POWER WAS TO CONVERT SOUND INTO OTHER FORMS OF ENERGY, CORRECT?
YEAH. THAT'S WHY I CARRIED THE RADIO.
YOU SEEN HOW SMALL THEY'VE GOTTEN THESE DAYS? THE SIZE OF A PACK OF GUM. I MEAN, HELL, THAT'S HANDY AND ALL...
...BUT IN MY DAY, WE KNEW HOW TO MAKE A STATEMENT, Y'KNO--GGH!
TZZAMM

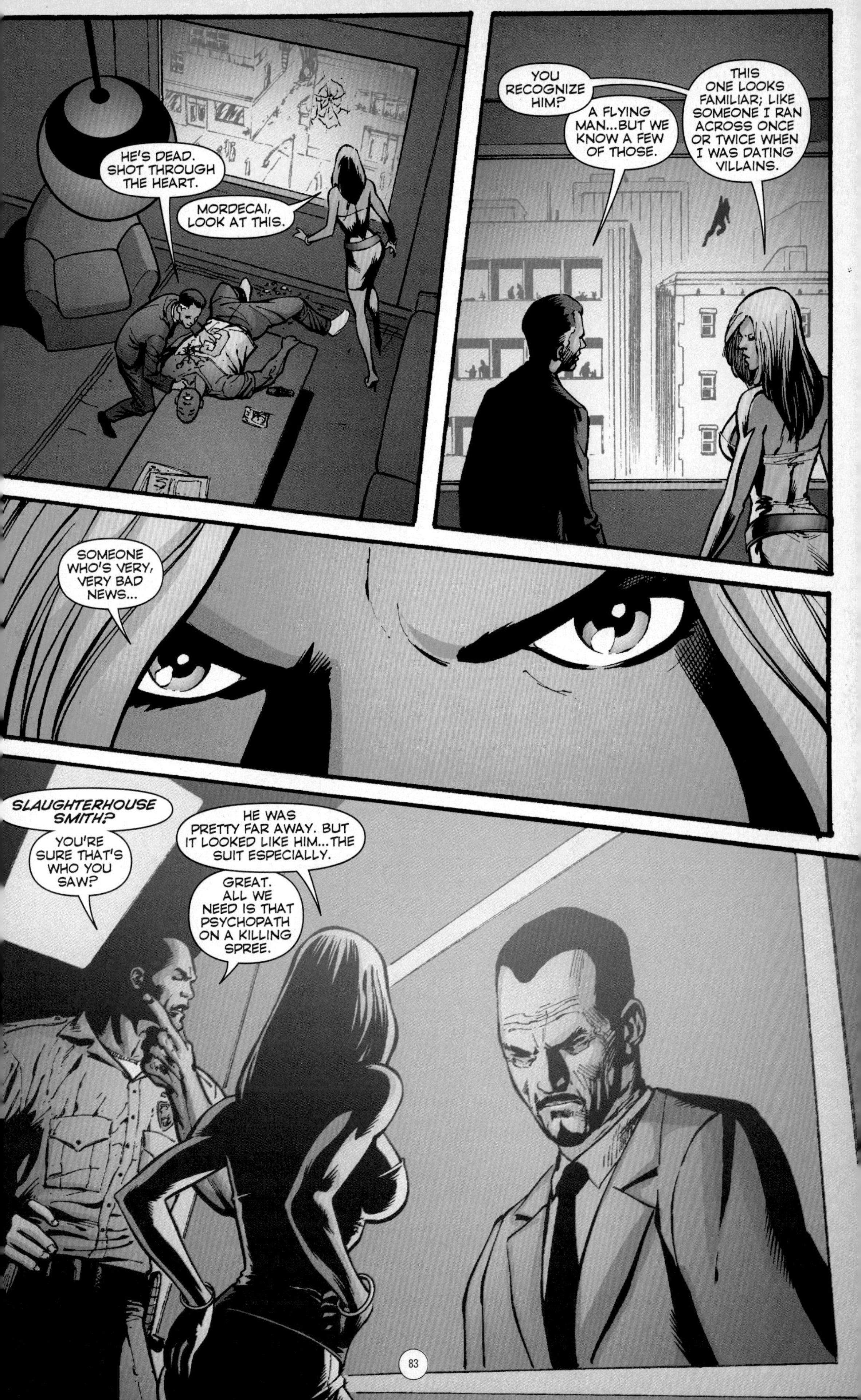
HE'S DEAD. SHOT THROUGH THE HEART.
MORDECAI, LOOK AT THIS.
YOU RECOGNIZE HIM?
A FLYING MAN...BUT WE KNOW A FEW OF THOSE.
THIS ONE LOOKS FAMILIAR; LIKE SOMEONE I RAN ACROSS ONCE OR TWICE WHEN I WAS DATING VILLAINS.
SOMEONE WHO'S VERY, VERY BAD NEWS...
SLAUGHTERHOUSE SMITH?
YOU'RE SURE THAT'S WHO YOU SAW?
HE WAS PRETTY FAR AWAY. BUT IT LOOKED LIKE HIM...THE SUIT ESPECIALLY.
GREAT. ALL WE NEED IS THAT PSYCHOPATH ON A KILLING SPREE.

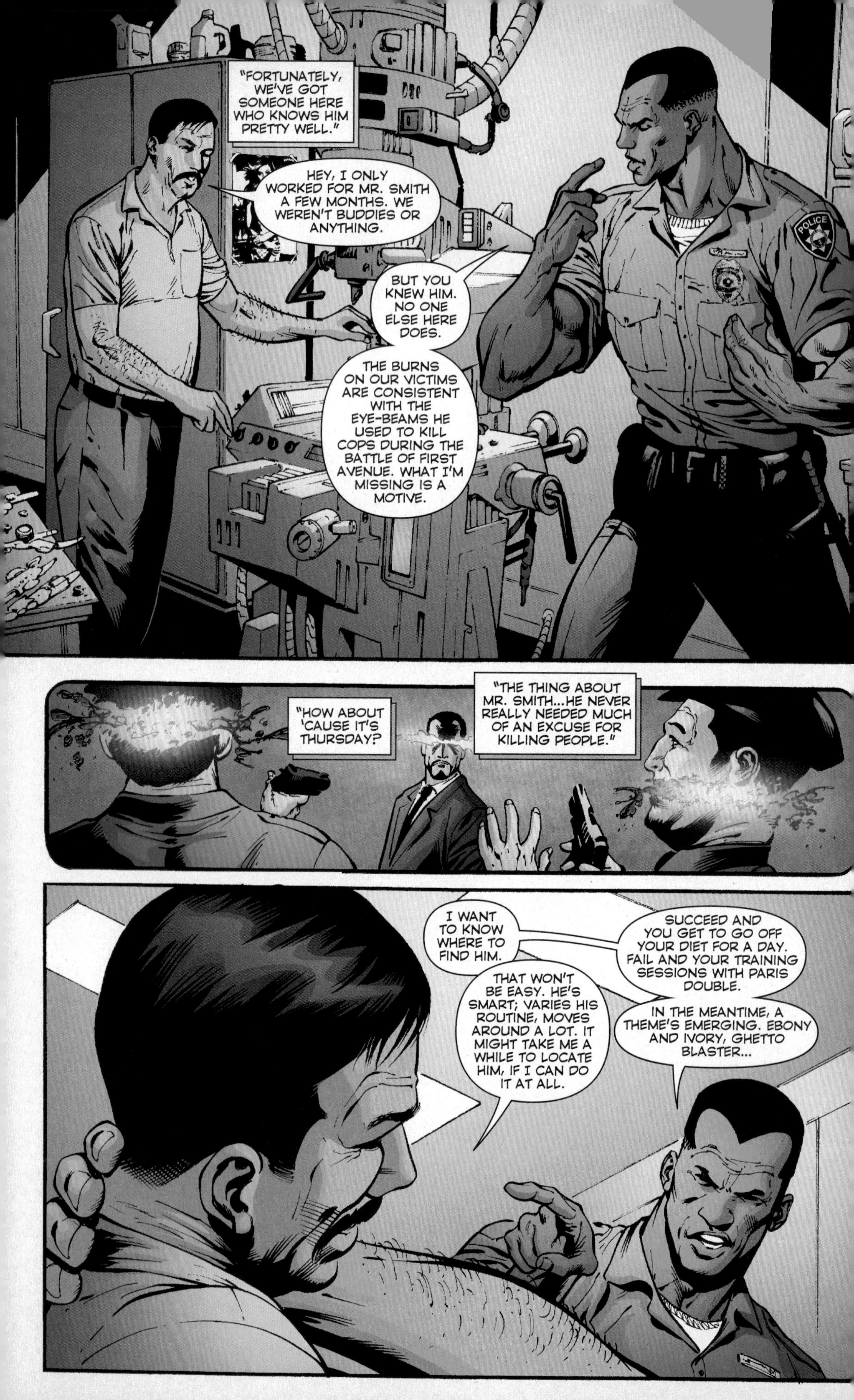
"FORTUNATELY, WE'VE GOT SOMEONE HERE WHO KNOWS HIM PRETTY WELL."
HEY, I ONLY WORKED FOR MR. SMITH A FEW MONTHS. WE WEREN'T BUDDIES OR ANYTHING.
BUT YOU KNEW HIM. NO ONE ELSE HERE DOES.
THE BURNS ON OUR VICTIMS ARE CONSISTENT WITH THE EYE-BEAMS HE USED TO KILL COPS DURING THE BATTLE OF FIRST AVENUE. WHAT I'M MISSING IS A MOTIVE.
"HOW ABOUT 'CAUSE IT'S THURSDAY?
"THE THING ABOUT MR. SMITH...HE NEVER REALLY NEEDED MUCH OF AN EXCUSE FOR KILLING PEOPLE."
I WANT TO KNOW WHERE TO FIND HIM.
THAT WON'T BE EASY. HE'S SMART; VARIES HIS ROUTINE, MOVES AROUND A LOT. IT MIGHT TAKE ME A WHILE TO LOCATE HIM, IF I CAN DO IT AT ALL.
SUCCEED AND YOU GET TO GO OFF YOUR DIET FOR A DAY. FAIL AND YOUR TRAINING SESSIONS WITH PARIS DOUBLE.
IN THE MEANTIME, A THEME'S EMERGING. EBONY AND IVORY, GHETTO BLASTER...

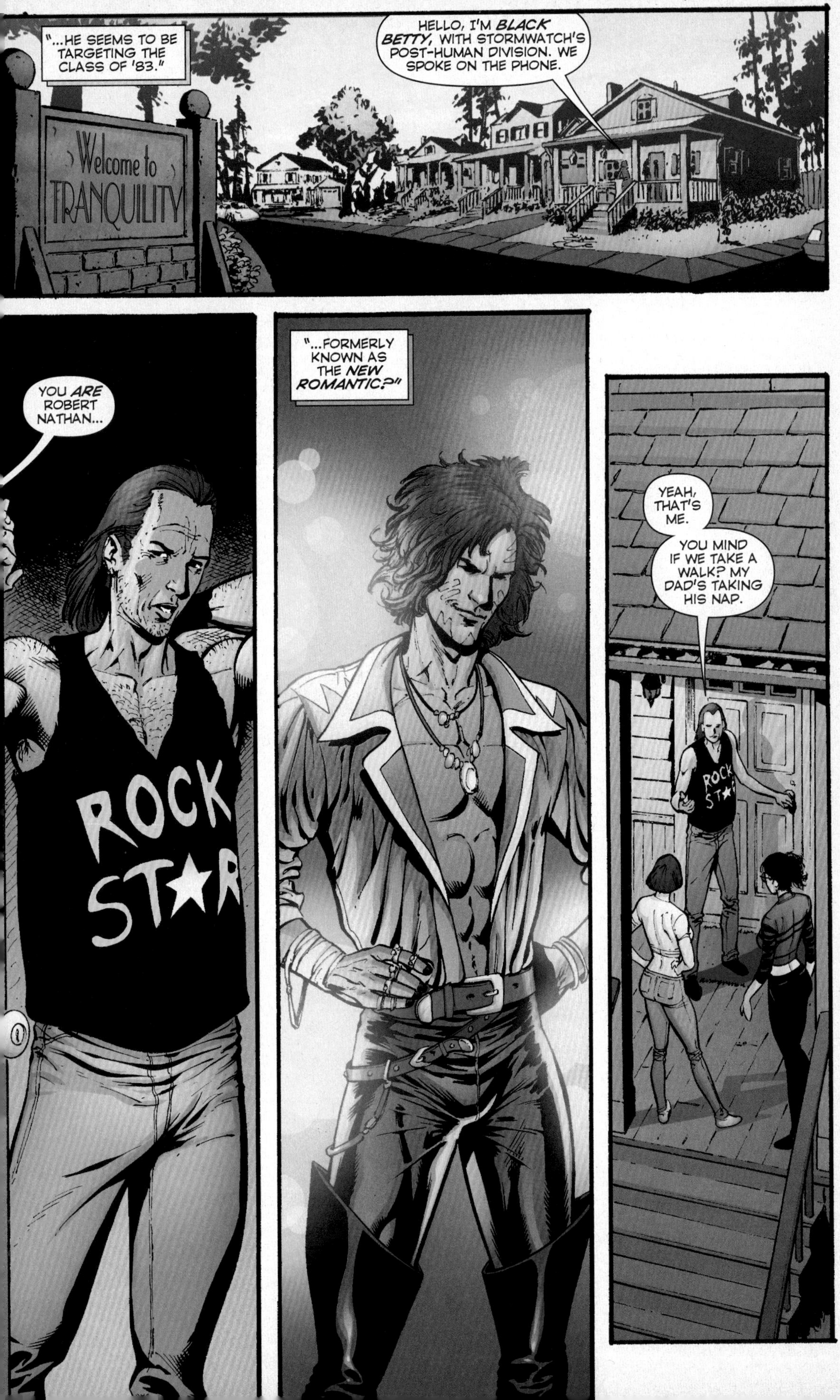
"...HE SEEMS TO BE TARGETING THE CLASS OF '83."
Welcome to TRANQUILITY
HELLO, I'M BLACK BETTY, WITH STORMWATCH'S POST-HUMAN DIVISION. WE SPOKE ON THE PHONE.
YOU ARE ROBERT NATHAN...
ROCK STAR
"...FORMERLY KNOWN AS THE NEW ROMANTIC?"
YEAH, THAT'S ME.
YOU MIND IF WE TAKE A WALK? MY DAD'S TAKING HIS NAP.
ROCK STAR

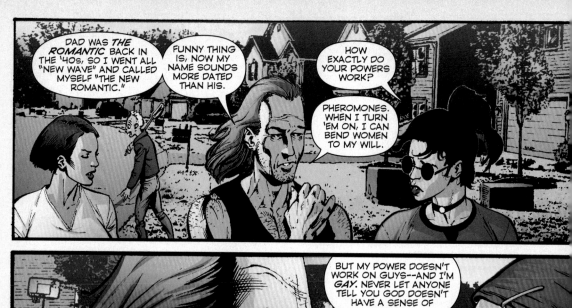

DAD WAS *THE ROMANTIC* BACK IN THE '40s, SO I WENT ALL "NEW WAVE" AND CALLED MYSELF "THE NEW ROMANTIC."

FUNNY THING IS, NOW MY NAME SOUNDS MORE DATED THAN HIS.

HOW EXACTLY DO YOUR POWERS WORK?

PHEROMONES. WHEN I TURN 'EM ON, I CAN BEND WOMEN TO MY WILL.

BUT MY POWER DOESN'T WORK ON GUYS--AND I'M *GAY.* NEVER LET ANYONE TELL YOU GOD DOESN'T HAVE A SENSE OF HUMOR...

NO OFFENSE, BUT THOSE AREN'T EXACTLY COMBAT-OPS TALENTS.

YOU'RE RIGHT. I MOSTLY WORKED INTEL, UNDERCOVER. BENDIX'S BLACK OPS SQUAD.

STORMWATCH BLACK? I THOUGHT HE ONLY FORMED THAT AFTER I WAS ON THE TEAM.

C'MON, YOU KNEW BENDIX. HE HAD MORE SECRET OPS THAN LEGIT ONES. THERE WAS ALWAYS A BLACK TEAM. PROBABLY SEVERAL.

WHO ELSE WAS IN THE UNIT WITH YOU?

OH, THEY'D ROTATE IN AND OUT DEPENDING ON THE MISSION. GHETTO BLASTER, DEATHRACE, EBONY AND IVORY...

...THE *URBAN COWBOY,* THAT POOR BASTARD...JUST DIED OF HEART FAILURE LAST YEAR. RED MEAT WITH EVERY MEAL, THAT GUY.

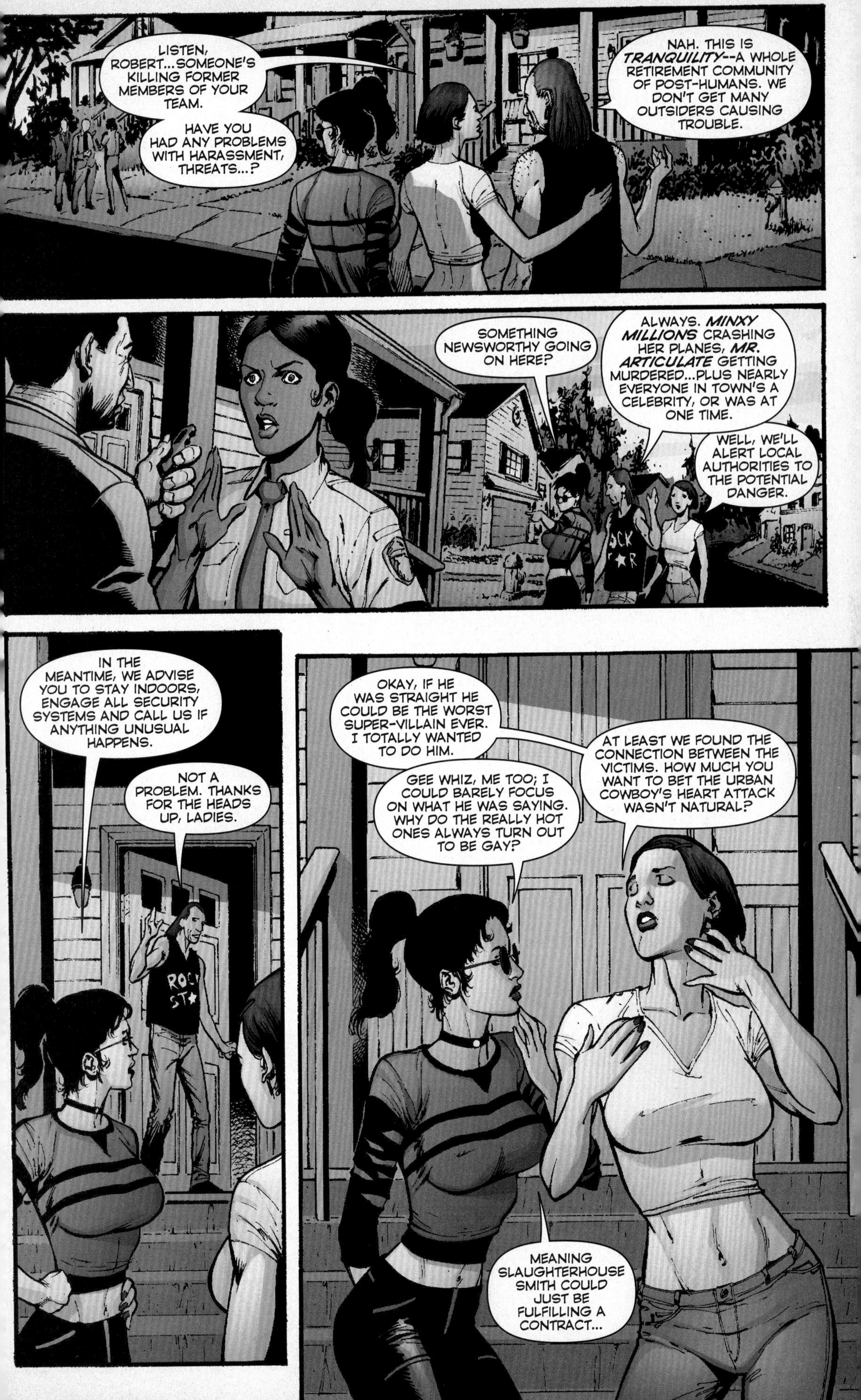
LISTEN, ROBERT...SOMEONE'S KILLING FORMER MEMBERS OF YOUR TEAM.
HAVE YOU HAD ANY PROBLEMS WITH HARASSMENT, THREATS...?
NAH. THIS IS TRANQUILITY--A WHOLE RETIREMENT COMMUNITY OF POST-HUMANS. WE DON'T GET MANY OUTSIDERS CAUSING TROUBLE.
SOMETHING NEWSWORTHY GOING ON HERE?
ALWAYS. MINXY MILLIONS CRASHING HER PLANES, MR. ARTICULATE GETTING MURDERED...PLUS NEARLY EVERYONE IN TOWN'S A CELEBRITY, OR WAS AT ONE TIME.
WELL, WE'LL ALERT LOCAL AUTHORITIES TO THE POTENTIAL DANGER.
IN THE MEANTIME, WE ADVISE YOU TO STAY INDOORS, ENGAGE ALL SECURITY SYSTEMS AND CALL US IF ANYTHING UNUSUAL HAPPENS.
NOT A PROBLEM. THANKS FOR THE HEADS UP, LADIES.
OKAY, IF HE WAS STRAIGHT HE COULD BE THE WORST SUPER-VILLAIN EVER. I TOTALLY WANTED TO DO HIM.
GEE WHIZ, ME TOO; I COULD BARELY FOCUS ON WHAT HE WAS SAYING. WHY DO THE REALLY HOT ONES ALWAYS TURN OUT TO BE GAY?
AT LEAST WE FOUND THE CONNECTION BETWEEN THE VICTIMS. HOW MUCH YOU WANT TO BET THE URBAN COWBOY'S HEART ATTACK WASN'T NATURAL?
MEANING SLAUGHTERHOUSE SMITH COULD JUST BE FULFILLING A CONTRACT...

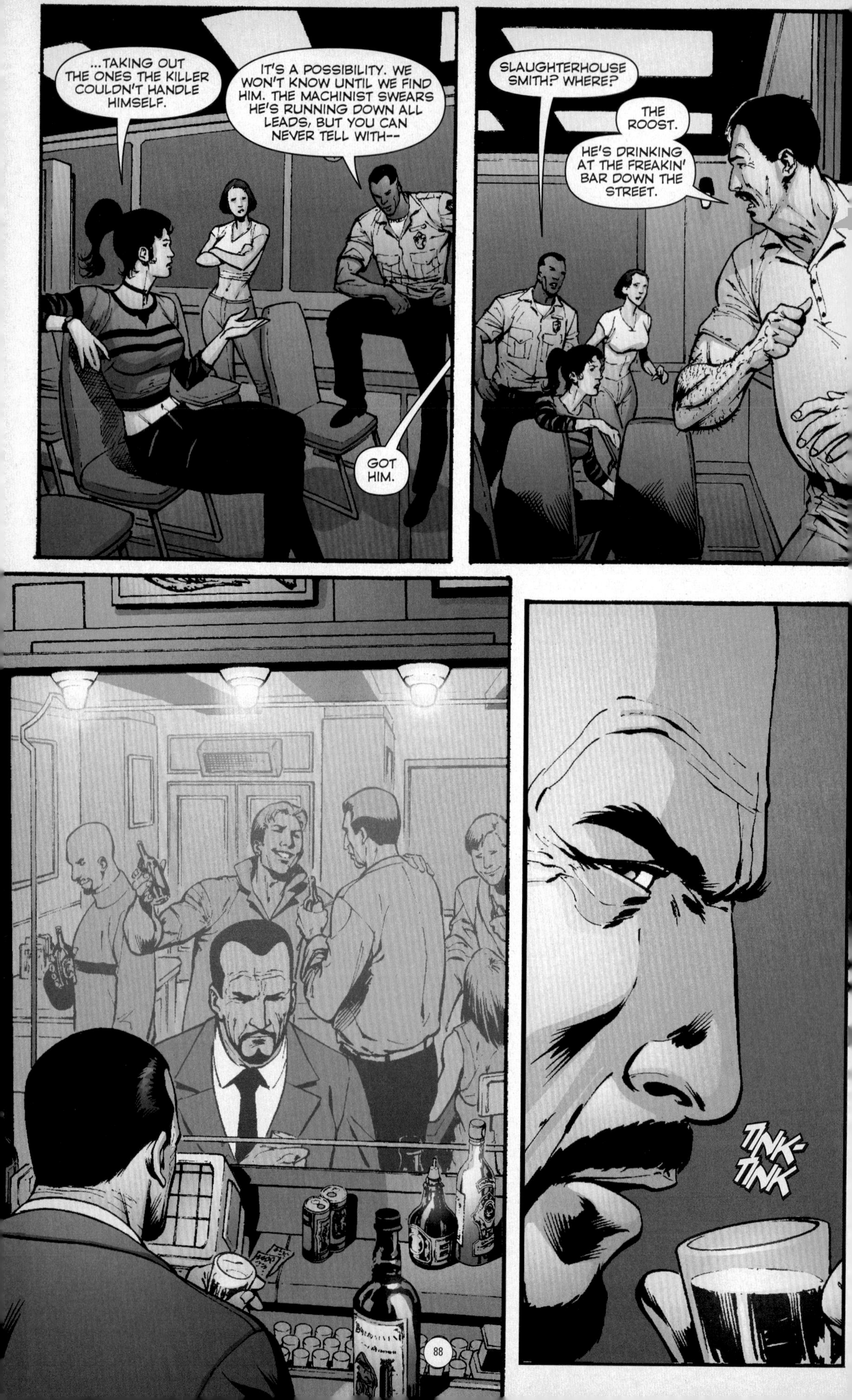

...TAKING OUT THE ONES THE KILLER COULDN'T HANDLE HIMSELF.
IT'S A POSSIBILITY. WE WON'T KNOW UNTIL WE FIND HIM. THE MACHINIST SWEARS HE'S RUNNING DOWN ALL LEADS, BUT YOU CAN NEVER TELL WITH--
GOT HIM.
SLAUGHTERHOUSE SMITH? WHERE?
THE ROOST.
HE'S DRINKING AT THE FREAKIN' BAR DOWN THE STREET.
TINK-TINK

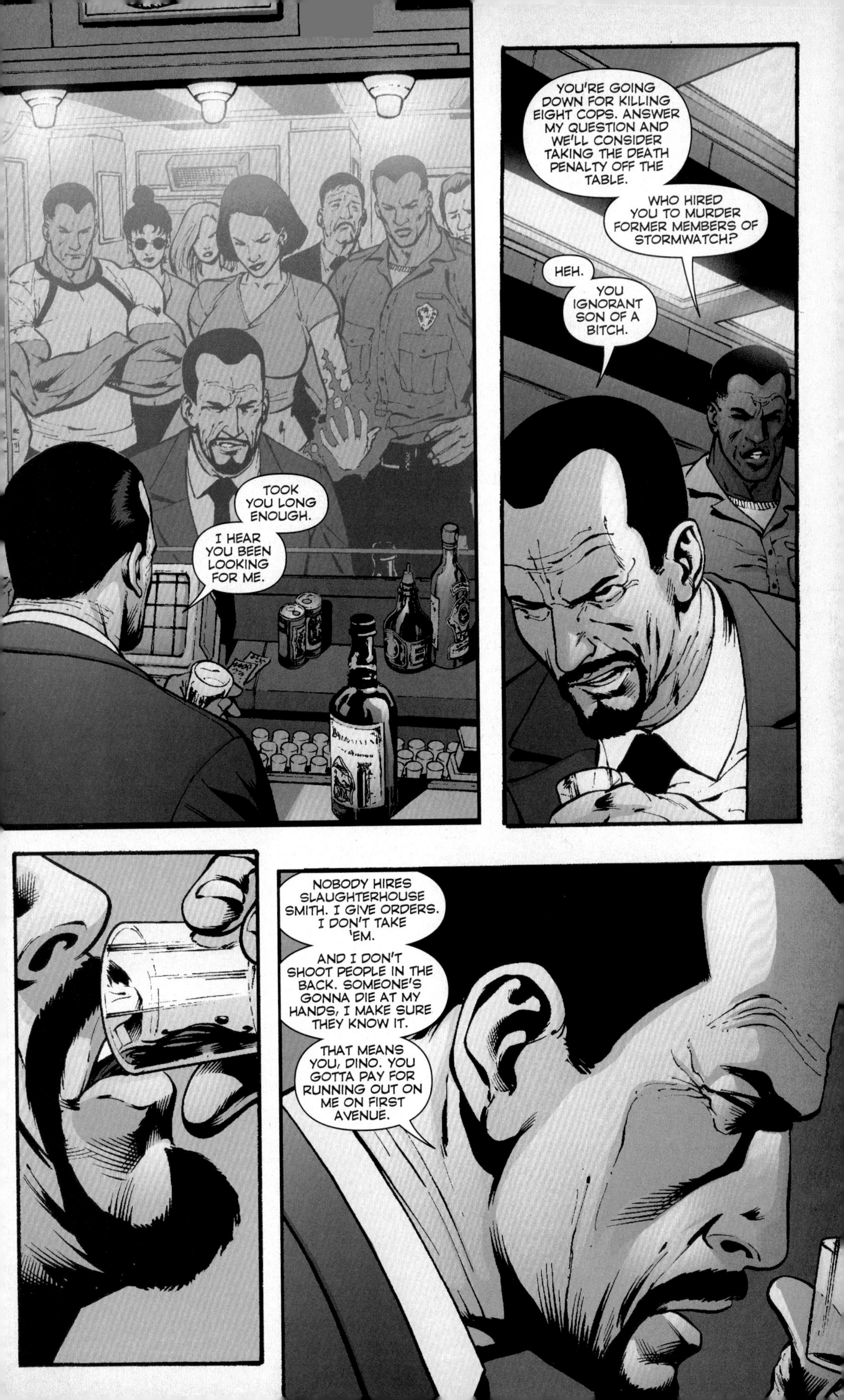
TOOK YOU LONG ENOUGH.
I HEAR YOU BEEN LOOKING FOR ME.
YOU'RE GOING DOWN FOR KILLING EIGHT COPS. ANSWER MY QUESTION AND WE'LL CONSIDER TAKING THE DEATH PENALTY OFF THE TABLE.
WHO HIRED YOU TO MURDER FORMER MEMBERS OF STORMWATCH?
HEH.
YOU IGNORANT SON OF A BITCH.
NOBODY HIRES SLAUGHTERHOUSE SMITH. I GIVE ORDERS. I DON'T TAKE 'EM.
AND I DON'T SHOOT PEOPLE IN THE BACK. SOMEONE'S GONNA DIE AT MY HANDS, I MAKE SURE THEY KNOW IT.
THAT MEANS YOU, DINO. YOU GOTTA PAY FOR RUNNING OUT ON ME ON FIRST AVENUE.

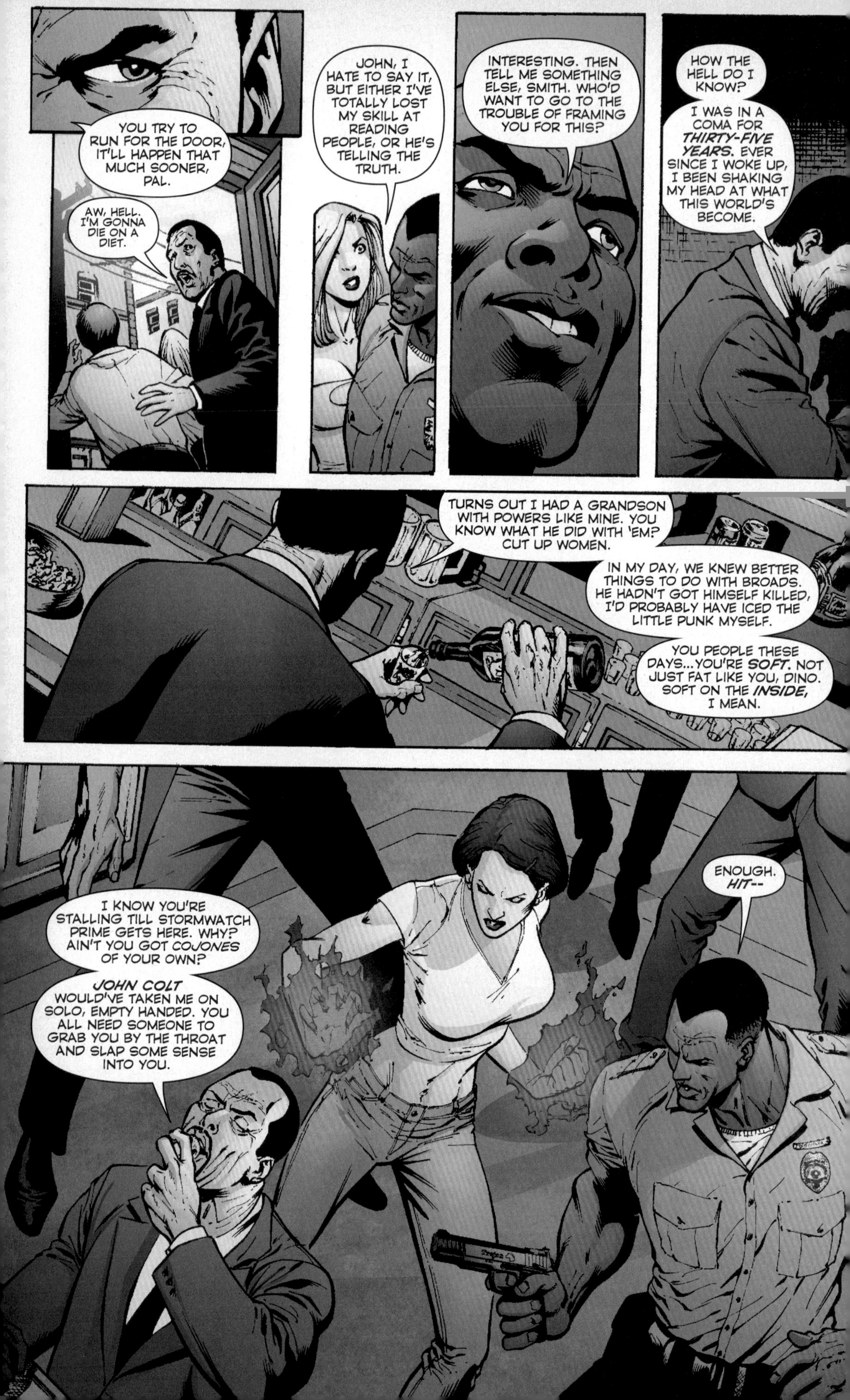
YOU TRY TO RUN FOR THE DOOR, IT'LL HAPPEN THAT MUCH SOONER, PAL.
AW, HELL. I'M GONNA DIE ON A DIET.
JOHN, I HATE TO SAY IT, BUT EITHER I'VE TOTALLY LOST MY SKILL AT READING PEOPLE, OR HE'S TELLING THE TRUTH.
INTERESTING. THEN TELL ME SOMETHING ELSE, SMITH. WHO'D WANT TO GO TO THE TROUBLE OF FRAMING YOU FOR THIS?
HOW THE HELL DO I KNOW?
I WAS IN A COMA FOR THIRTY-FIVE YEARS. EVER SINCE I WOKE UP, I BEEN SHAKING MY HEAD AT WHAT THIS WORLD'S BECOME.
TURNS OUT I HAD A GRANDSON WITH POWERS LIKE MINE. YOU KNOW WHAT HE DID WITH 'EM? CUT UP WOMEN.
IN MY DAY, WE KNEW BETTER THINGS TO DO WITH BROADS. HE HADN'T GOT HIMSELF KILLED, I'D PROBABLY HAVE ICED THE LITTLE PUNK MYSELF.
YOU PEOPLE THESE DAYS...YOU'RE SOFT. NOT JUST FAT LIKE YOU, DINO. SOFT ON THE INSIDE, I MEAN.
I KNOW YOU'RE STALLING TILL STORMWATCH PRIME GETS HERE. WHY? AIN'T YOU GOT COJONES OF YOUR OWN?
JOHN COLT WOULD'VE TAKEN ME ON SOLO, EMPTY HANDED. YOU ALL NEED SOMEONE TO GRAB YOU BY THE THROAT AND SLAP SOME SENSE INTO YOU.
ENOUGH. HIT--

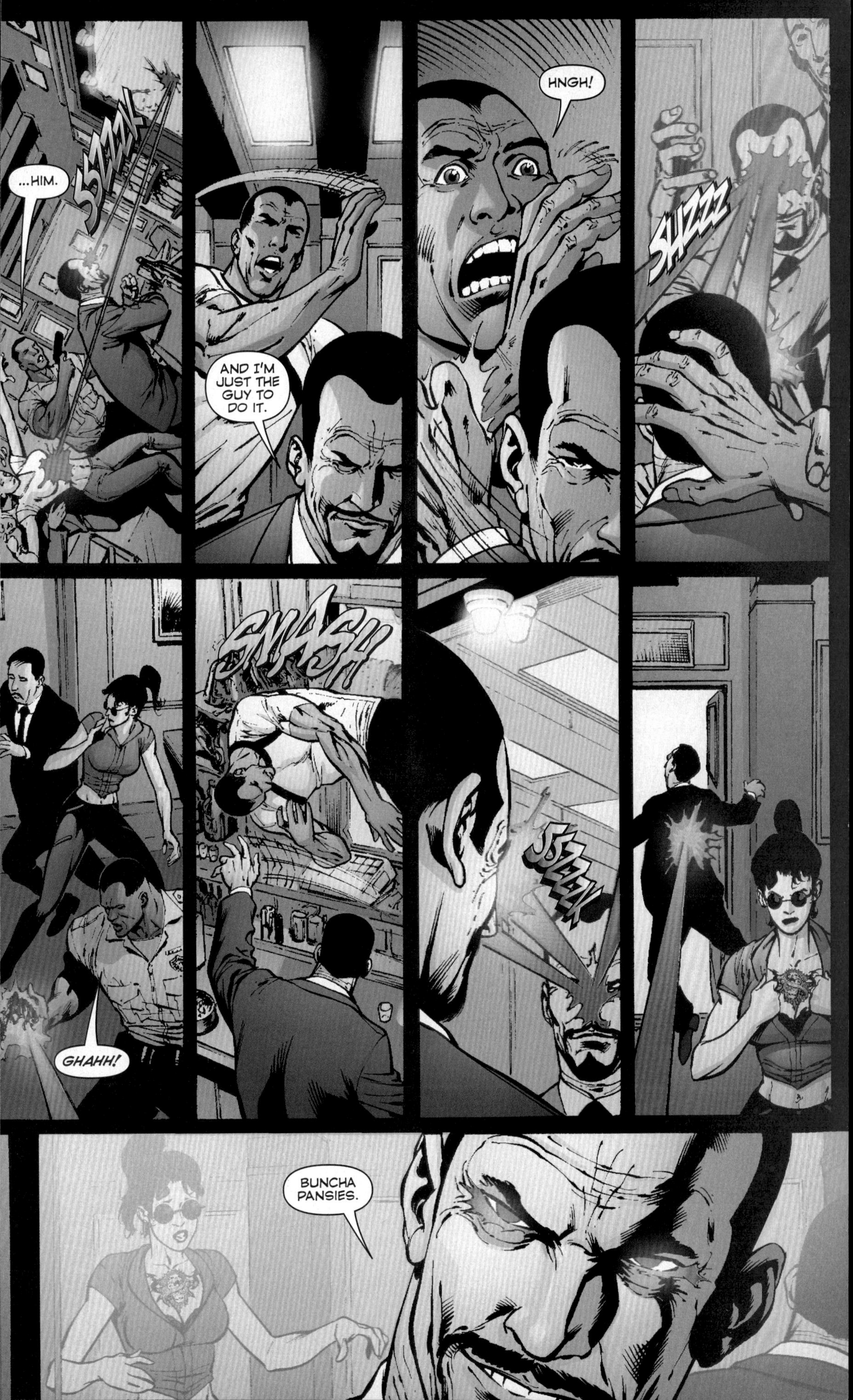
...HIM.
SSZZZK
AND I'M JUST THE GUY TO DO IT.
HNGH!
SHZZZZ
SMASH
GHAHH!
SSZZZK
BUNCHA PANSIES.

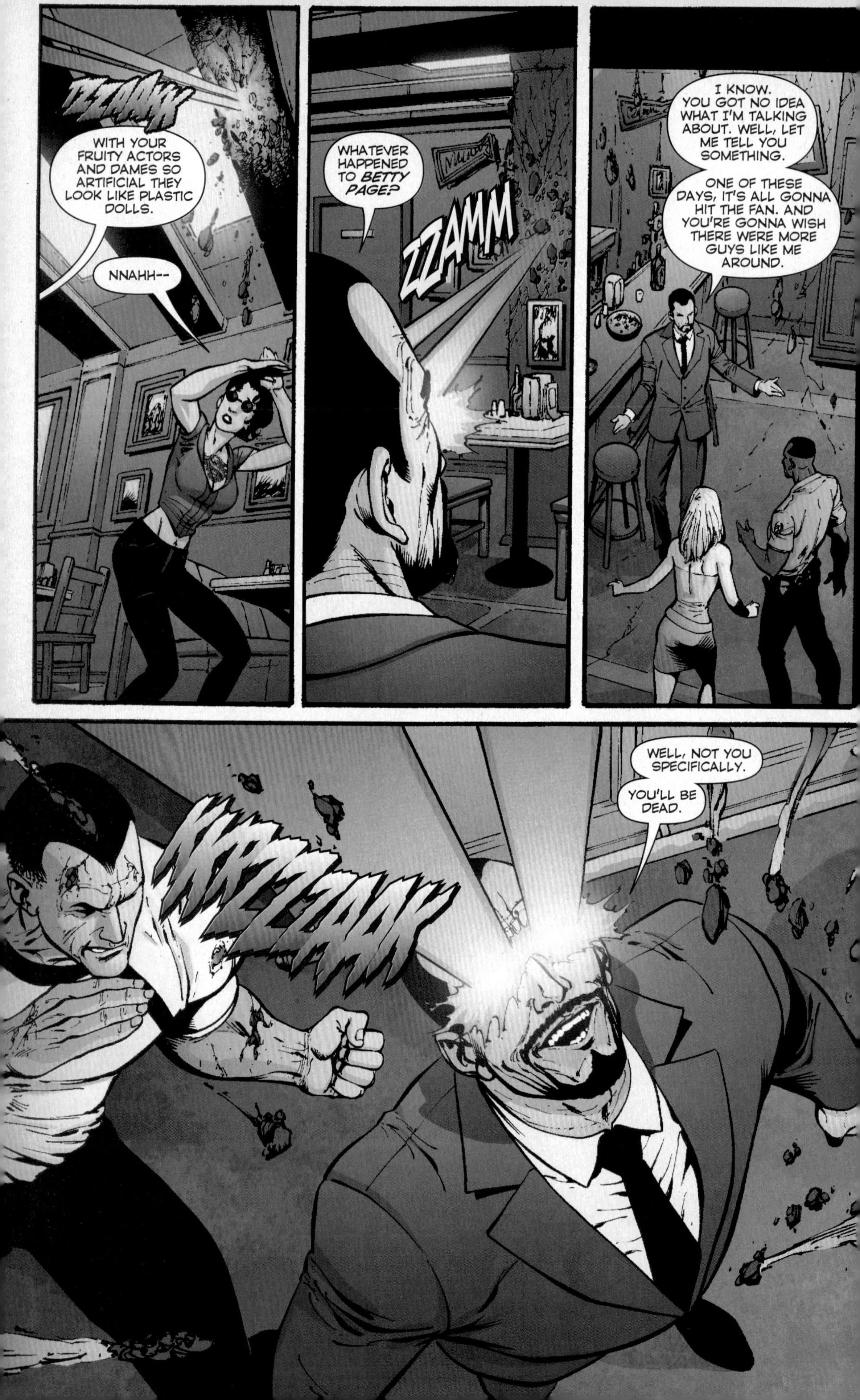
TZZAAKK
WITH YOUR FRUITY ACTORS AND DAMES SO ARTIFICIAL THEY LOOK LIKE PLASTIC DOLLS.
NNAHH--
WHATEVER HAPPENED TO *BETTY PAGE?*
ZZAMM
I KNOW. YOU GOT NO IDEA WHAT I'M TALKING ABOUT. WELL, LET ME TELL YOU SOMETHING.
ONE OF THESE DAYS, IT'S ALL GONNA HIT THE FAN. AND YOU'RE GONNA WISH THERE WERE MORE GUYS LIKE ME AROUND.
WELL, NOT YOU SPECIFICALLY.
YOU'LL BE DEAD.
KRZZAAK

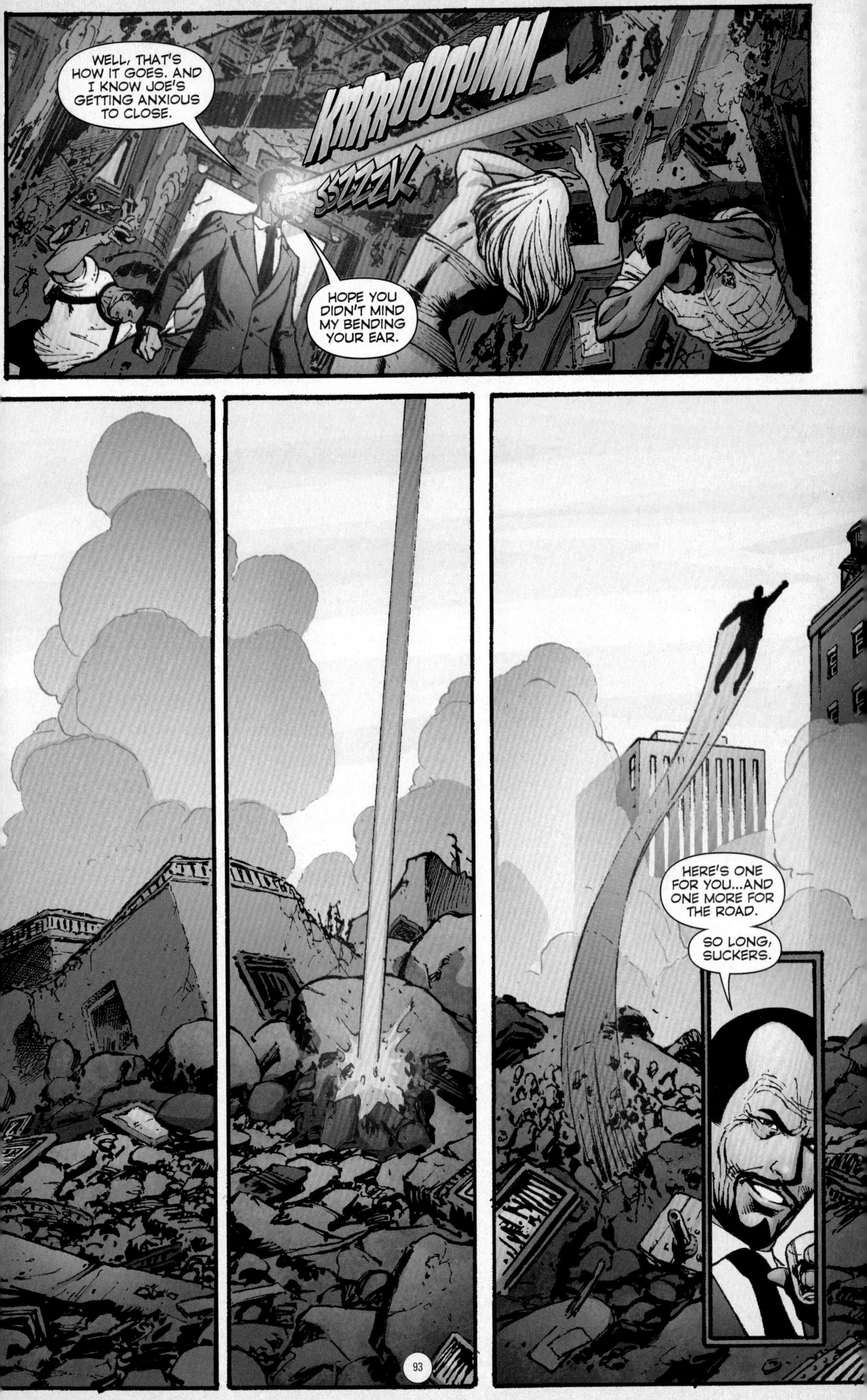

WELL, THAT'S HOW IT GOES. AND I KNOW JOE'S GETTING ANXIOUS TO CLOSE.
KRRRROOOOOMM
SSZZZZK
HOPE YOU DIDN'T MIND MY BENDING YOUR EAR.
HERE'S ONE FOR YOU...AND ONE MORE FOR THE ROAD.
SO LONG, SUCKERS.

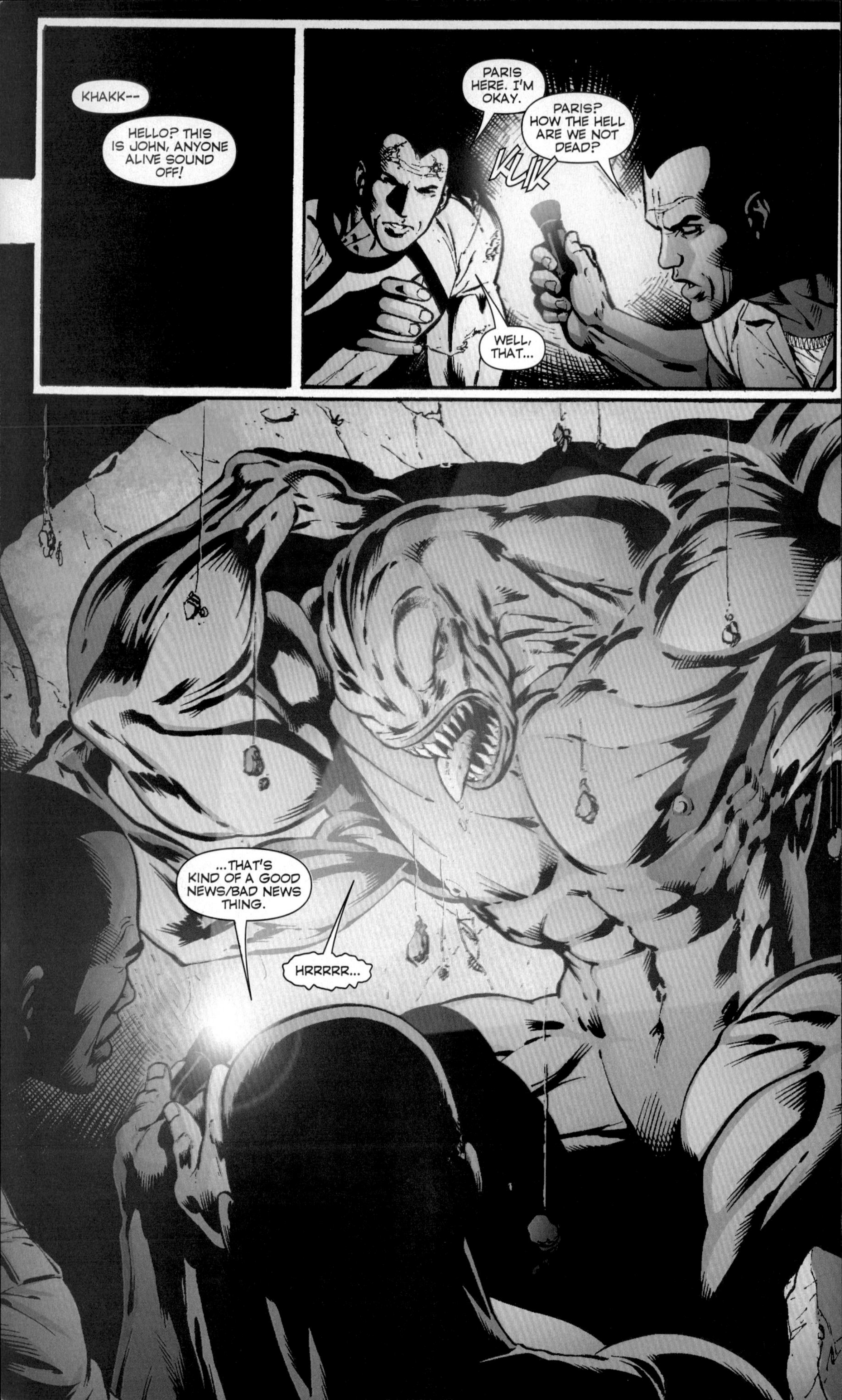
KHAKK--
HELLO? THIS IS JOHN, ANYONE ALIVE SOUND OFF!
PARIS HERE. I'M OKAY.
PARIS? HOW THE HELL ARE WE NOT DEAD?
KLIK
WELL, THAT...
...THAT'S KIND OF A GOOD NEWS/BAD NEWS THING.
HRRRRR...

Mike McKone & David Baron

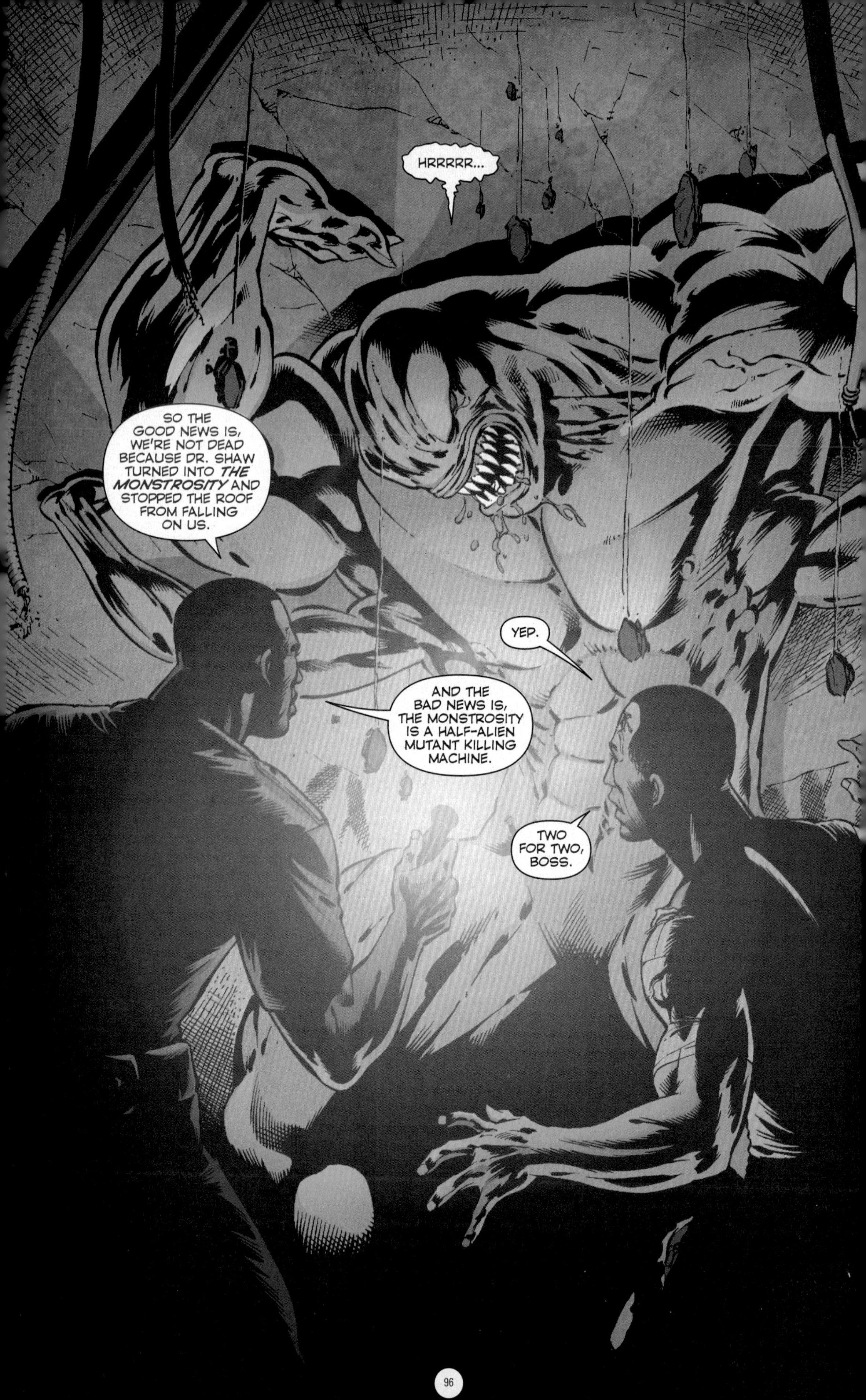
HRRRRR...
SO THE GOOD NEWS IS, WE'RE NOT DEAD BECAUSE DR. SHAW TURNED INTO *THE MONSTROSITY* AND STOPPED THE ROOF FROM FALLING ON US.
YEP.
AND THE BAD NEWS IS, THE MONSTROSITY IS A HALF-ALIEN MUTANT KILLING MACHINE.
TWO FOR TWO, BOSS.

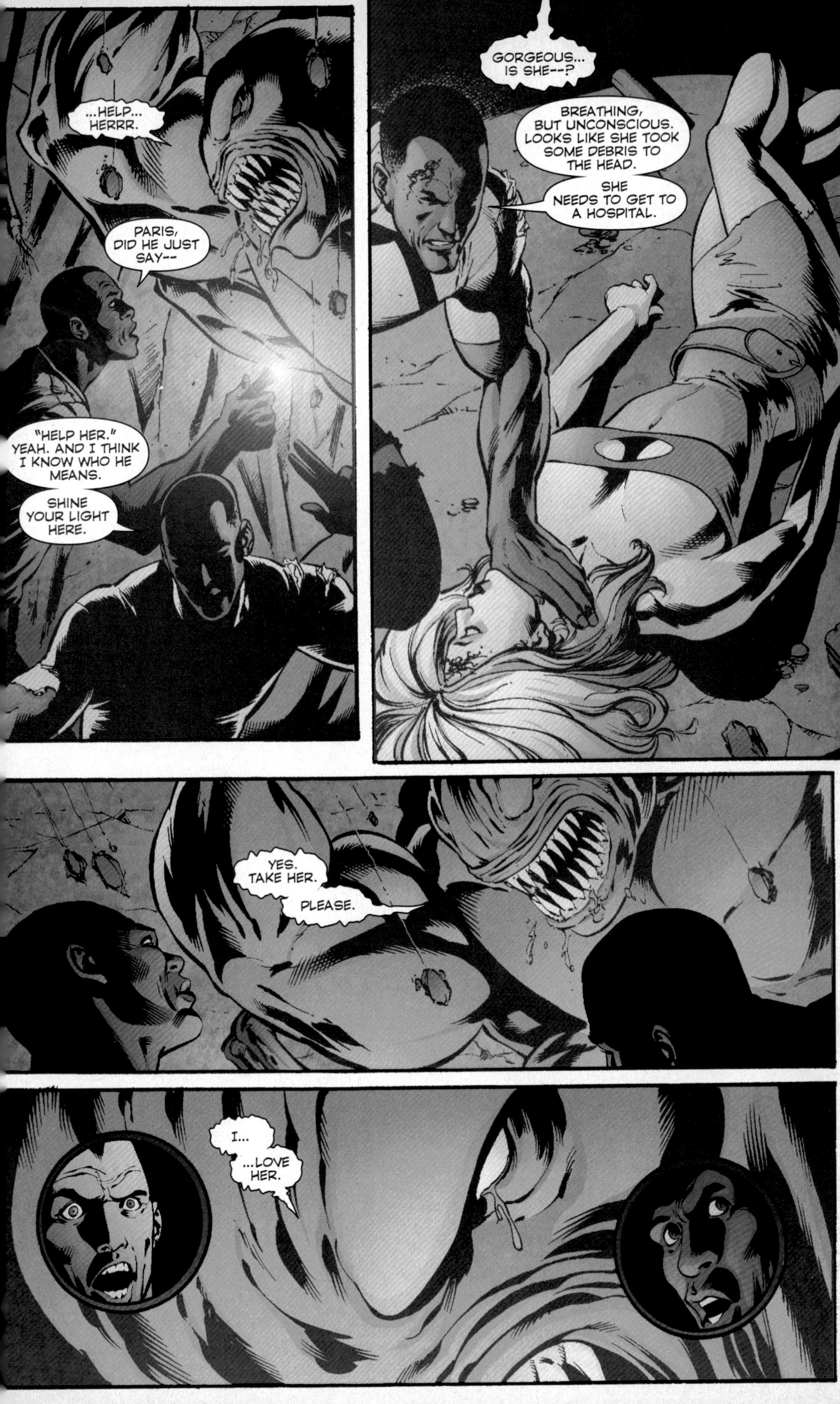
...HELP... HERRR.
PARIS, DID HE JUST SAY--
"HELP HER." YEAH. AND I THINK I KNOW WHO HE MEANS.
SHINE YOUR LIGHT HERE.
GORGEOUS... IS SHE--?
BREATHING, BUT UNCONSCIOUS. LOOKS LIKE SHE TOOK SOME DEBRIS TO THE HEAD.
SHE NEEDS TO GET TO A HOSPITAL.
YES. TAKE HER.
PLEASE.
I...
...LOVE HER.

UM, OKAY. THERE'S NOTHING I'D LIKE BETTER THAN TO GET GORGEOUS TO A HOSPITAL, BUT WE'RE TRAPPED UNDER A BUILDING HERE.

CAN YOU GET IT OFF OF US?

NO...IT'S HEAVY. CAN BARELY...HOLD IT UP.

MACHINIST! YOU'RE ALIVE!

USE YOUR TECH VEST. WHIP UP SOMETHING TO GET US OUT OF HERE.

YEAH, I'M GLAD YOU'RE ALIVE TOO. JERK.

AND AS FOR MY VEST...

THE REASON I'M ALIVE IS 'CAUSE *IT* TOOK *SLAUGHTERHOUSE SMITH'S* EYE-BEAMS INSTEAD OF MY ACHING BACK.

I MIGHT BE ABLE TO MAKE SOMETHING OUT OF THE PARTS, BUT IT'LL BE A WHILE.

WE DON'T HAVE THAT KIND OF TIME.

JOHN, TURN YOUR BEAM IN A 360. LET'S SEE WHO ELSE IS--

UNNNH...

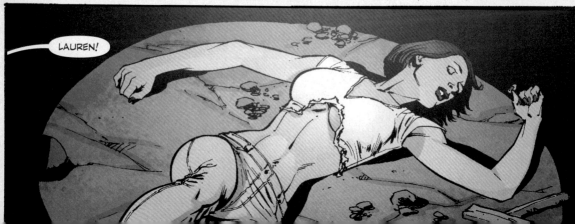

LAUREN!

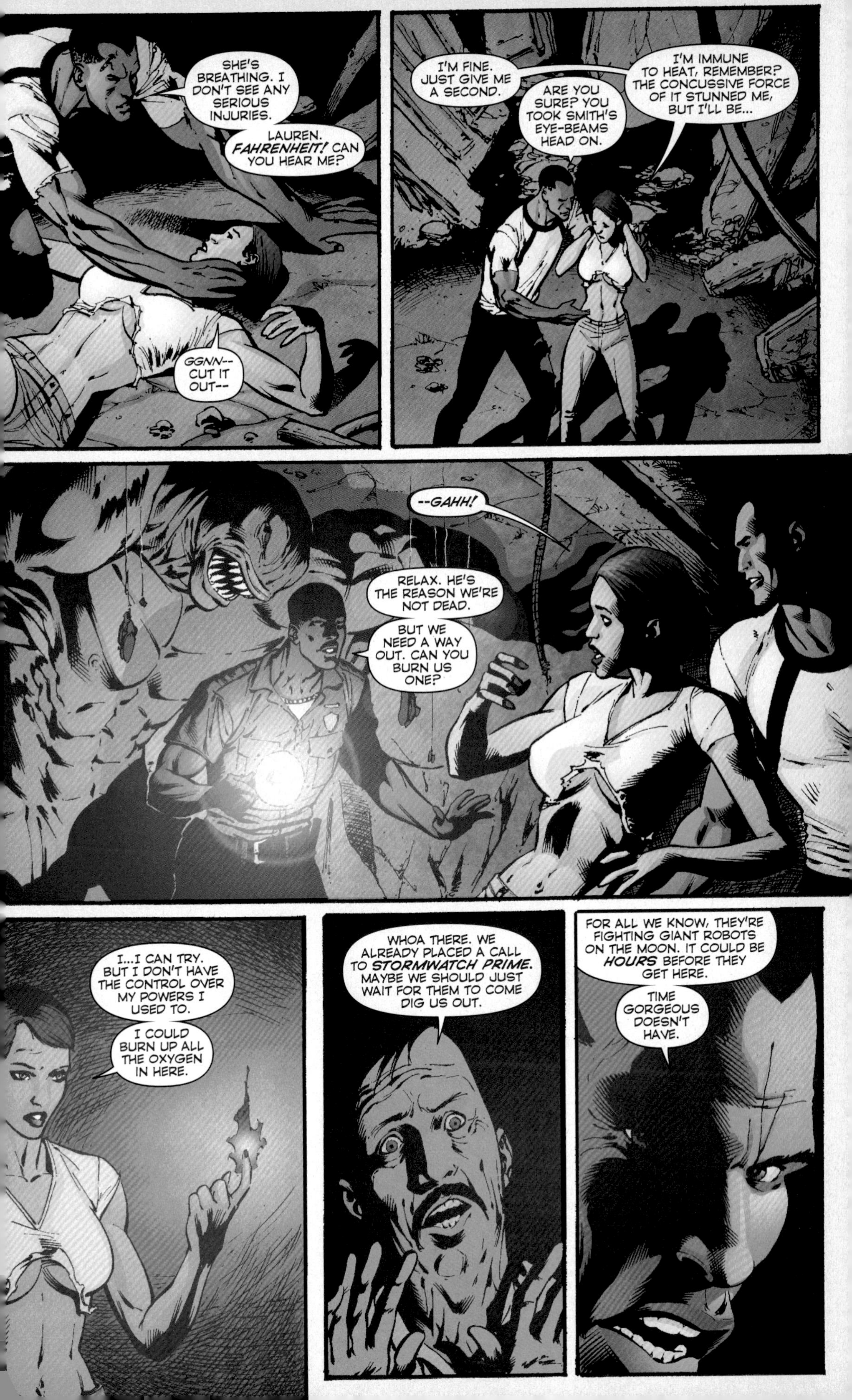
SHE'S BREATHING. I DON'T SEE ANY SERIOUS INJURIES.
LAUREN. *FAHRENHEIT!* CAN YOU HEAR ME?
GGNN-- CUT IT OUT--
I'M FINE. JUST GIVE ME A SECOND.
ARE YOU SURE? YOU TOOK SMITH'S EYE-BEAMS HEAD ON.
I'M IMMUNE TO HEAT, REMEMBER? THE CONCUSSIVE FORCE OF IT STUNNED ME, BUT I'LL BE...
--GAHH!
RELAX. HE'S THE REASON WE'RE NOT DEAD.
BUT WE NEED A WAY OUT. CAN YOU BURN US ONE?
I...I CAN TRY. BUT I DON'T HAVE THE CONTROL OVER MY POWERS I USED TO.
I COULD BURN UP ALL THE OXYGEN IN HERE.
WHOA THERE. WE ALREADY PLACED A CALL TO *STORMWATCH PRIME.* MAYBE WE SHOULD JUST WAIT FOR THEM TO COME DIG US OUT.
FOR ALL WE KNOW, THEY'RE FIGHTING GIANT ROBOTS ON THE MOON. IT COULD BE *HOURS* BEFORE THEY GET HERE.
TIME GORGEOUS DOESN'T HAVE.

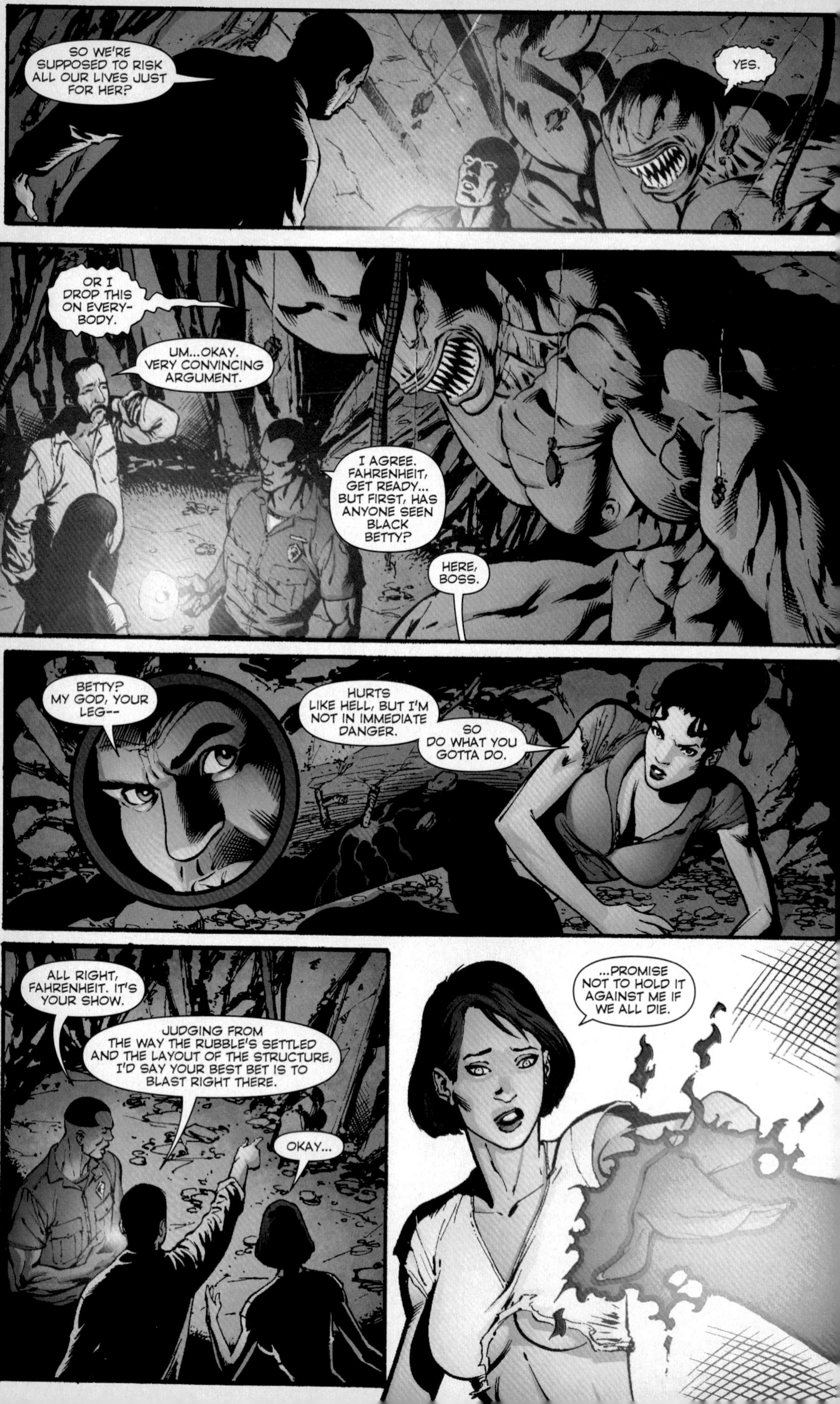
SO WE'RE SUPPOSED TO RISK ALL OUR LIVES JUST FOR HER?
YES.
OR I DROP THIS ON EVERY-BODY.
UM...OKAY. VERY CONVINCING ARGUMENT.
I AGREE. FAHRENHEIT, GET READY... BUT FIRST, HAS ANYONE SEEN BLACK BETTY?
HERE, BOSS.
BETTY? MY GOD, YOUR LEG--
HURTS LIKE HELL, BUT I'M NOT IN IMMEDIATE DANGER.
SO DO WHAT YOU GOTTA DO.
ALL RIGHT, FAHRENHEIT. IT'S YOUR SHOW.
JUDGING FROM THE WAY THE RUBBLE'S SETTLED AND THE LAYOUT OF THE STRUCTURE, I'D SAY YOUR BEST BET IS TO BLAST RIGHT THERE.
OKAY...
...PROMISE NOT TO HOLD IT AGAINST ME IF WE ALL DIE.

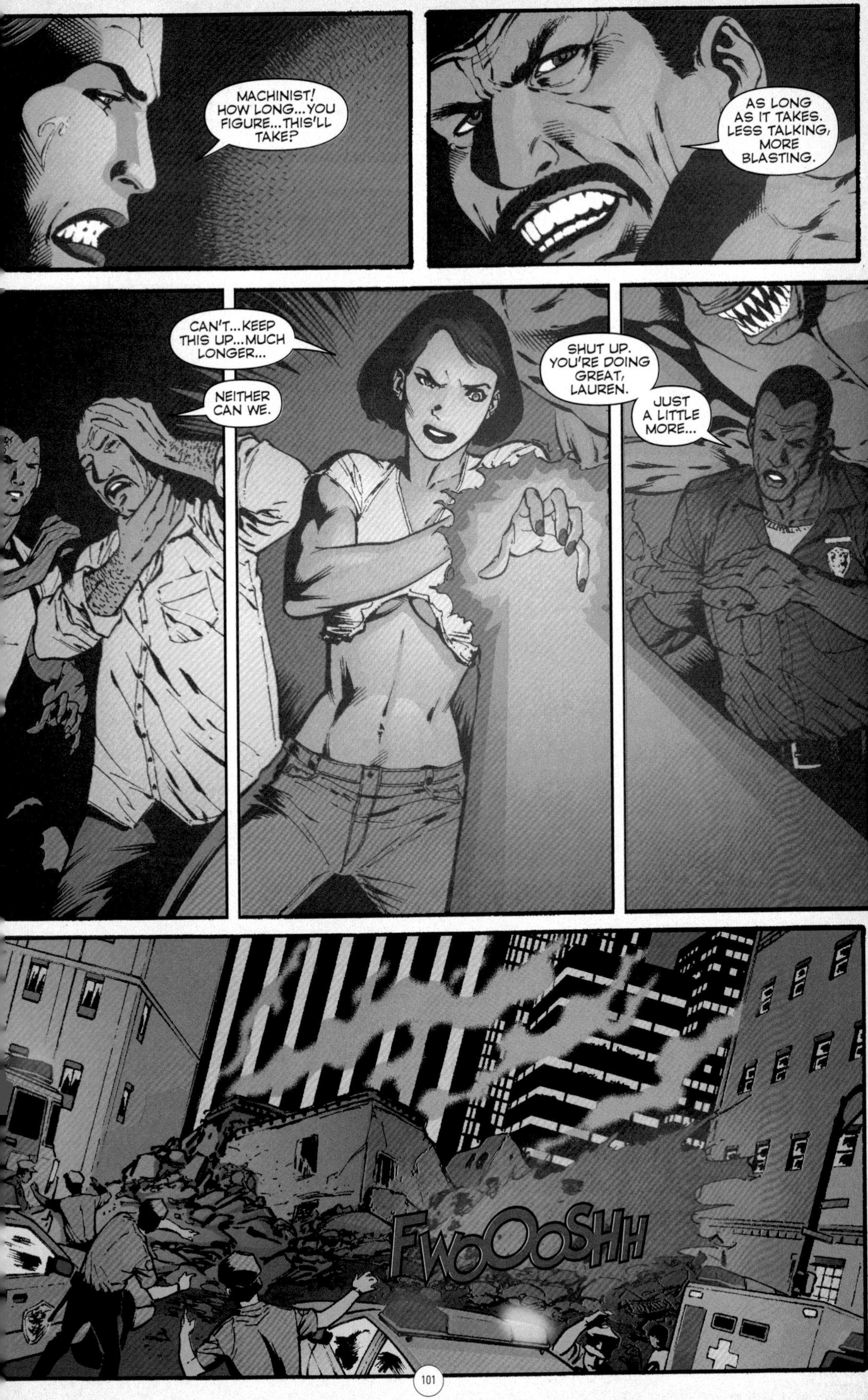

MACHINIST! HOW LONG...YOU FIGURE...THIS'LL TAKE?
AS LONG AS IT TAKES. LESS TALKING, MORE BLASTING.
CAN'T...KEEP THIS UP...MUCH LONGER...
NEITHER CAN WE.
SHUT UP. YOU'RE DOING GREAT, LAUREN.
JUST A LITTLE MORE...
FWOOOOSHH

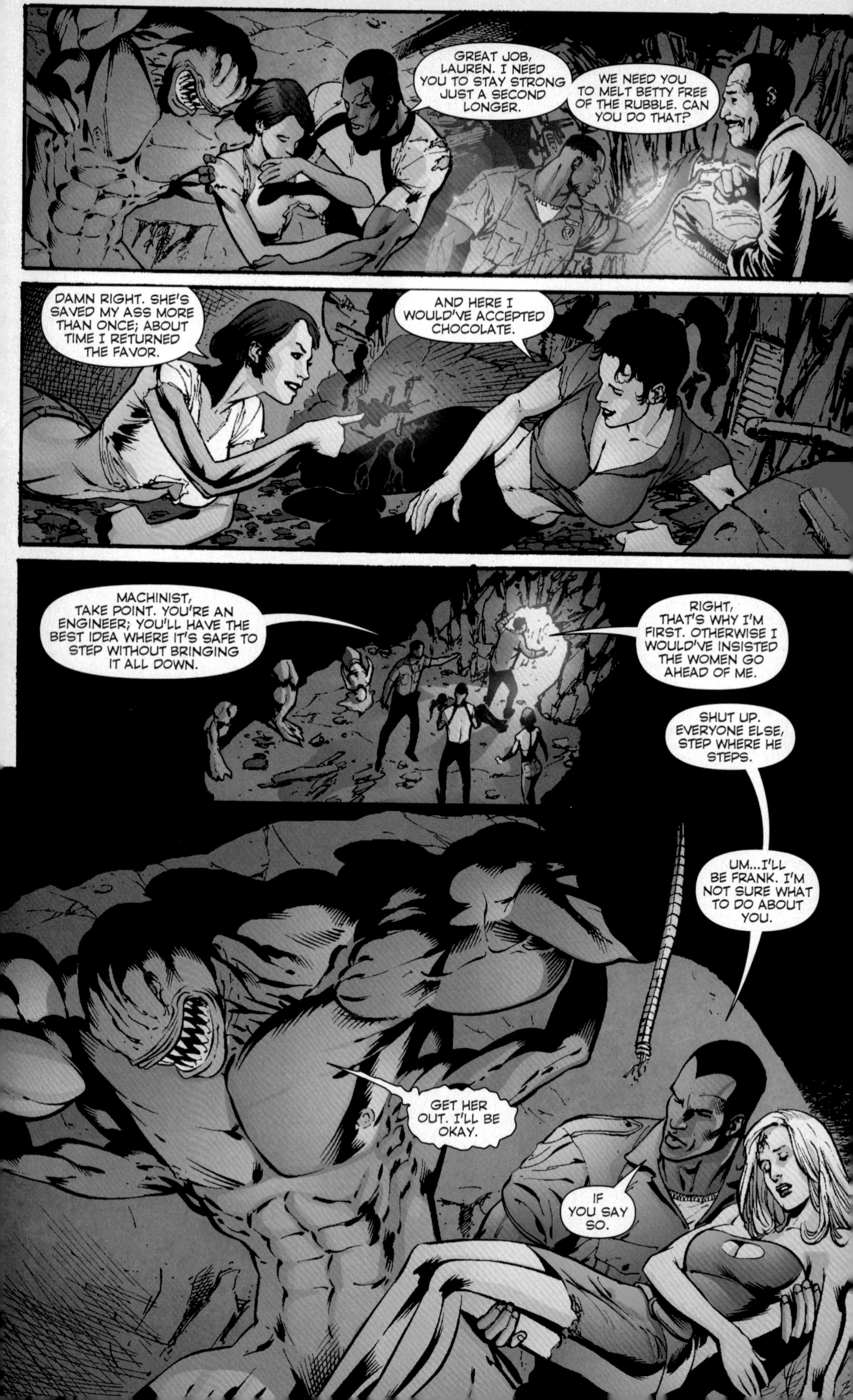

GREAT JOB, LAUREN. I NEED YOU TO STAY STRONG JUST A SECOND LONGER.
WE NEED YOU TO MELT BETTY FREE OF THE RUBBLE. CAN YOU DO THAT?
DAMN RIGHT. SHE'S SAVED MY ASS MORE THAN ONCE; ABOUT TIME I RETURNED THE FAVOR.
AND HERE I WOULD'VE ACCEPTED CHOCOLATE.
MACHINIST, TAKE POINT. YOU'RE AN ENGINEER; YOU'LL HAVE THE BEST IDEA WHERE IT'S SAFE TO STEP WITHOUT BRINGING IT ALL DOWN.
RIGHT, THAT'S WHY I'M FIRST. OTHERWISE I WOULD'VE INSISTED THE WOMEN GO AHEAD OF ME.
SHUT UP. EVERYONE ELSE, STEP WHERE HE STEPS.
UM...I'LL BE FRANK. I'M NOT SURE WHAT TO DO ABOUT YOU.
GET HER OUT. I'LL BE OKAY.
IF YOU SAY SO.

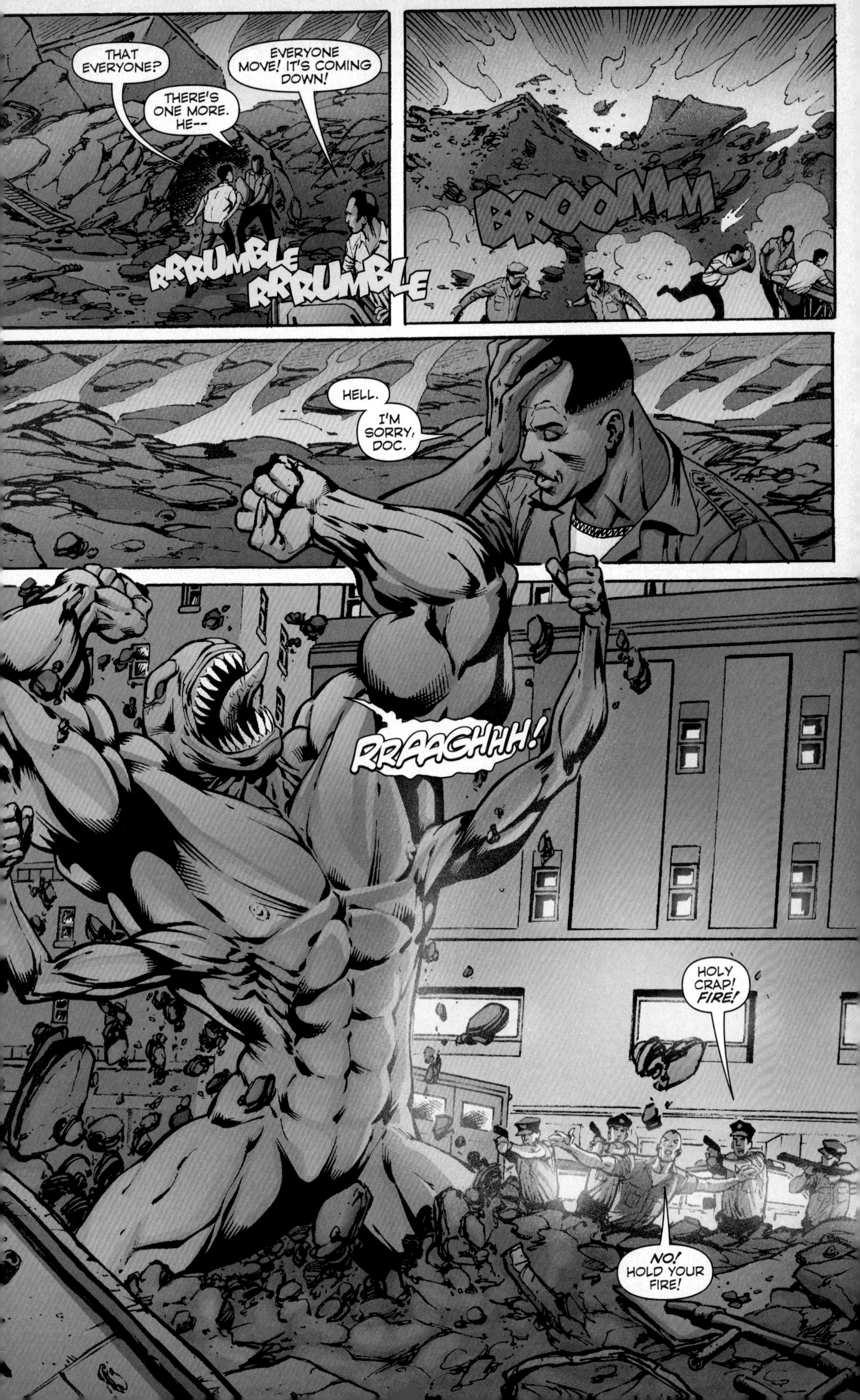
THAT EVERYONE?
THERE'S ONE MORE. HE--
EVERYONE MOVE! IT'S COMING DOWN!
RRRUMBLE RRRUMBLE
BROOMM
HELL.
I'M SORRY, DOC.
RRAAGHHH!
HOLY CRAP! FIRE!
NO! HOLD YOUR FIRE!

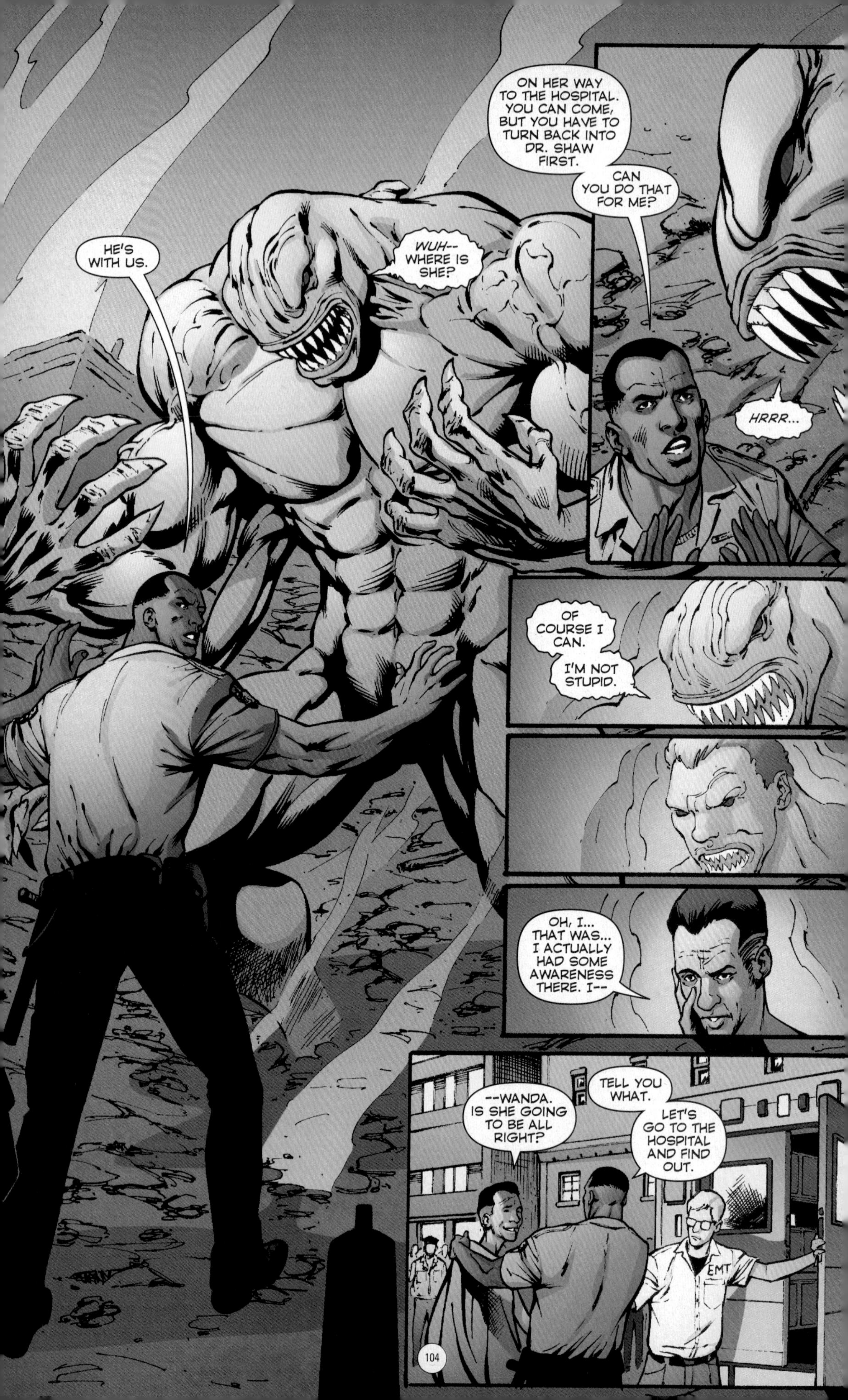
HE'S WITH US.
WUH-- WHERE IS SHE?
ON HER WAY TO THE HOSPITAL. YOU CAN COME, BUT YOU HAVE TO TURN BACK INTO DR. SHAW FIRST.
CAN YOU DO THAT FOR ME?
HRRR...
OF COURSE I CAN.
I'M NOT STUPID.
OH, I... THAT WAS... I ACTUALLY HAD SOME AWARENESS THERE. I--
--WANDA. IS SHE GOING TO BE ALL RIGHT?
TELL YOU WHAT.
LET'S GO TO THE HOSPITAL AND FIND OUT.
EMT

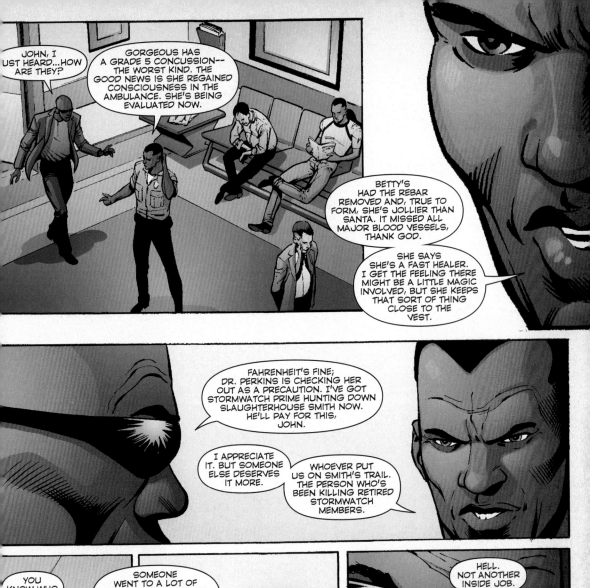

JOHN, I JUST HEARD...HOW ARE THEY?

GORGEOUS HAS A GRADE 5 CONCUSSION--THE WORST KIND. THE GOOD NEWS IS SHE REGAINED CONSCIOUSNESS IN THE AMBULANCE. SHE'S BEING EVALUATED NOW.

BETTY'S HAD THE REBAR REMOVED AND, TRUE TO FORM, SHE'S JOLLIER THAN SANTA. IT MISSED ALL MAJOR BLOOD VESSELS, THANK GOD.

SHE SAYS SHE'S A FAST HEALER. I GET THE FEELING THERE MIGHT BE A LITTLE MAGIC INVOLVED, BUT SHE KEEPS THAT SORT OF THING CLOSE TO THE VEST.

FAHRENHEIT'S FINE; DR. PERKINS IS CHECKING HER OUT AS A PRECAUTION. I'VE GOT STORMWATCH PRIME HUNTING DOWN SLAUGHTERHOUSE SMITH NOW. HE'LL PAY FOR THIS, JOHN.

I APPRECIATE IT. BUT SOMEONE ELSE DESERVES IT MORE.

WHOEVER PUT US ON SMITH'S TRAIL. THE PERSON WHO'S BEEN KILLING RETIRED STORMWATCH MEMBERS.

YOU KNOW WHO IT IS?

I HAVE A THEORY.

SOMEONE WENT TO A LOT OF TROUBLE TO MAKE US THINK SLAUGHTERHOUSE SMITH KILLED THOSE PEOPLE.

FROM WEARING CLOTHES LIKE HIS WHEN THEY KILLED *GHETTO BLASTER* TO MAKING SURE THE LETHAL LASER BLASTS FORENSICALLY RESEMBLED SMITH'S EYE BEAMS.

THIS SOMEONE KNOWS A LOT ABOUT OUR OPERATIONS. AND HAS ACCESS TO TECH LIKE HOVER-PACKS AND LASER GUNS.

HELL. NOT ANOTHER INSIDE JOB.

LET'S FIND OUT.

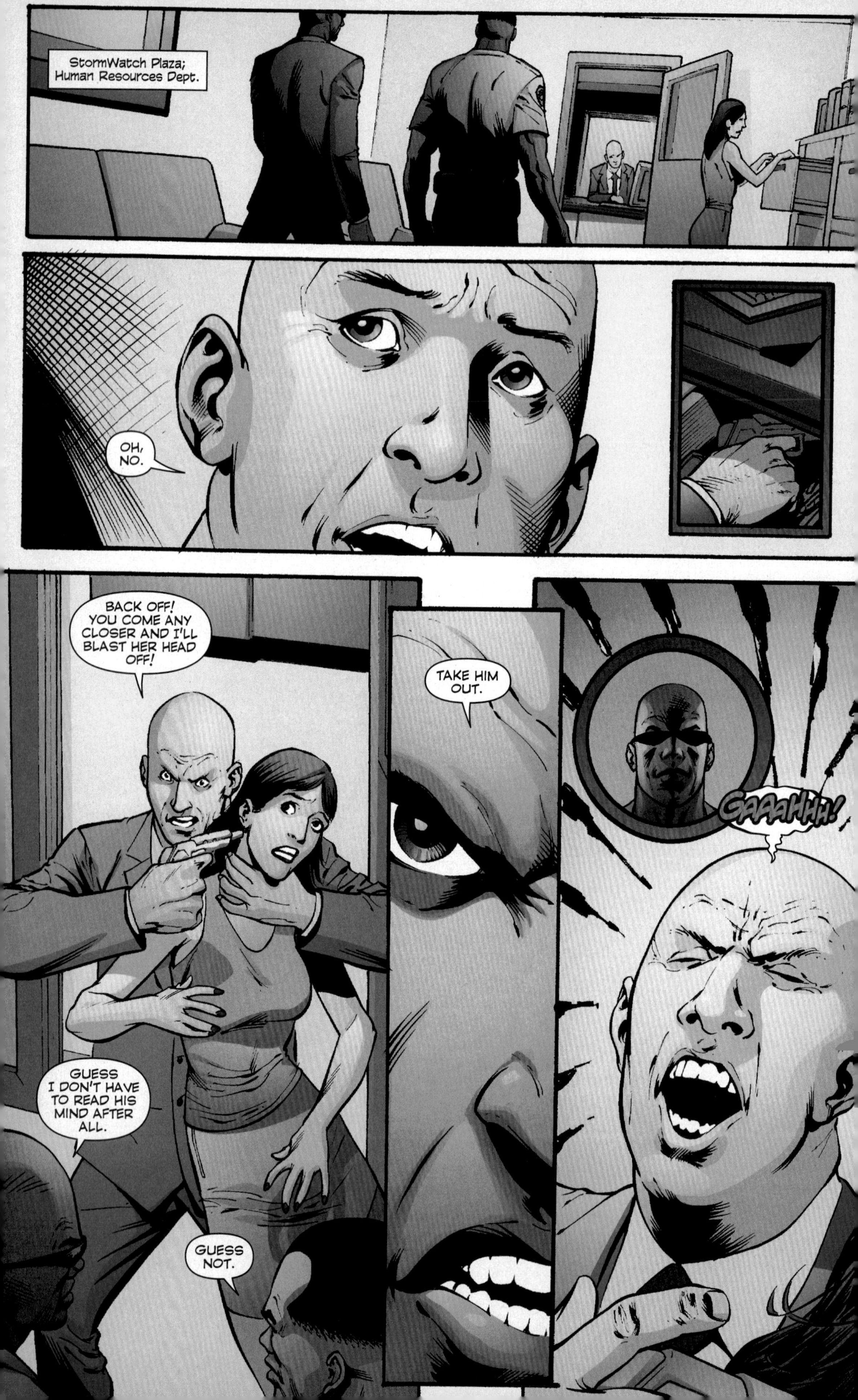
StormWatch Plaza; Human Resources Dept.
OH, NO.
BACK OFF! YOU COME ANY CLOSER AND I'LL BLAST HER HEAD OFF!
GUESS I DON'T HAVE TO READ HIS MIND AFTER ALL.
GUESS NOT.
TAKE HIM OUT.
GAAAHHH!

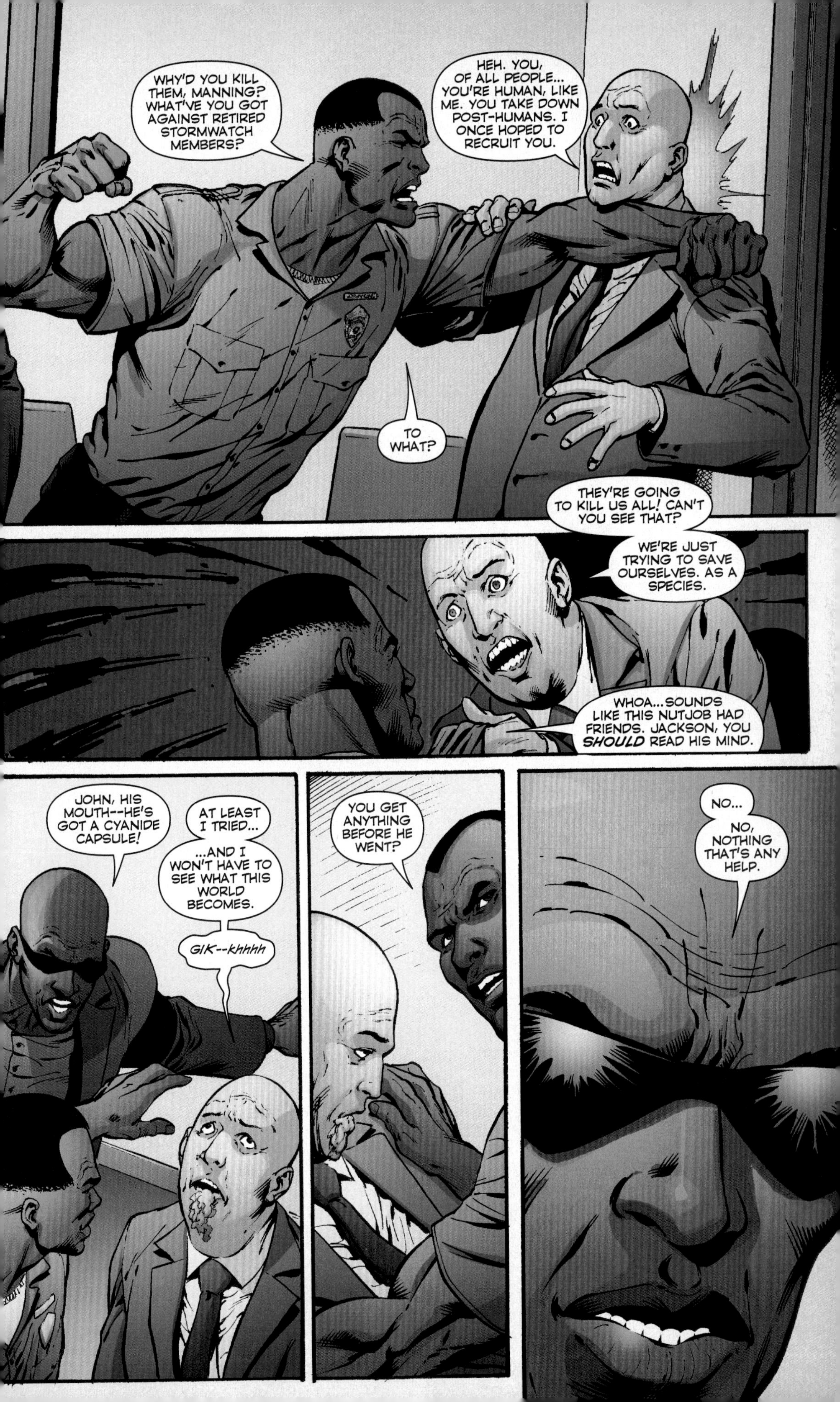

WHY'D YOU KILL THEM, MANNING? WHAT'VE YOU GOT AGAINST RETIRED STORMWATCH MEMBERS?
HEH. YOU, OF ALL PEOPLE... YOU'RE HUMAN, LIKE ME. YOU TAKE DOWN POST-HUMANS. I ONCE HOPED TO RECRUIT YOU.
TO WHAT?
THEY'RE GOING TO KILL US ALL! CAN'T YOU SEE THAT?
WE'RE JUST TRYING TO SAVE OURSELVES. AS A SPECIES.
WHOA...SOUNDS LIKE THIS NUTJOB HAD FRIENDS. JACKSON, YOU *SHOULD* READ HIS MIND.
JOHN, HIS MOUTH--HE'S GOT A CYANIDE CAPSULE!
AT LEAST I TRIED...
...AND I WON'T HAVE TO SEE WHAT THIS WORLD BECOMES.
GIK--khhhh
YOU GET ANYTHING BEFORE HE WENT?
NO...
NO, NOTHING THAT'S ANY HELP.

I'M HAPPY TO SAY MS. DURST DOESN'T SHOW ANY SIGNS OF NEUROLOGICAL DAMAGE. SHE'S STILL GROGGY, BUT SHE SHOULD BE ABLE TO RECEIVE VISITORS SOON.

OH, THANK GOD.

THANKS, DOC.

HEY. SHAW.

THIS WHOLE THING ABOUT BEING IN LOVE WITH GORGEOUS...IS THAT JUST THE MONSTER, OR IS IT YOU?

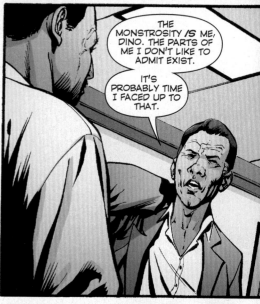

THE MONSTROSITY *IS* ME, DINO. THE PARTS OF ME I DON'T LIKE TO ADMIT EXIST.

IT'S PROBABLY TIME I FACED UP TO THAT.

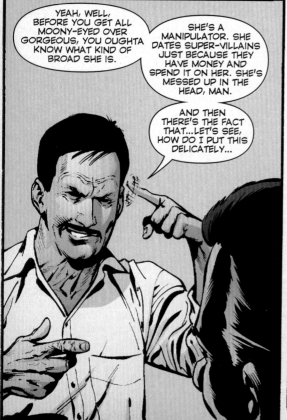

YEAH, WELL, BEFORE YOU GET ALL MOONY-EYED OVER GORGEOUS, YOU OUGHTA KNOW WHAT KIND OF BROAD SHE IS.

SHE'S A MANIPULATOR. SHE DATES SUPER-VILLAINS JUST BECAUSE THEY HAVE MONEY AND SPEND IT ON HER. SHE'S MESSED UP IN THE HEAD, MAN.

AND THEN THERE'S THE FACT THAT...LET'S SEE, HOW DO I PUT THIS DELICATELY...

SHE'S BEEN SAMPLED MORE TIMES THAN JAMES BROWN.

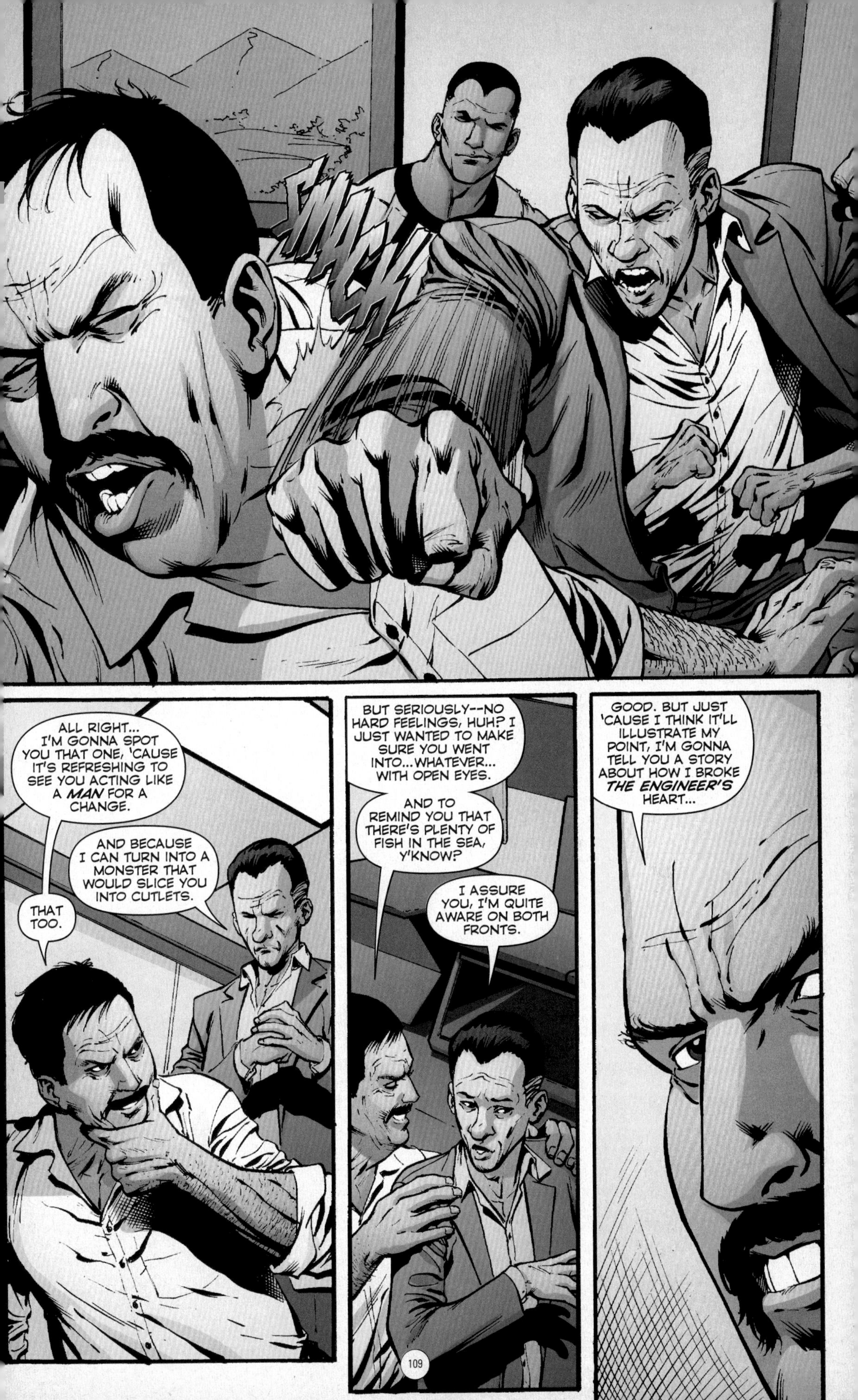
SMACK
ALL RIGHT... I'M GONNA SPOT YOU THAT ONE, 'CAUSE IT'S REFRESHING TO SEE YOU ACTING LIKE A *MAN* FOR A CHANGE.
AND BECAUSE I CAN TURN INTO A MONSTER THAT WOULD SLICE YOU INTO CUTLETS.
THAT TOO.
BUT SERIOUSLY--NO HARD FEELINGS, HUH? I JUST WANTED TO MAKE SURE YOU WENT INTO...WHATEVER... WITH OPEN EYES.
AND TO REMIND YOU THAT THERE'S PLENTY OF FISH IN THE SEA, Y'KNOW?
I ASSURE YOU, I'M QUITE AWARE ON BOTH FRONTS.
GOOD. BUT JUST 'CAUSE I THINK IT'LL ILLUSTRATE MY POINT, I'M GONNA TELL YOU A STORY ABOUT HOW I BROKE ***THE ENGINEER'S*** HEART...

THAT WAS STORMWATCH SECURITY. TURNS OUT CRAIG MANNING'S BROTHER WAS PART OF A SECRET I.O. BLACK OPS CELL CALLED *THE PURITANS*.

DEDICATED TO WIPING ALL ALIENS AND SUPERHUMANS FROM THE PLANET. "EARTH FOR HUMANITY" AND ALL THAT. THEY WERE SHUT DOWN YEARS AGO.

NOT HARD TO IMAGINE HE'D BE A SYMPATHIZER. THIS COME UP IN MANNING'S BACKGROUND CHECK?

SURE, BUT HIS OWN RECORD WAS SPOTLESS. AND HIS BROTHER'S ACTIVITIES WERE TOP SECRET, SO WE HAD NO REASON TO BELIEVE HE EVER KNEW ABOUT THEM.

SO THE QUESTION IS, WAS HE ACTING ALONE--CARRYING ON THE FAMILY LEGACY? OR ARE THE PURITANS STILL AROUND IN SOME CAPACITY?

ALREADY BEING LOOKED INTO.

AND WHAT POSSIBLE THREAT DID HE THINK A BUNCH OF MIDDLE-AGED, RETIRED SUPERHUMANS POSED, ANYWAY?

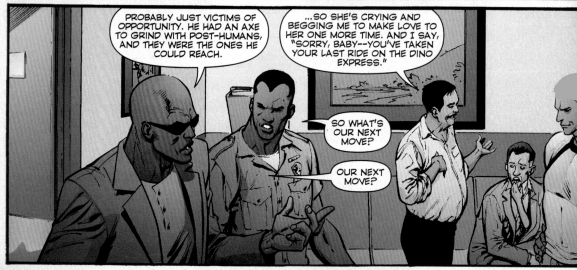

PROBABLY JUST VICTIMS OF OPPORTUNITY. HE HAD AN AXE TO GRIND WITH POST-HUMANS, AND THEY WERE THE ONES HE COULD REACH.

...SO SHE'S CRYING AND BEGGING ME TO MAKE LOVE TO HER ONE MORE TIME. AND I SAY, "SORRY, BABY--YOU'VE TAKEN YOUR LAST RIDE ON THE DINO EXPRESS."

SO WHAT'S OUR NEXT MOVE?

OUR NEXT MOVE?

WE TAKE CARE OF OUR OWN.

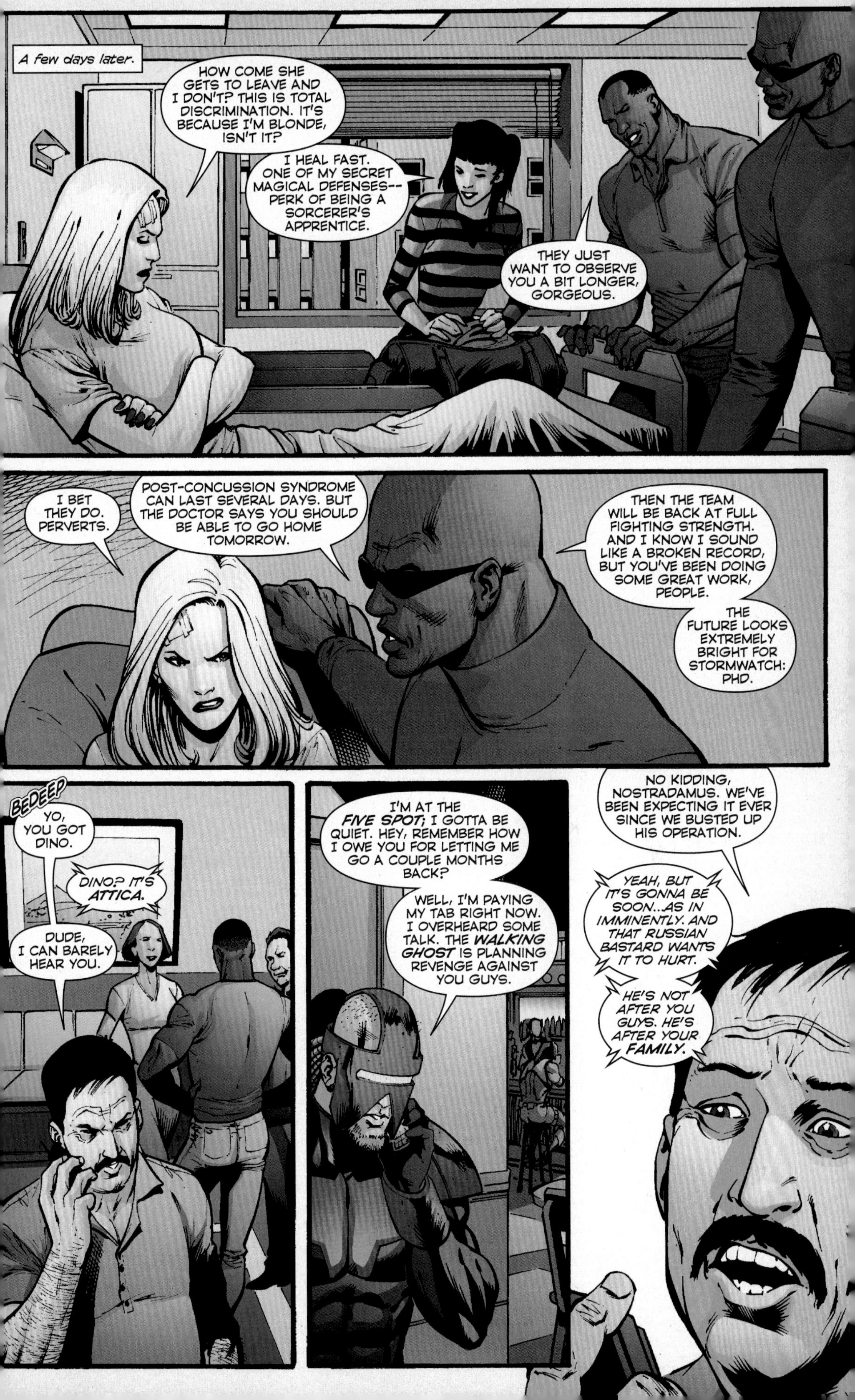

A few days later.
HOW COME SHE GETS TO LEAVE AND I DON'T? THIS IS TOTAL DISCRIMINATION. IT'S BECAUSE I'M BLONDE, ISN'T IT?
I HEAL FAST. ONE OF MY SECRET MAGICAL DEFENSES-- PERK OF BEING A SORCERER'S APPRENTICE.
THEY JUST WANT TO OBSERVE YOU A BIT LONGER, GORGEOUS.
I BET THEY DO. PERVERTS.
POST-CONCUSSION SYNDROME CAN LAST SEVERAL DAYS. BUT THE DOCTOR SAYS YOU SHOULD BE ABLE TO GO HOME TOMORROW.
THEN THE TEAM WILL BE BACK AT FULL FIGHTING STRENGTH. AND I KNOW I SOUND LIKE A BROKEN RECORD, BUT YOU'VE BEEN DOING SOME GREAT WORK, PEOPLE.
THE FUTURE LOOKS EXTREMELY BRIGHT FOR STORMWATCH: PHD.
BEDEEP
YO, YOU GOT DINO.
DINO? IT'S ATTICA.
DUDE, I CAN BARELY HEAR YOU.
I'M AT THE FIVE SPOT; I GOTTA BE QUIET. HEY, REMEMBER HOW I OWE YOU FOR LETTING ME GO A COUPLE MONTHS BACK?
WELL, I'M PAYING MY TAB RIGHT NOW. I OVERHEARD SOME TALK. THE WALKING GHOST IS PLANNING REVENGE AGAINST YOU GUYS.
NO KIDDING, NOSTRADAMUS. WE'VE BEEN EXPECTING IT EVER SINCE WE BUSTED UP HIS OPERATION.
YEAH, BUT IT'S GONNA BE SOON...AS IN IMMINENTLY. AND THAT RUSSIAN BASTARD WANTS IT TO HURT.
HE'S NOT AFTER YOU GUYS. HE'S AFTER YOUR FAMILY.

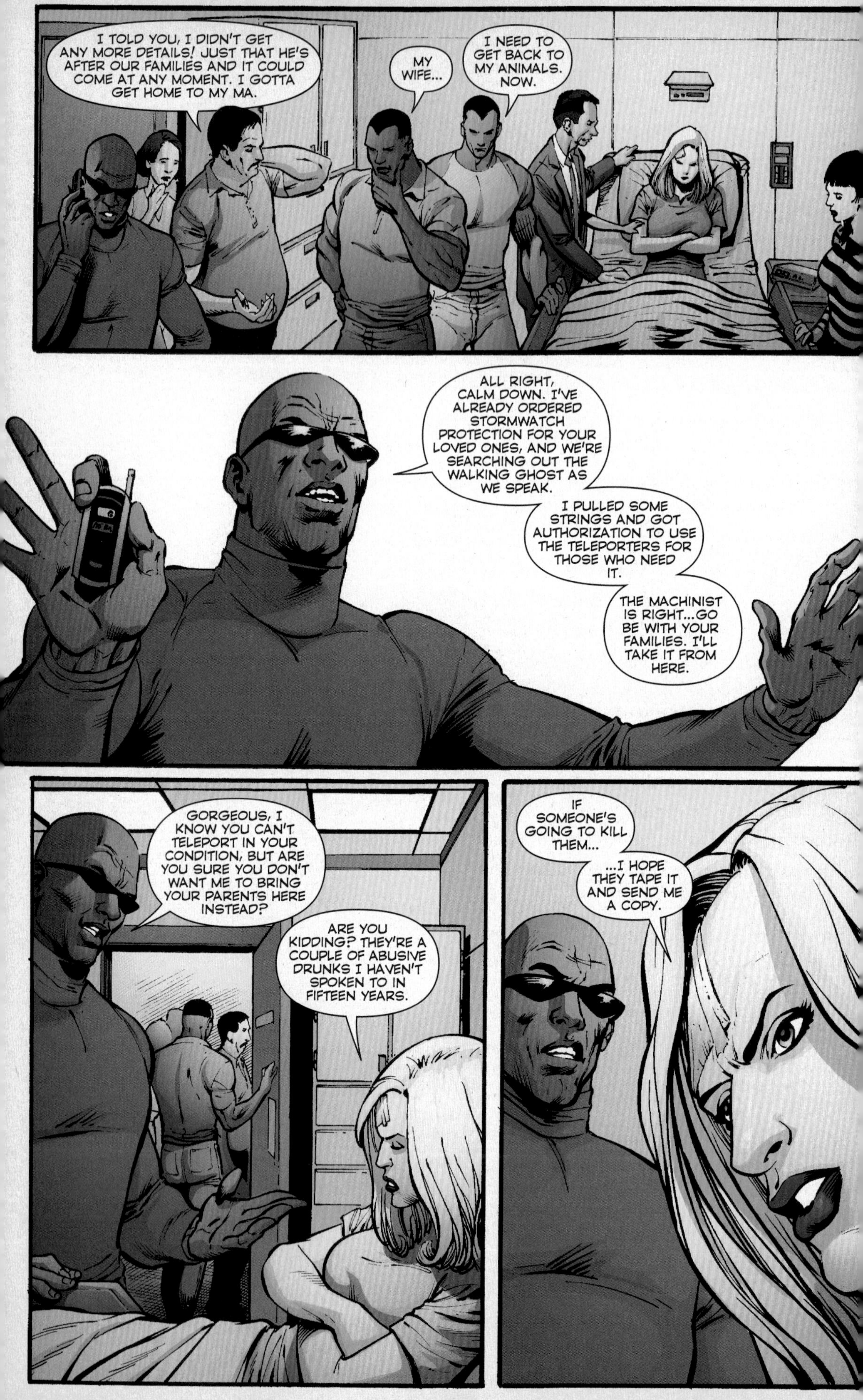
I TOLD YOU, I DIDN'T GET ANY MORE DETAILS! JUST THAT HE'S AFTER OUR FAMILIES AND IT COULD COME AT ANY MOMENT. I GOTTA GET HOME TO MY MA.
MY WIFE...
I NEED TO GET BACK TO MY ANIMALS. NOW.
ALL RIGHT, CALM DOWN. I'VE ALREADY ORDERED STORMWATCH PROTECTION FOR YOUR LOVED ONES, AND WE'RE SEARCHING OUT THE WALKING GHOST AS WE SPEAK.
I PULLED SOME STRINGS AND GOT AUTHORIZATION TO USE THE TELEPORTERS FOR THOSE WHO NEED IT.
THE MACHINIST IS RIGHT...GO BE WITH YOUR FAMILIES. I'LL TAKE IT FROM HERE.
GORGEOUS, I KNOW YOU CAN'T TELEPORT IN YOUR CONDITION, BUT ARE YOU SURE YOU DON'T WANT ME TO BRING YOUR PARENTS HERE INSTEAD?
ARE YOU KIDDING? THEY'RE A COUPLE OF ABUSIVE DRUNKS I HAVEN'T SPOKEN TO IN FIFTEEN YEARS.
IF SOMEONE'S GOING TO KILL THEM...
...I HOPE THEY TAPE IT AND SEND ME A COPY.

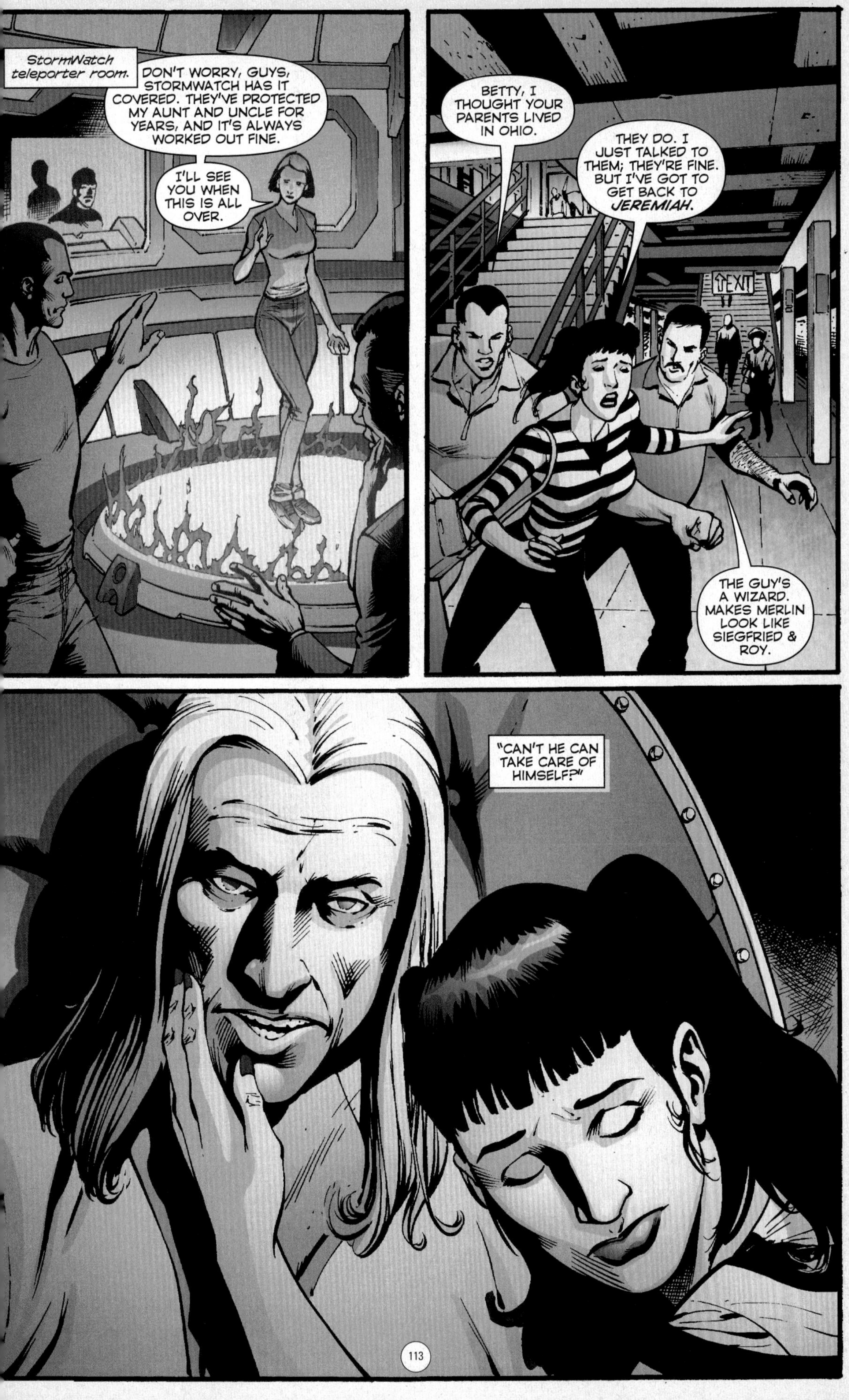
StormWatch teleporter room.
DON'T WORRY, GUYS, STORMWATCH HAS IT COVERED. THEY'VE PROTECTED MY AUNT AND UNCLE FOR YEARS, AND IT'S ALWAYS WORKED OUT FINE.
I'LL SEE YOU WHEN THIS IS ALL OVER.
BETTY, I THOUGHT YOUR PARENTS LIVED IN OHIO.
THEY DO. I JUST TALKED TO THEM; THEY'RE FINE. BUT I'VE GOT TO GET BACK TO *JEREMIAH*.
EXIT
THE GUY'S A WIZARD. MAKES MERLIN LOOK LIKE SIEGFRIED & ROY.
"CAN'T HE CAN TAKE CARE OF HIMSELF?"

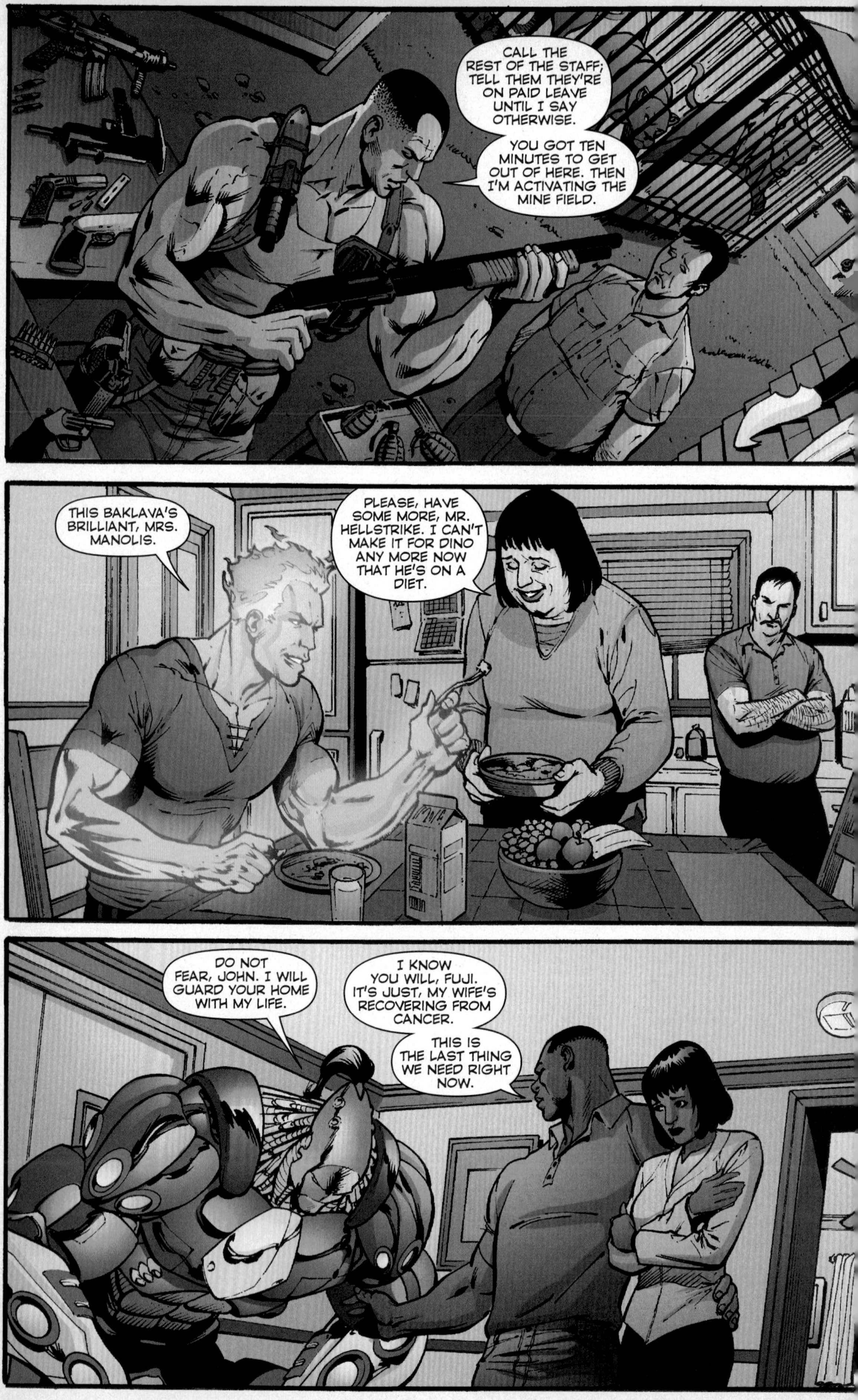
CALL THE REST OF THE STAFF; TELL THEM THEY'RE ON PAID LEAVE UNTIL I SAY OTHERWISE.
YOU GOT TEN MINUTES TO GET OUT OF HERE. THEN I'M ACTIVATING THE MINE FIELD.
THIS BAKLAVA'S BRILLIANT, MRS. MANOLIS.
PLEASE, HAVE SOME MORE, MR. HELLSTRIKE. I CAN'T MAKE IT FOR DINO ANY MORE NOW THAT HE'S ON A DIET.
DO NOT FEAR, JOHN. I WILL GUARD YOUR HOME WITH MY LIFE.
I KNOW YOU WILL, FUJI. IT'S JUST, MY WIFE'S RECOVERING FROM CANCER.
THIS IS THE LAST THING WE NEED RIGHT NOW.

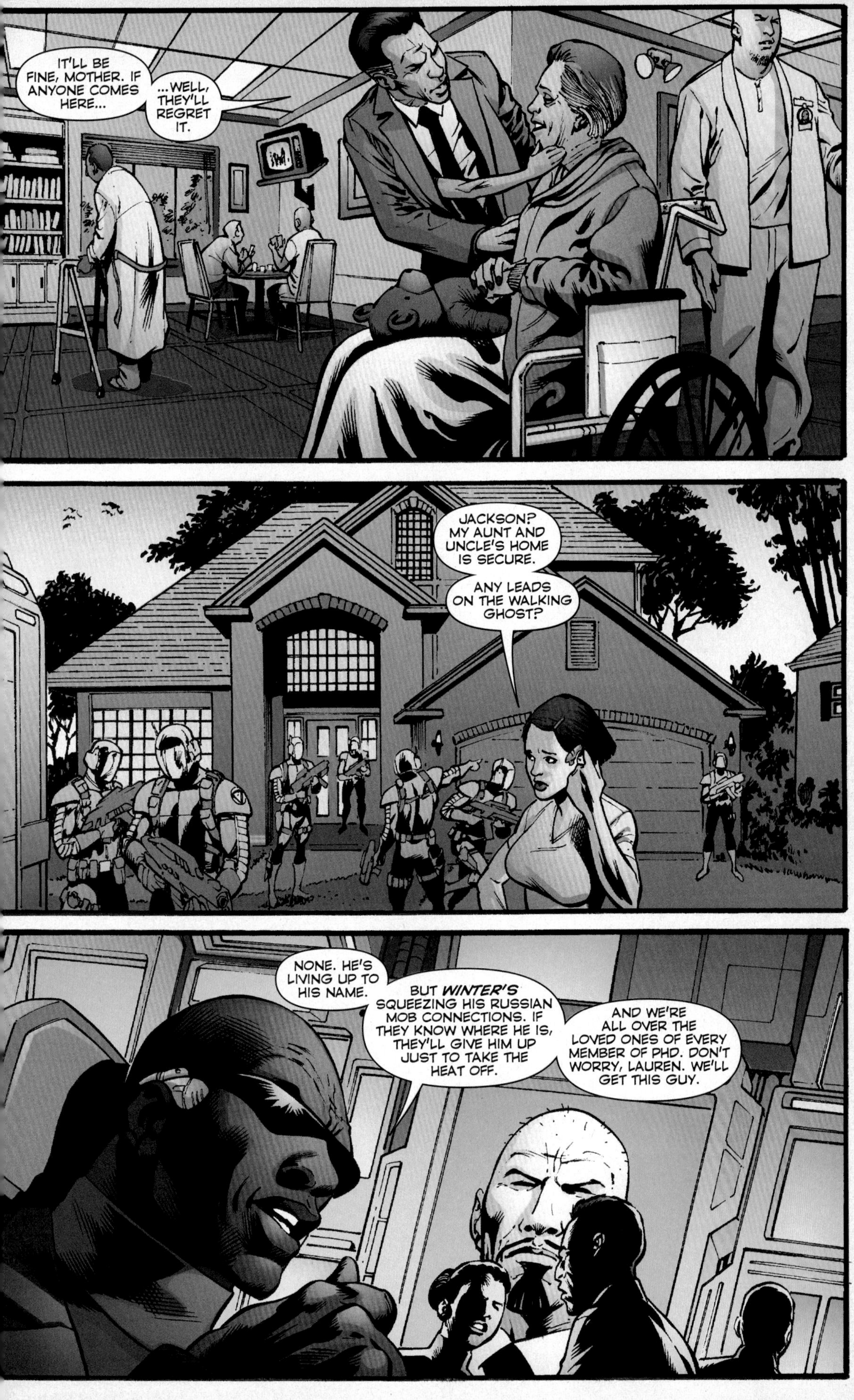
IT'LL BE FINE, MOTHER. IF ANYONE COMES HERE...
...WELL, THEY'LL REGRET IT.
JACKSON? MY AUNT AND UNCLE'S HOME IS SECURE.
ANY LEADS ON THE WALKING GHOST?
NONE. HE'S LIVING UP TO HIS NAME.
BUT *WINTER'S* SQUEEZING HIS RUSSIAN MOB CONNECTIONS. IF THEY KNOW WHERE HE IS, THEY'LL GIVE HIM UP JUST TO TAKE THE HEAT OFF.
AND WE'RE ALL OVER THE LOVED ONES OF EVERY MEMBER OF PHD. DON'T WORRY, LAUREN. WE'LL GET THIS GUY.

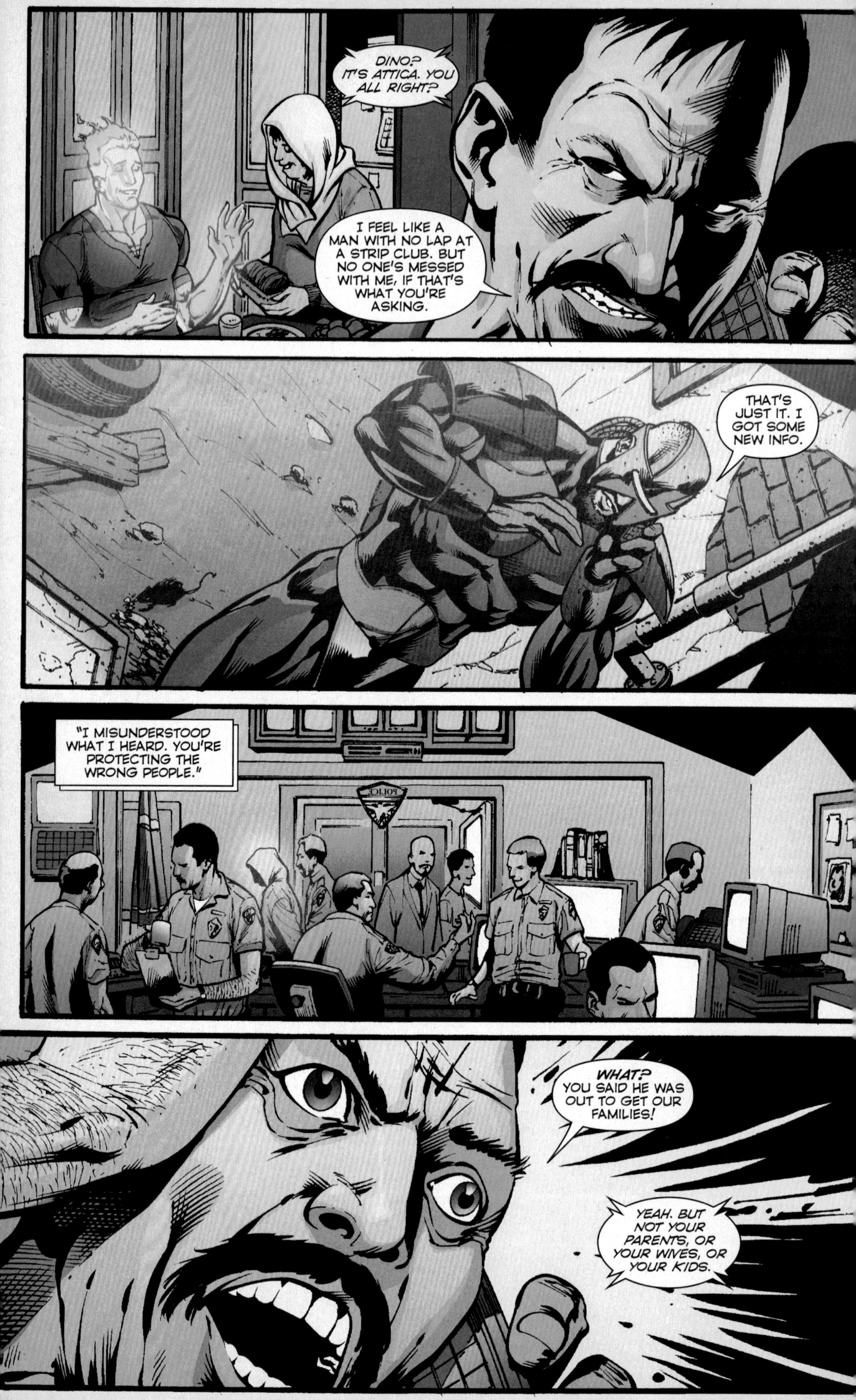
DINO? IT'S ATTICA. YOU ALL RIGHT?
I FEEL LIKE A MAN WITH NO LAP AT A STRIP CLUB. BUT NO ONE'S MESSED WITH ME, IF THAT'S WHAT YOU'RE ASKING.
THAT'S JUST IT. I GOT SOME NEW INFO.
"I MISUNDERSTOOD WHAT I HEARD. YOU'RE PROTECTING THE WRONG PEOPLE."
WHAT? YOU SAID HE WAS OUT TO GET OUR FAMILIES!
YEAH. BUT NOT YOUR PARENTS, OR YOUR WIVES, OR YOUR KIDS.

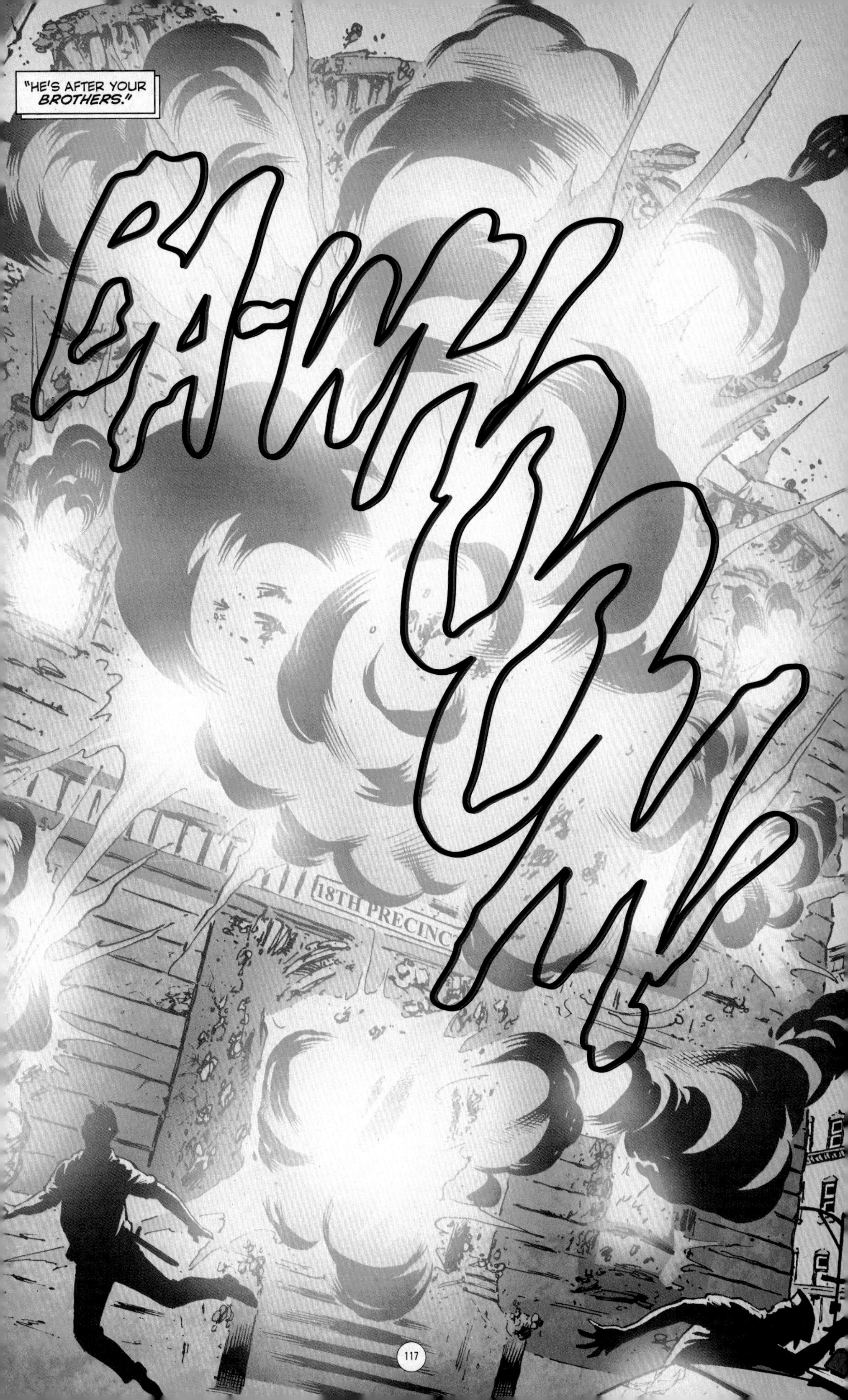
"HE'S AFTER YOUR *BROTHERS*."
18TH PRECINC

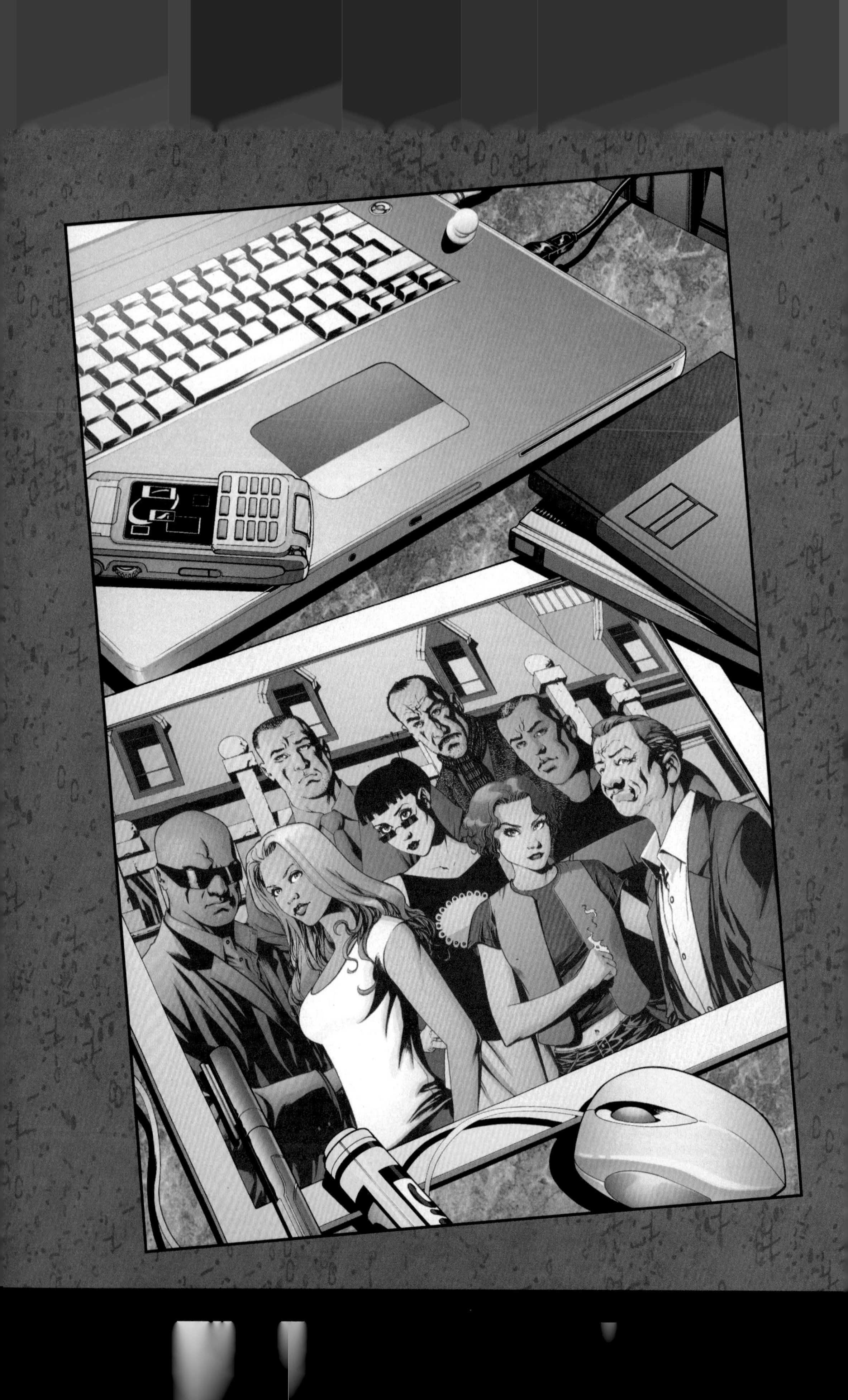

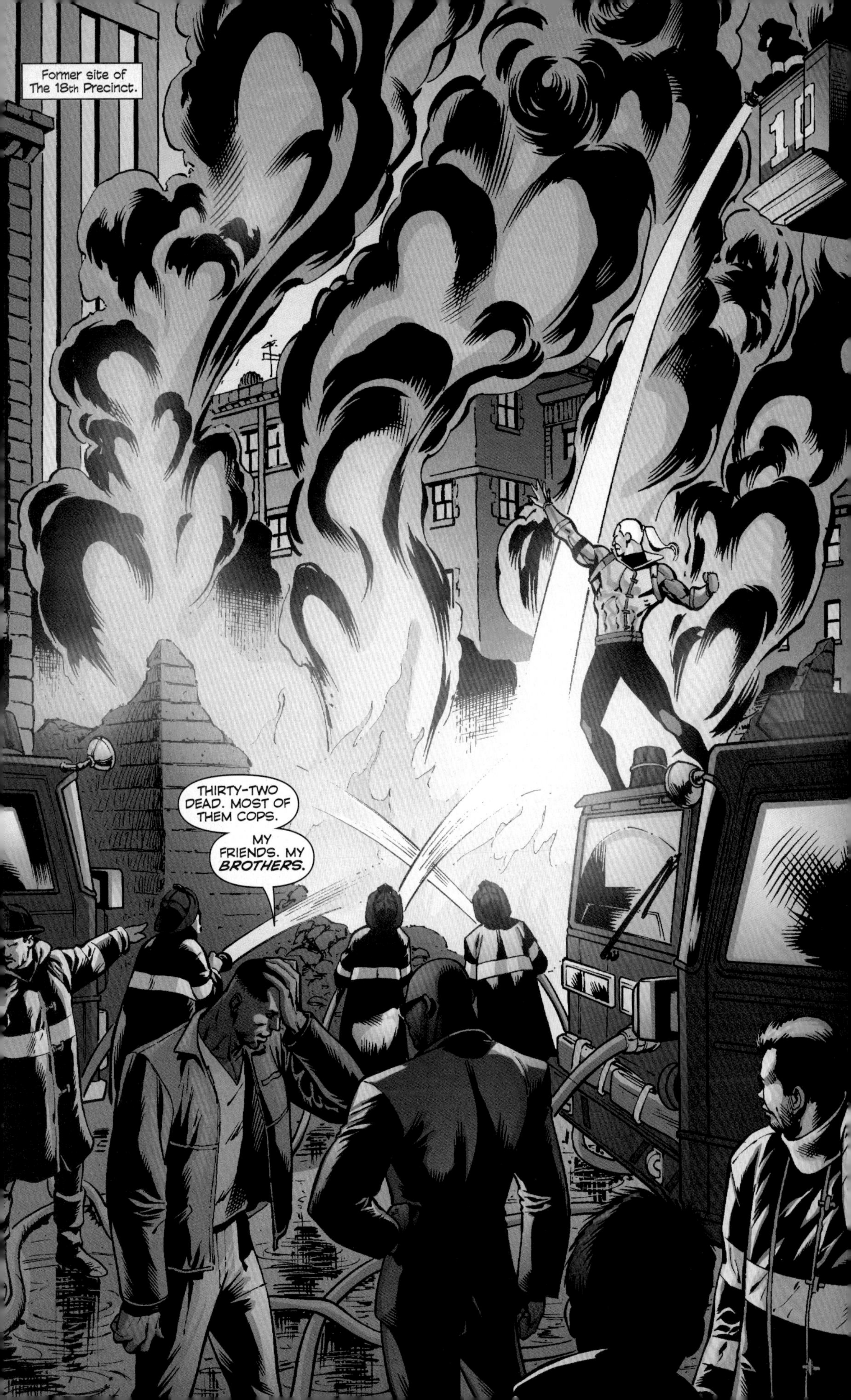
Former site of The 18th Precinct.
10
THIRTY-TWO DEAD. MOST OF THEM COPS.
MY FRIENDS. MY BROTHERS.

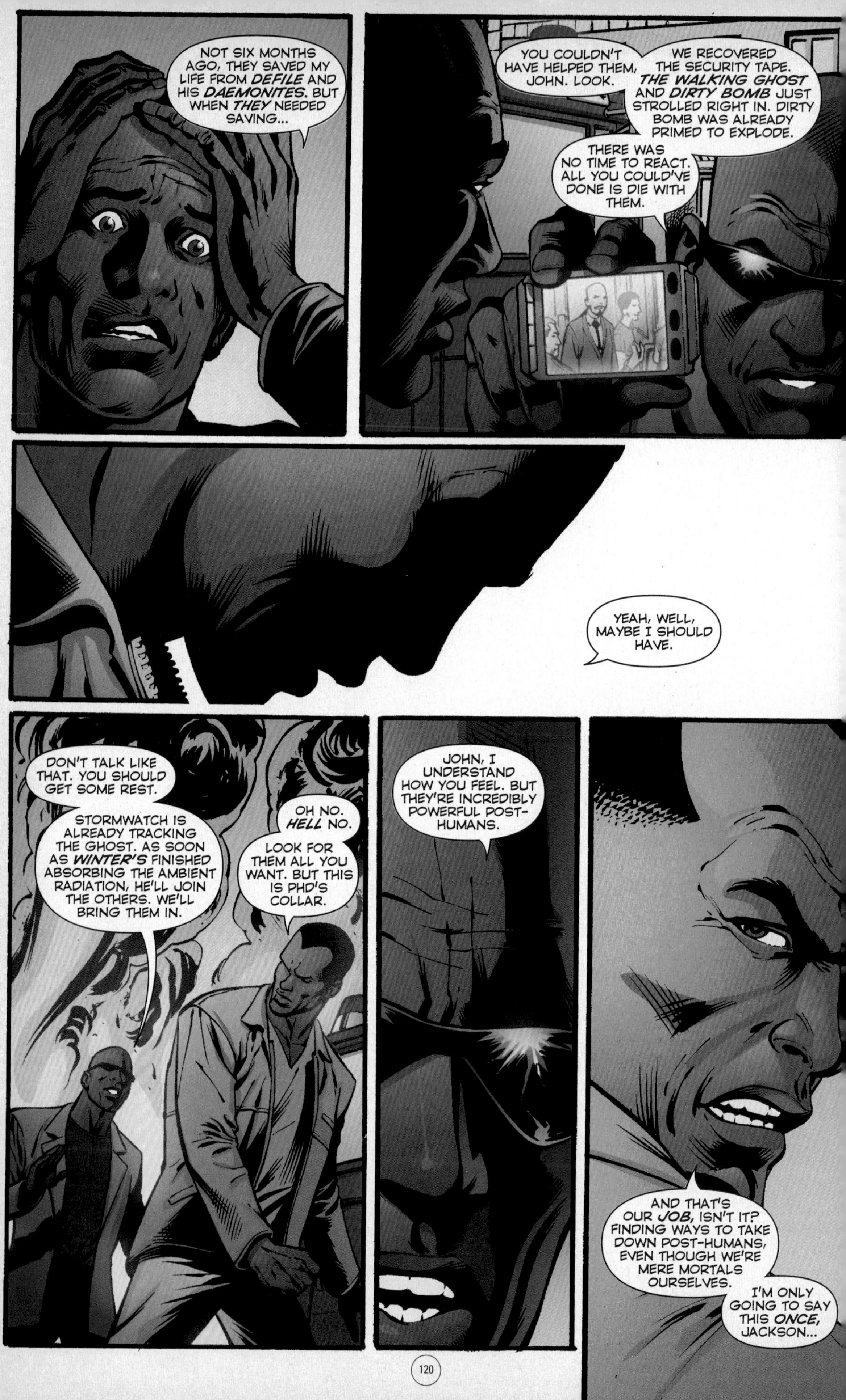
NOT SIX MONTHS AGO, THEY SAVED MY LIFE FROM DEFILE AND HIS DAEMONITES. BUT WHEN THEY NEEDED SAVING...
YOU COULDN'T HAVE HELPED THEM, JOHN. LOOK.
WE RECOVERED THE SECURITY TAPE. THE WALKING GHOST AND DIRTY BOMB JUST STROLLED RIGHT IN. DIRTY BOMB WAS ALREADY PRIMED TO EXPLODE.
THERE WAS NO TIME TO REACT. ALL YOU COULD'VE DONE IS DIE WITH THEM.
YEAH, WELL, MAYBE I SHOULD HAVE.
DON'T TALK LIKE THAT. YOU SHOULD GET SOME REST.
STORMWATCH IS ALREADY TRACKING THE GHOST. AS SOON AS WINTER'S FINISHED ABSORBING THE AMBIENT RADIATION, HE'LL JOIN THE OTHERS. WE'LL BRING THEM IN.
OH NO. HELL NO.
LOOK FOR THEM ALL YOU WANT. BUT THIS IS PHD'S COLLAR.
JOHN, I UNDERSTAND HOW YOU FEEL. BUT THEY'RE INCREDIBLY POWERFUL POST-HUMANS.
AND THAT'S OUR JOB, ISN'T IT? FINDING WAYS TO TAKE DOWN POST-HUMANS, EVEN THOUGH WE'RE MERE MORTALS OURSELVES.
I'M ONLY GOING TO SAY THIS ONCE, JACKSON...

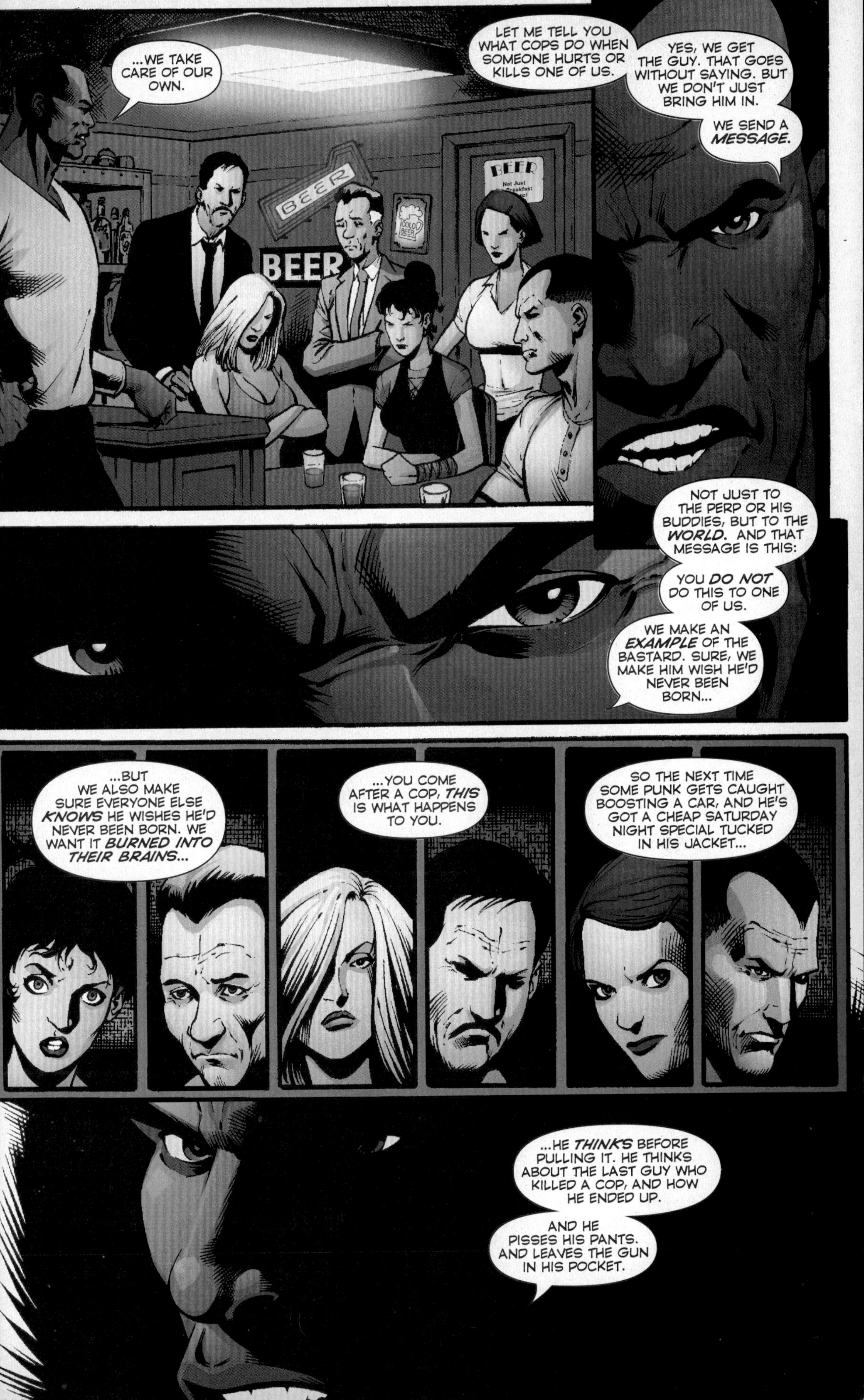
...WE TAKE CARE OF OUR OWN.
LET ME TELL YOU WHAT COPS DO WHEN SOMEONE HURTS OR KILLS ONE OF US.
YES, WE GET THE GUY. THAT GOES WITHOUT SAYING. BUT WE DON'T JUST BRING HIM IN.
WE SEND A MESSAGE.
BEER
BEER
BEER
NOT JUST TO THE PERP OR HIS BUDDIES, BUT TO THE WORLD. AND THAT MESSAGE IS THIS:
YOU DO NOT DO THIS TO ONE OF US.
WE MAKE AN EXAMPLE OF THE BASTARD. SURE, WE MAKE HIM WISH HE'D NEVER BEEN BORN...
...BUT WE ALSO MAKE SURE EVERYONE ELSE KNOWS HE WISHES HE'D NEVER BEEN BORN. WE WANT IT BURNED INTO THEIR BRAINS...
...YOU COME AFTER A COP, THIS IS WHAT HAPPENS TO YOU.
SO THE NEXT TIME SOME PUNK GETS CAUGHT BOOSTING A CAR, AND HE'S GOT A CHEAP SATURDAY NIGHT SPECIAL TUCKED IN HIS JACKET...
...HE THINKS BEFORE PULLING IT. HE THINKS ABOUT THE LAST GUY WHO KILLED A COP, AND HOW HE ENDED UP.
AND HE PISSES HIS PANTS. AND LEAVES THE GUN IN HIS POCKET.

NOW. I KNOW SOME OF YOU ARE CIVILIANS. YOU MIGHT NOT WANT TO BE A PART OF THIS.

SO I WON'T THINK ANY LESS OF YOU IF YOU--

BOSS...

...I HOPE YOU DIDN'T BRING US HERE TO INSULT US.

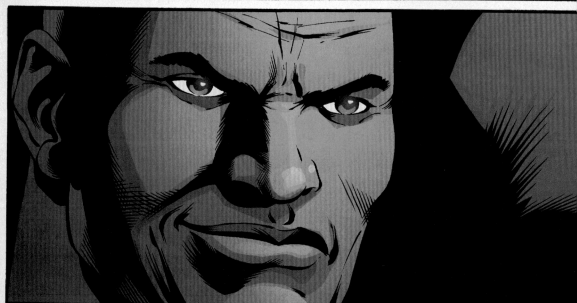

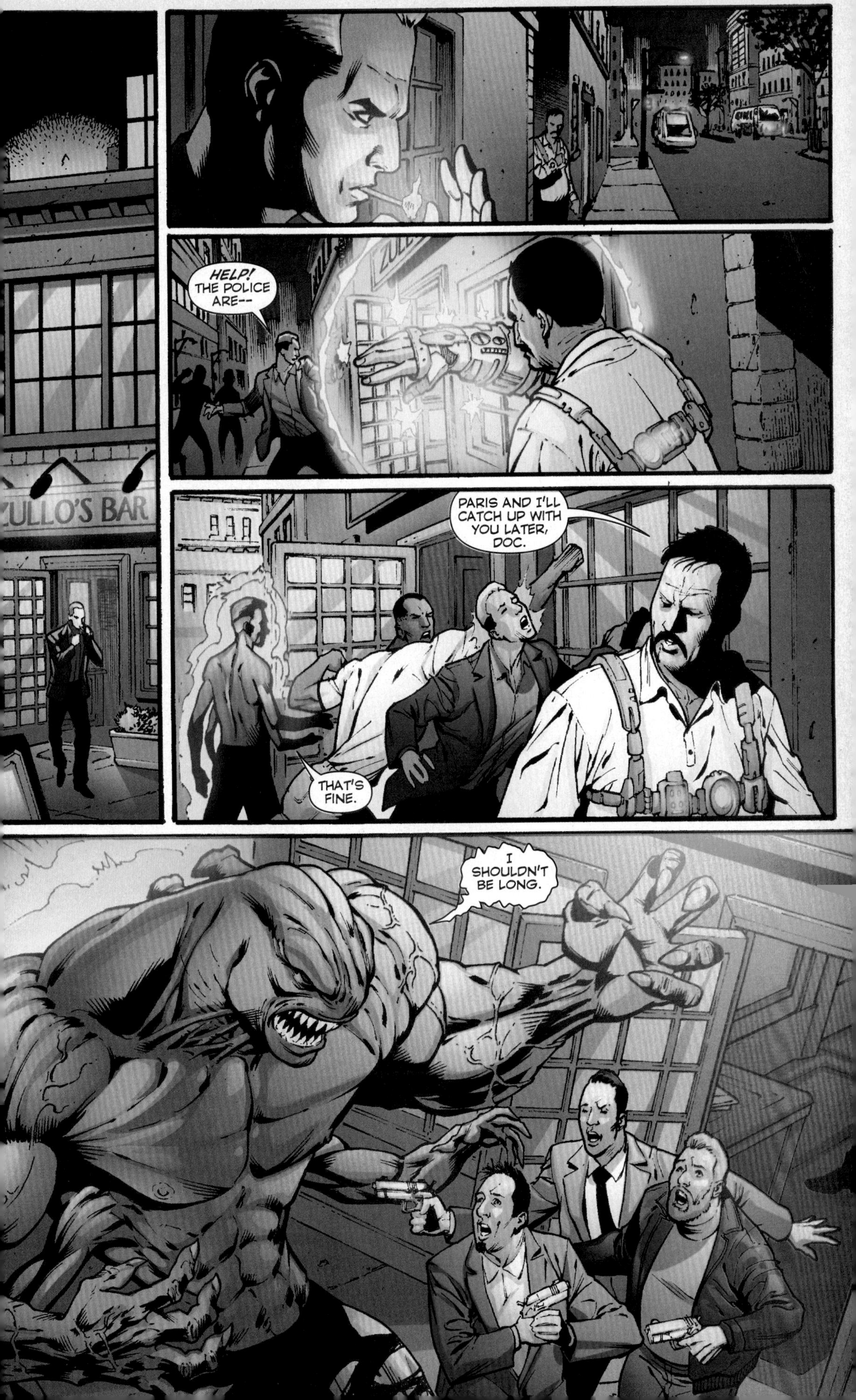
ZULLO'S BAR
HELP! THE POLICE ARE--
PARIS AND I'LL CATCH UP WITH YOU LATER, DOC.
THAT'S FINE.
I SHOULDN'T BE LONG.

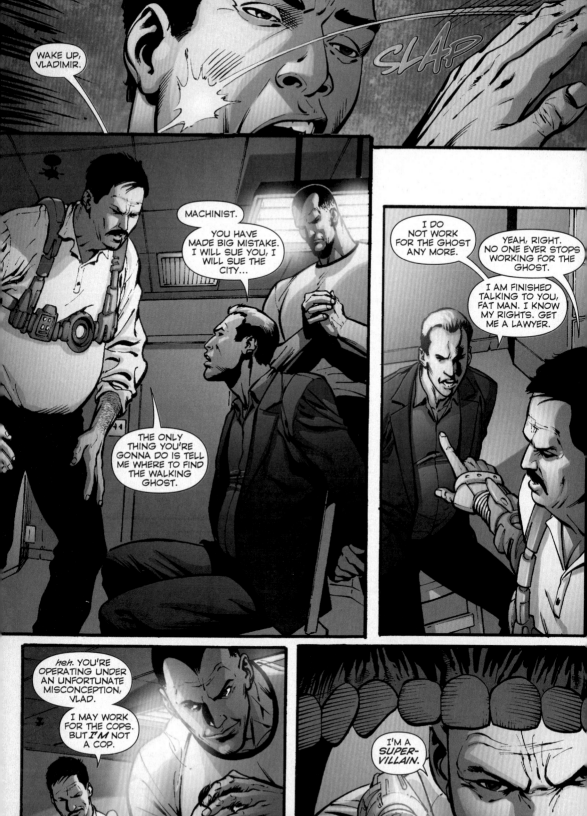

SLAP

WAKE UP, VLADIMIR.

MACHINIST. YOU HAVE MADE BIG MISTAKE. I WILL SUE YOU, I WILL SUE THE CITY...

THE ONLY THING YOU'RE GONNA DO IS TELL ME WHERE TO FIND THE WALKING GHOST.

I DO NOT WORK FOR THE GHOST ANY MORE.

YEAH, RIGHT. NO ONE EVER STOPS WORKING FOR THE GHOST.

I AM FINISHED TALKING TO YOU, FAT MAN. I KNOW MY RIGHTS. GET ME A LAWYER.

heh. YOU'RE OPERATING UNDER AN UNFORTUNATE MISCONCEPTION, VLAD.

I MAY WORK FOR THE COPS. BUT I'M NOT A COP.

I'M A SUPER-VILLAIN.

VREEEE

--EEEARRGHH!

WELL, WE GOT SOMETHING.

AFTER HOW MUCH TORTURE?

DON'T TELL ME YOU'RE GETTING SQUEAMISH.

HELL NO. I JUST WANT TO BE SURE WHAT HE GAVE US IS SOLID, NOT A LIE TO MAKE YOU STOP HURTING HIM.

I TOLD HIM IF HE LIED, WE'D BE BACK AND IT'D BE TWICE AS BAD. HE SEEMED TO BELIEVE ME.

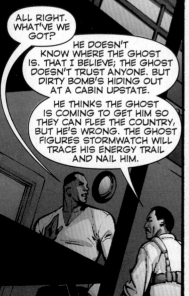

ALL RIGHT. WHAT'VE WE GOT?

HE DOESN'T KNOW WHERE THE GHOST IS. THAT I BELIEVE; THE GHOST DOESN'T TRUST ANYONE. BUT DIRTY BOMB'S HIDING OUT AT A CABIN UPSTATE.

HE THINKS THE GHOST IS COMING TO GET HIM SO THEY CAN FLEE THE COUNTRY, BUT HE'S WRONG. THE GHOST FIGURES STORMWATCH WILL TRACE HIS ENERGY TRAIL AND NAIL HIM.

SO HE HUNG DIRTY BOMB OUT TO DRY TO COVER HIS OWN ESCAPE.

IF WE GO AFTER DIRTY BOMB WE'RE PLAYING INTO HIS HANDS.

TRUE. BUT DIRTY BOMB'S THE ONE WHO EXPLODED AND KILLED ALL OUR BROTHERS.

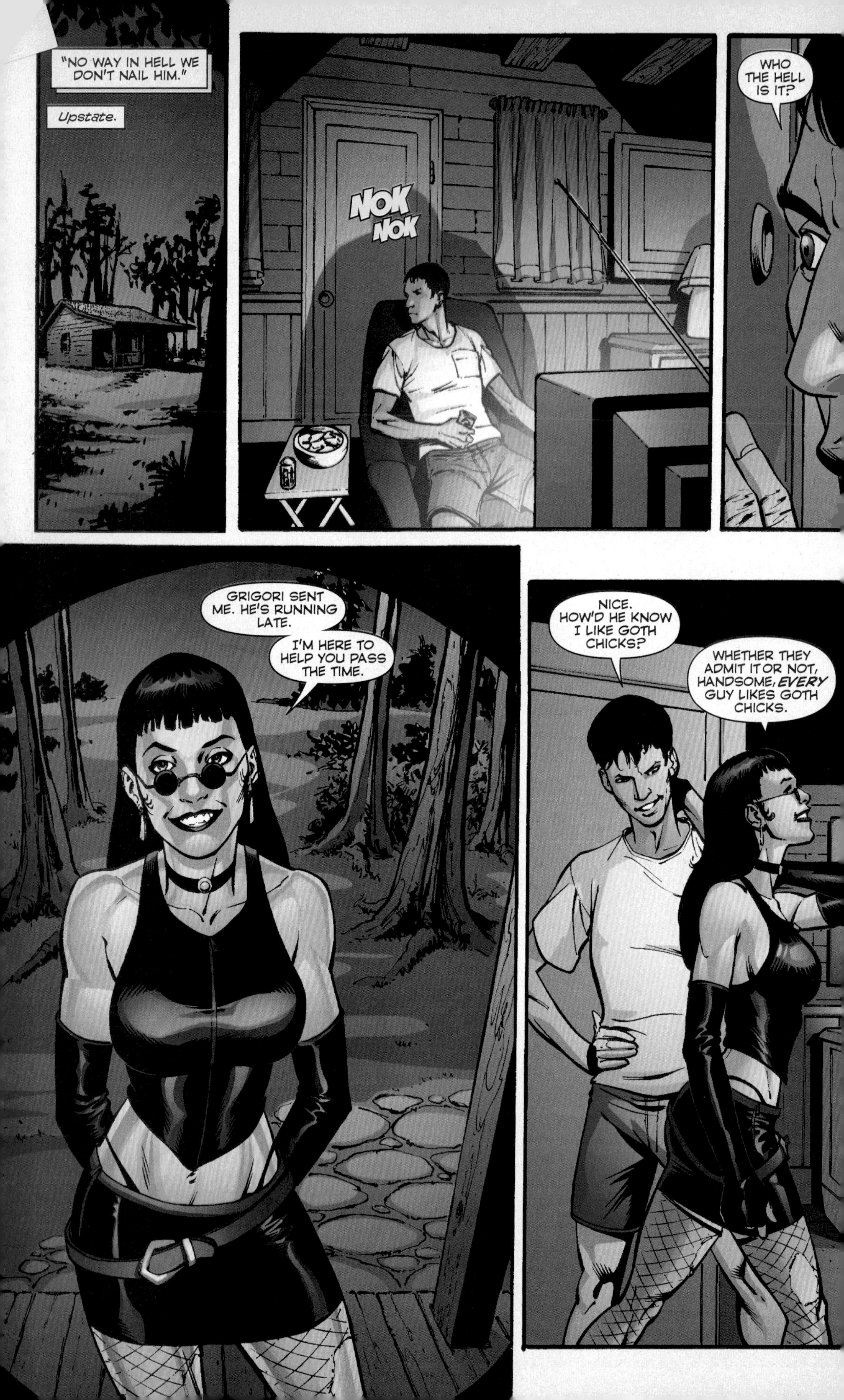
"NO WAY IN HELL WE DON'T NAIL HIM."
Upstate.
NOK NOK
WHO THE HELL IS IT?
GRIGORI SENT ME. HE'S RUNNING LATE.
I'M HERE TO HELP YOU PASS THE TIME.
NICE. HOW'D HE KNOW I LIKE GOTH CHICKS?
WHETHER THEY ADMIT IT OR NOT, HANDSOME, EVERY GUY LIKES GOTH CHICKS.

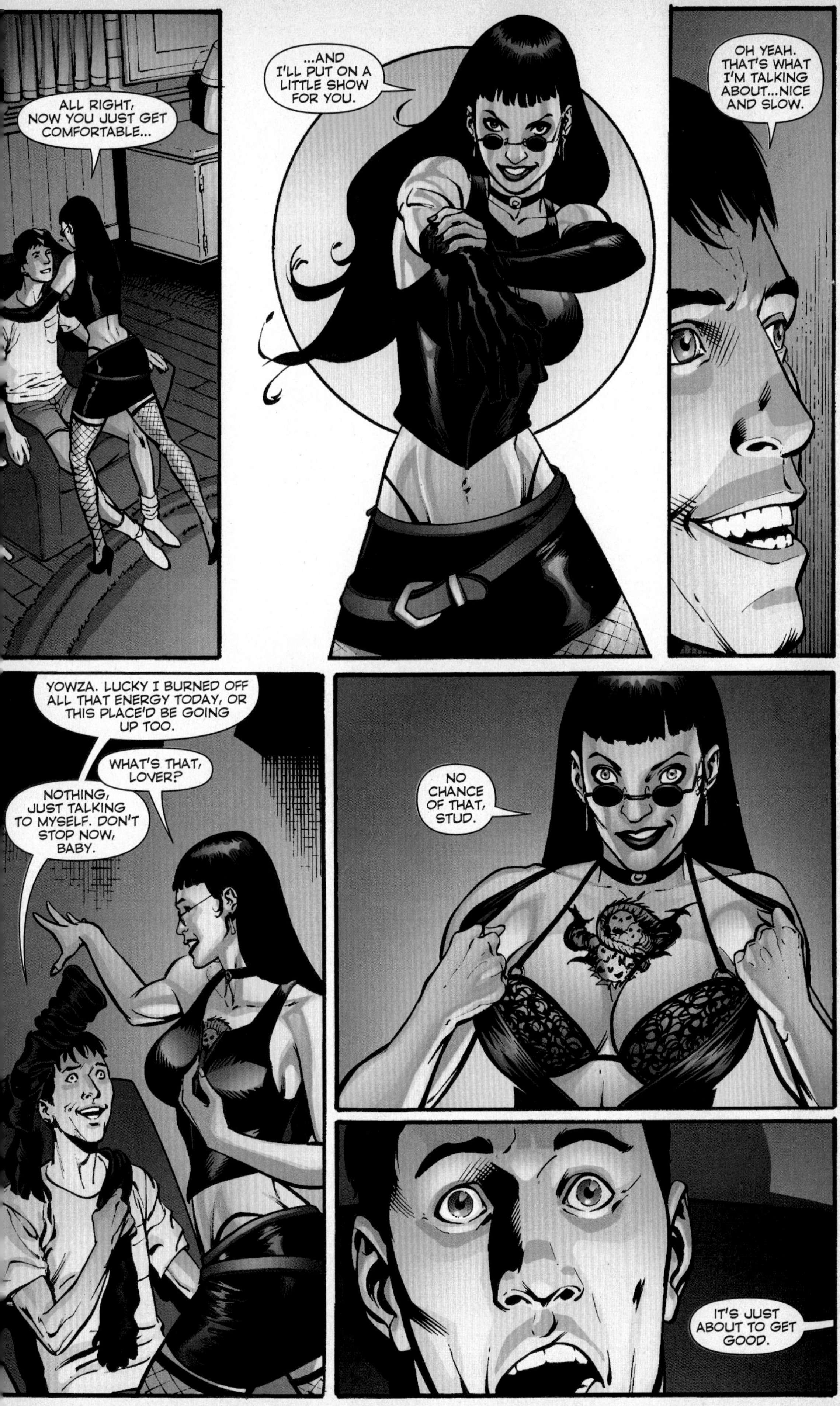
ALL RIGHT, NOW YOU JUST GET COMFORTABLE...
...AND I'LL PUT ON A LITTLE SHOW FOR YOU.
OH YEAH. THAT'S WHAT I'M TALKING ABOUT...NICE AND SLOW.
YOWZA. LUCKY I BURNED OFF ALL THAT ENERGY TODAY, OR THIS PLACE'D BE GOING UP TOO.
WHAT'S THAT, LOVER?
NOTHING, JUST TALKING TO MYSELF. DON'T STOP NOW, BABY.
NO CHANCE OF THAT, STUD.
IT'S JUST ABOUT TO GET GOOD.

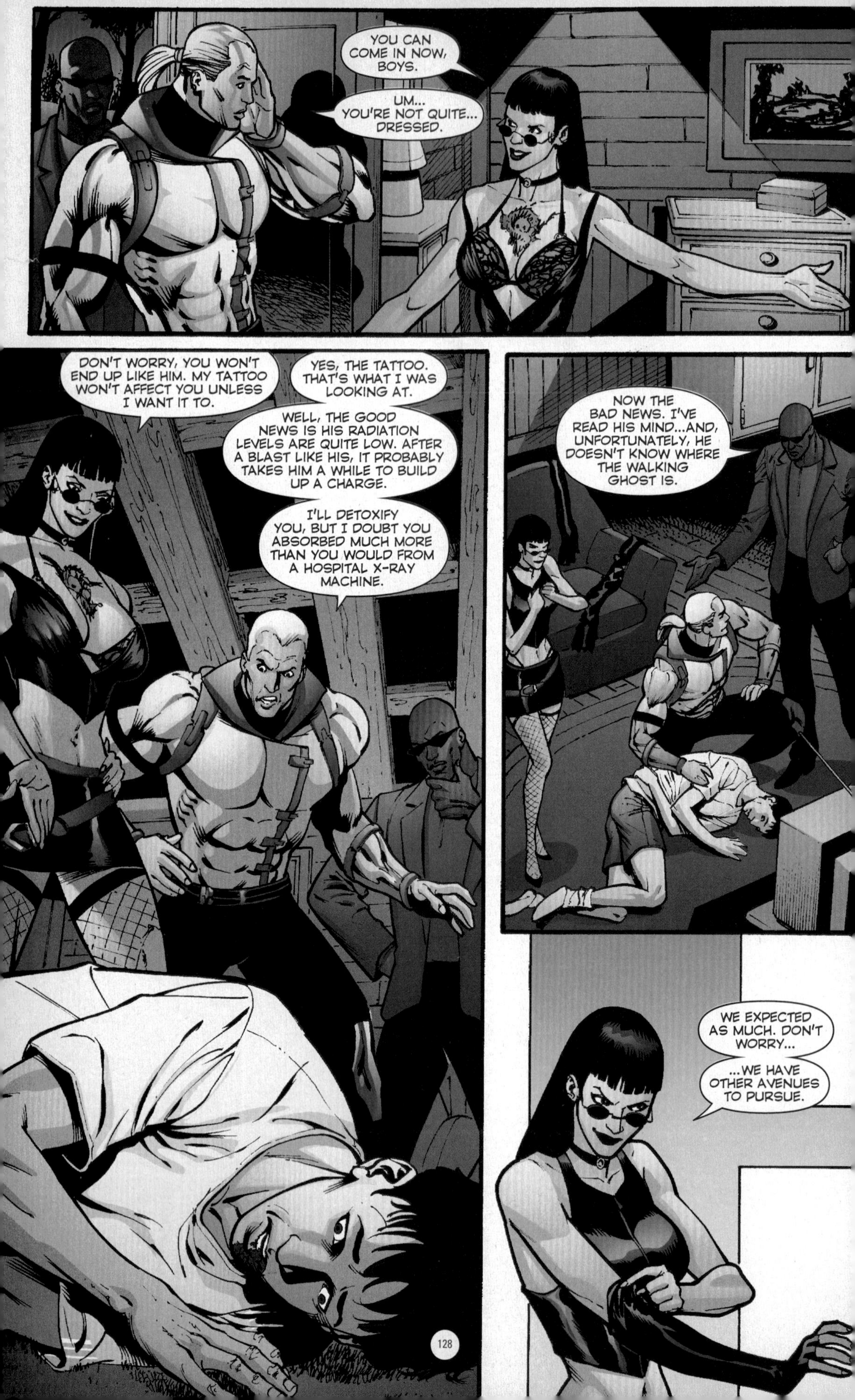
YOU CAN COME IN NOW, BOYS.
UM... YOU'RE NOT QUITE... DRESSED.
DON'T WORRY, YOU WON'T END UP LIKE HIM. MY TATTOO WON'T AFFECT YOU UNLESS I WANT IT TO.
YES, THE TATTOO. THAT'S WHAT I WAS LOOKING AT.
WELL, THE GOOD NEWS IS HIS RADIATION LEVELS ARE QUITE LOW. AFTER A BLAST LIKE HIS, IT PROBABLY TAKES HIM A WHILE TO BUILD UP A CHARGE.
I'LL DETOXIFY YOU, BUT I DOUBT YOU ABSORBED MUCH MORE THAN YOU WOULD FROM A HOSPITAL X-RAY MACHINE.
NOW THE BAD NEWS. I'VE READ HIS MIND...AND, UNFORTUNATELY, HE DOESN'T KNOW WHERE THE WALKING GHOST IS.
WE EXPECTED AS MUCH. DON'T WORRY...
...WE HAVE OTHER AVENUES TO PURSUE.

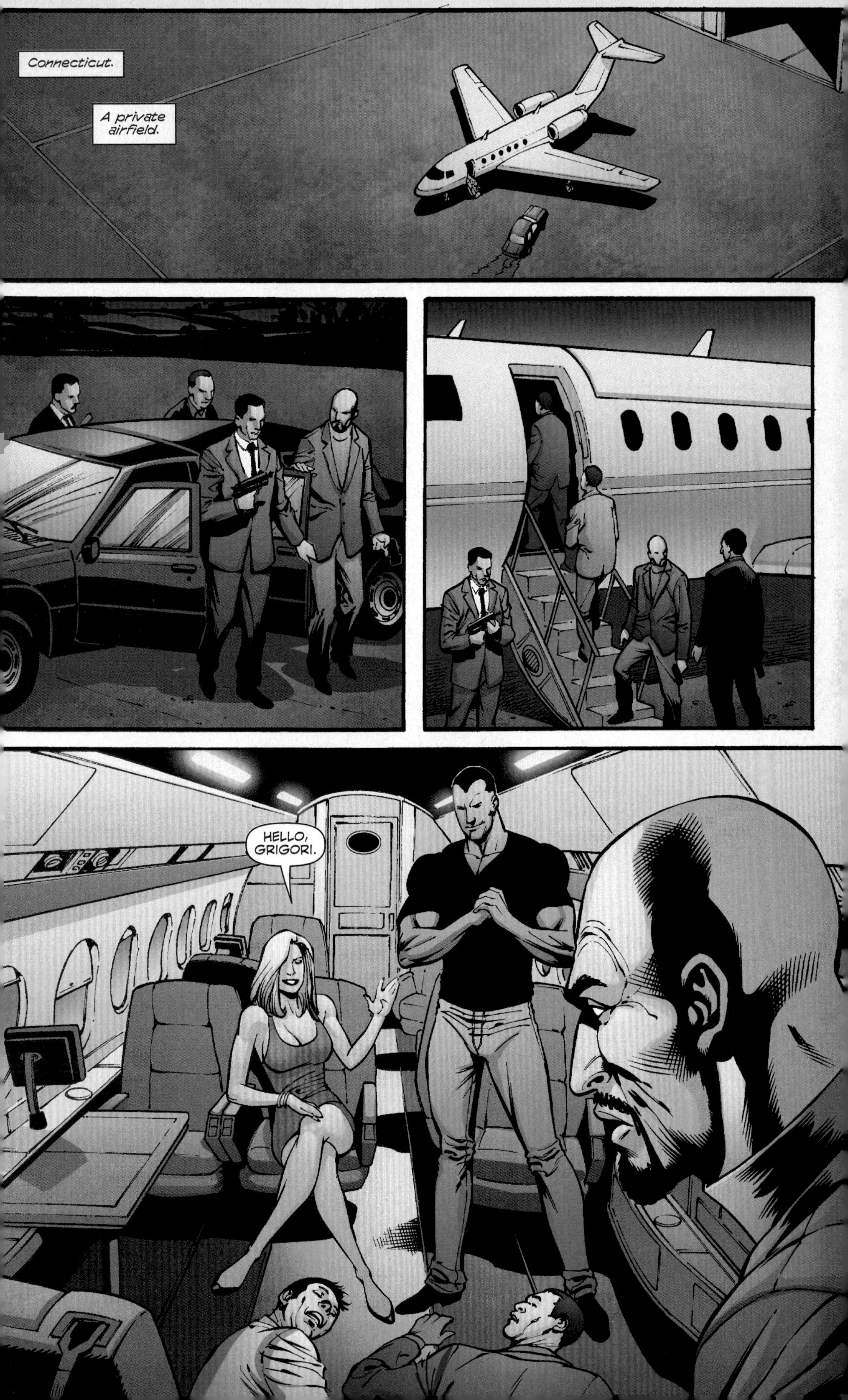

Connecticut.
A private airfield.
HELLO, GRIGORI.

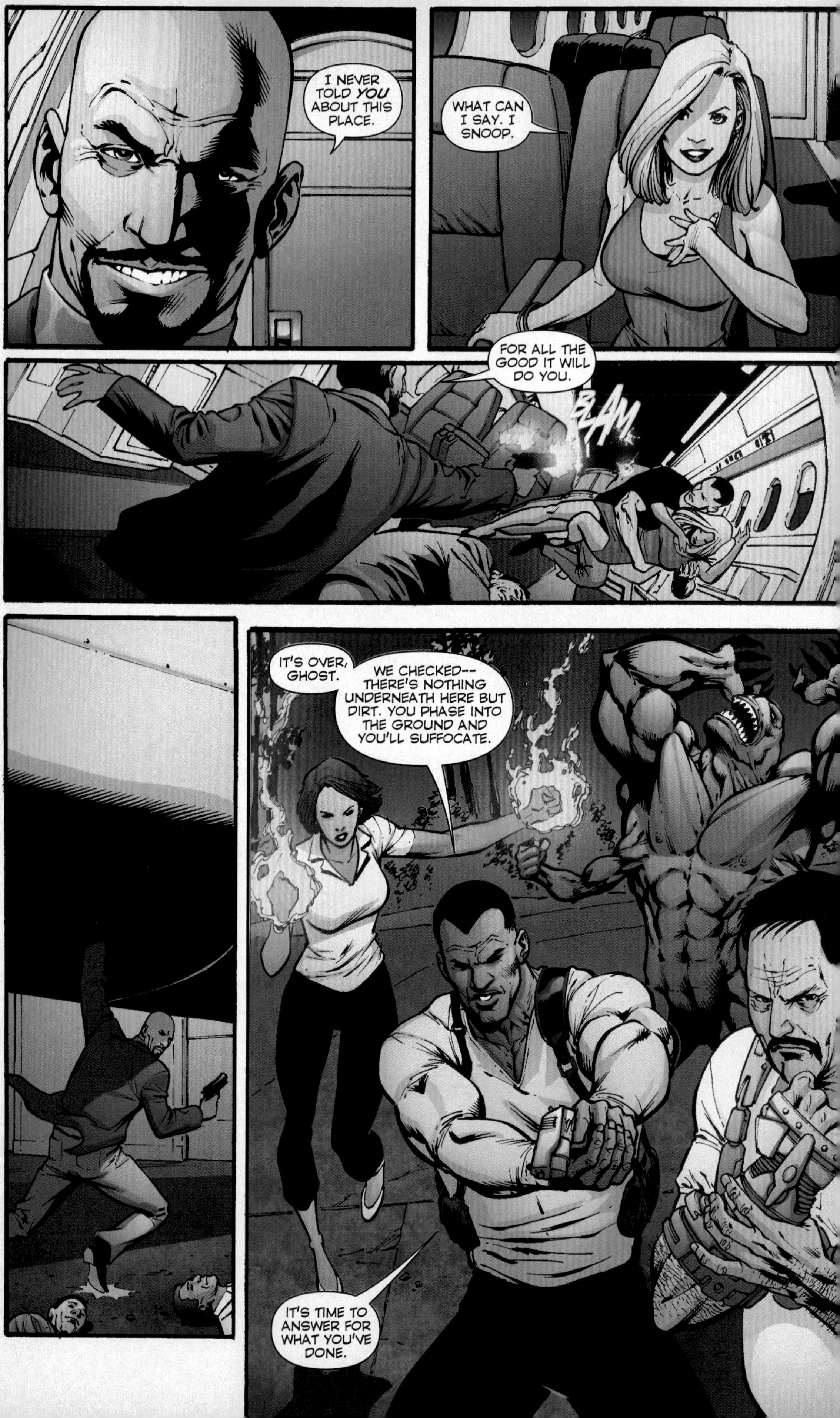
I NEVER TOLD *YOU* ABOUT THIS PLACE.
WHAT CAN I SAY. I SNOOP.
FOR ALL THE GOOD IT WILL DO YOU.
BLAM
IT'S OVER, GHOST.
WE CHECKED-- THERE'S NOTHING UNDERNEATH HERE BUT DIRT. YOU PHASE INTO THE GROUND AND YOU'LL SUFFOCATE.
IT'S TIME TO ANSWER FOR WHAT YOU'VE DONE.

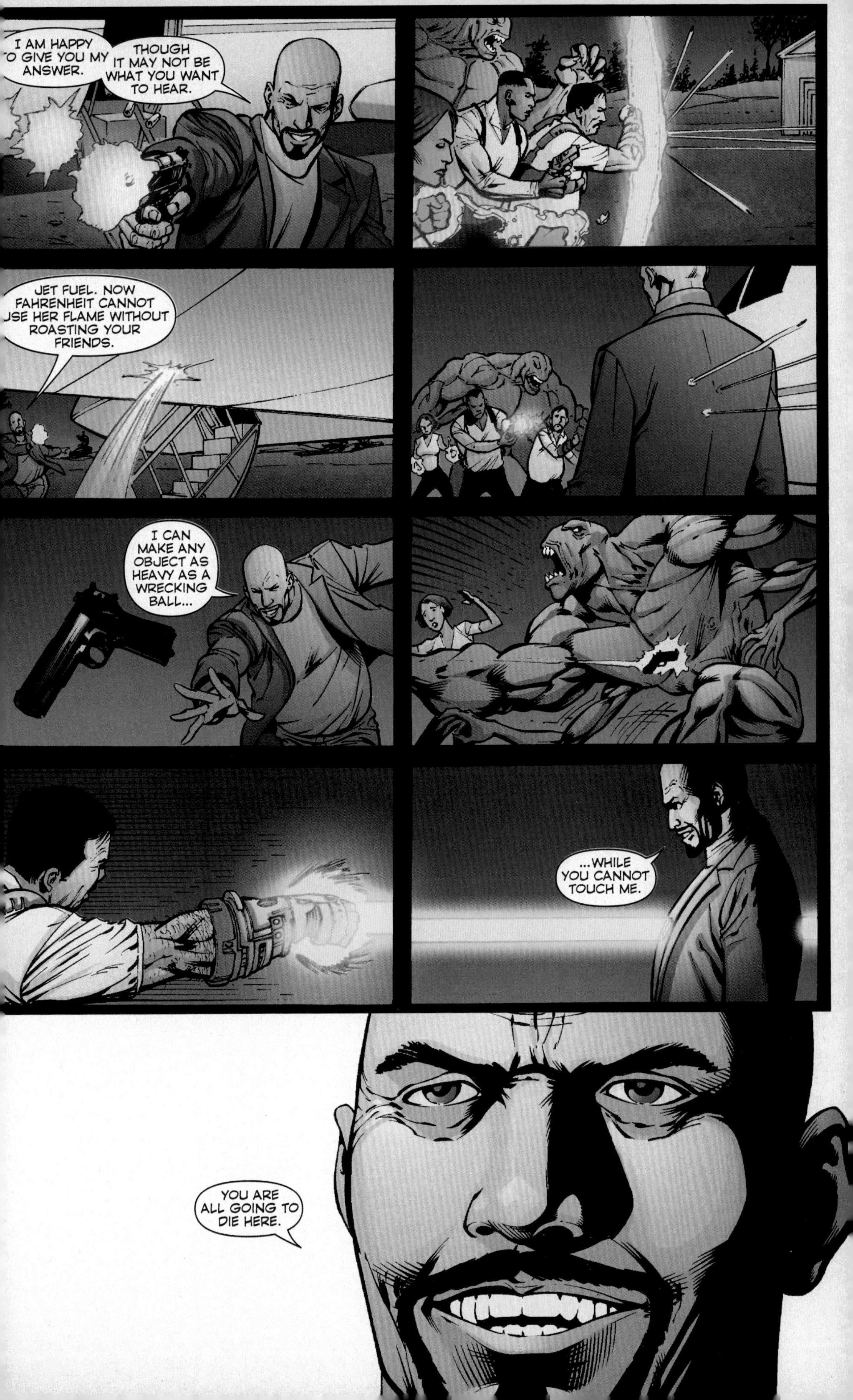
I AM HAPPY TO GIVE YOU MY ANSWER.
THOUGH IT MAY NOT BE WHAT YOU WANT TO HEAR.
JET FUEL. NOW FAHRENHEIT CANNOT USE HER FLAME WITHOUT ROASTING YOUR FRIENDS.
I CAN MAKE ANY OBJECT AS HEAVY AS A WRECKING BALL...
...WHILE YOU CANNOT TOUCH ME.
YOU ARE ALL GOING TO DIE HERE.

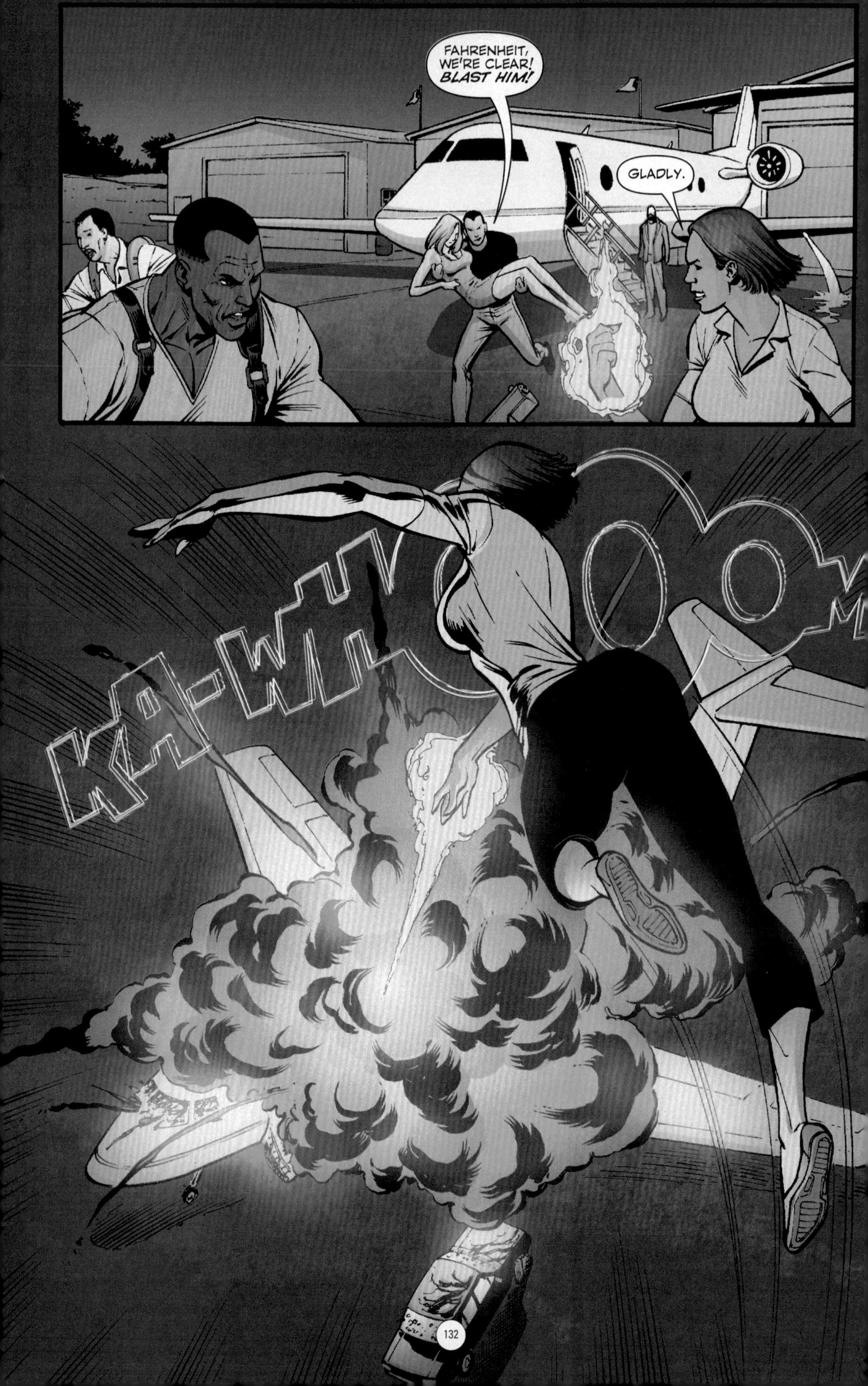
FAHRENHEIT, WE'RE CLEAR! *BLAST HIM!*
GLADLY.
KA-WHOOOM

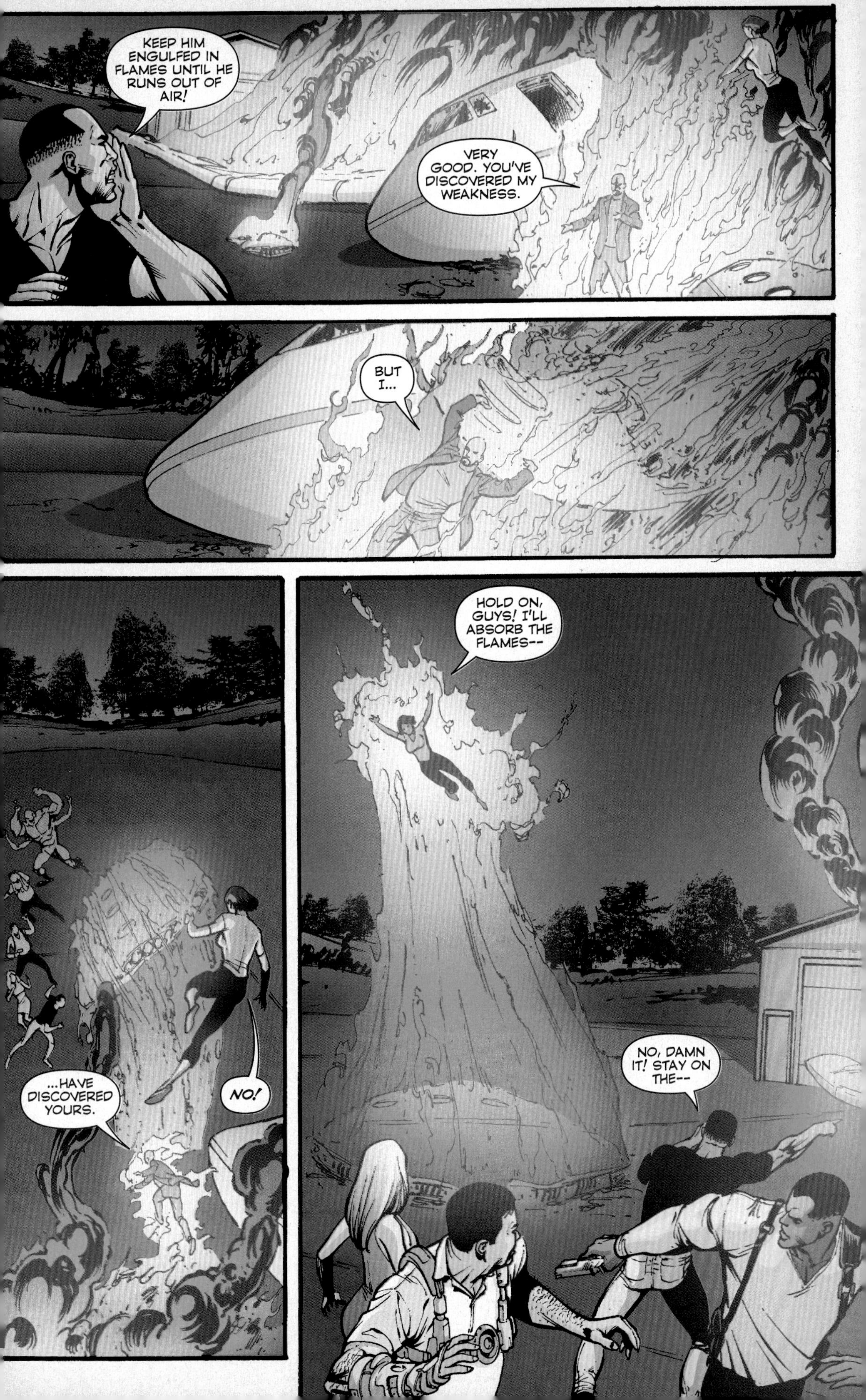
KEEP HIM ENGULFED IN FLAMES UNTIL HE RUNS OUT OF AIR!
VERY GOOD. YOU'VE DISCOVERED MY WEAKNESS.
BUT I...
...HAVE DISCOVERED YOURS.
NO!
HOLD ON, GUYS! I'LL ABSORB THE FLAMES--
NO, DAMN IT! STAY ON THE--

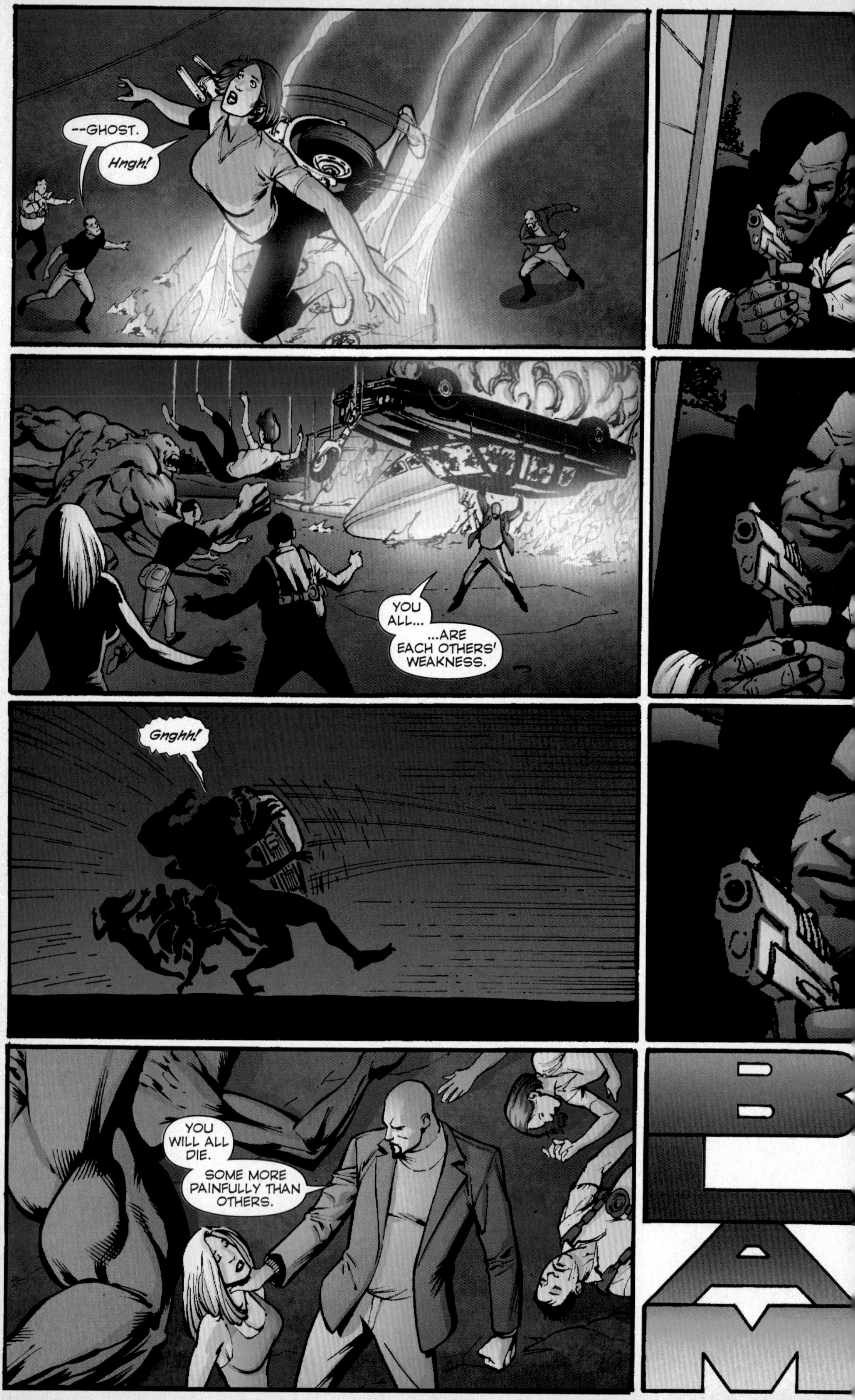
--GHOST.
Hngh!
YOU ALL...
...ARE EACH OTHERS' WEAKNESS.
Gnghh!
YOU WILL ALL DIE.
SOME MORE PAINFULLY THAN OTHERS.
BLAM

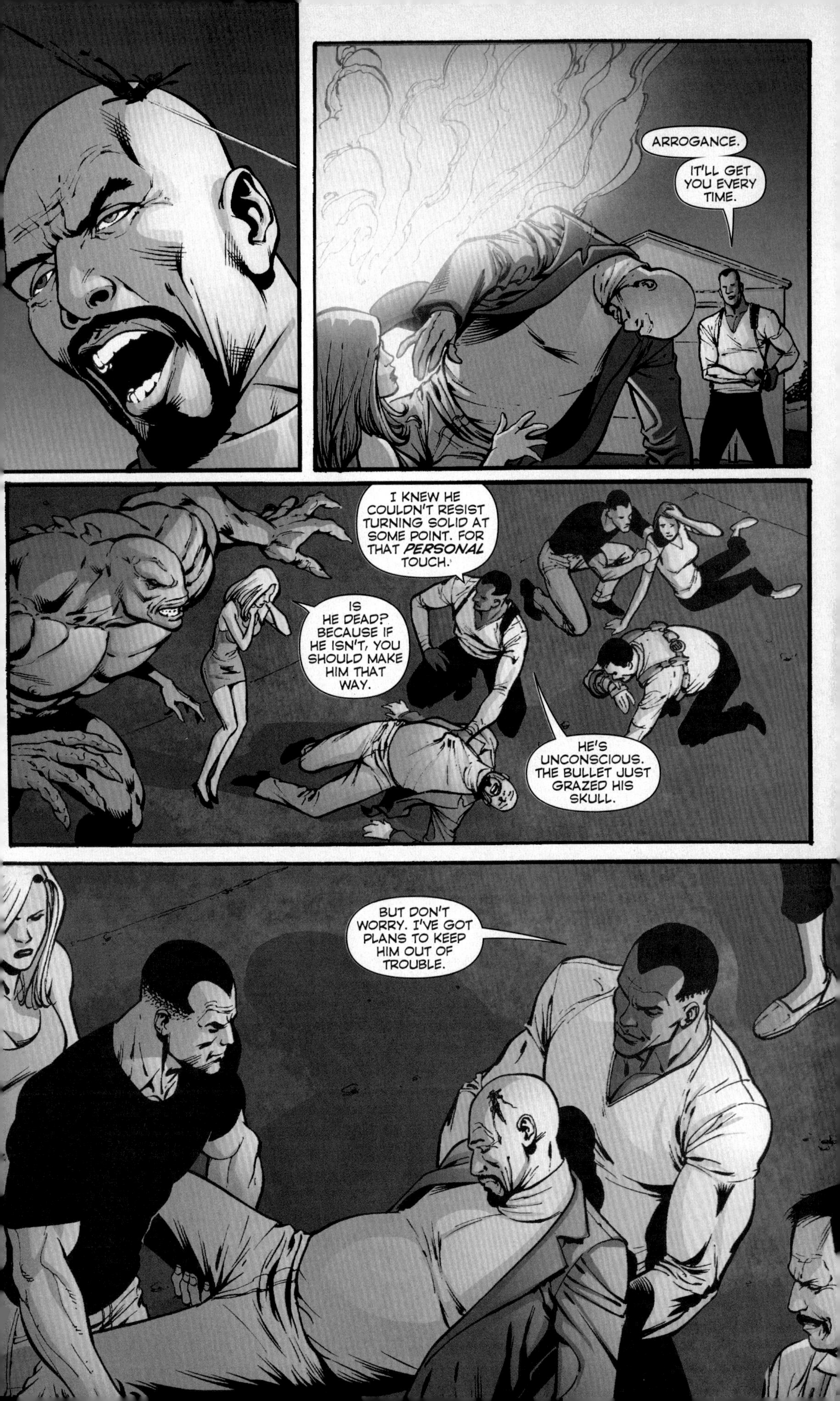
ARROGANCE.
IT'LL GET YOU EVERY TIME.
I KNEW HE COULDN'T RESIST TURNING SOLID AT SOME POINT. FOR THAT *PERSONAL* TOUCH.
IS HE DEAD? BECAUSE IF HE ISN'T, YOU SHOULD MAKE HIM THAT WAY.
HE'S UNCONSCIOUS. THE BULLET JUST GRAZED HIS SKULL.
BUT DON'T WORRY. I'VE GOT PLANS TO KEEP HIM OUT OF TROUBLE.

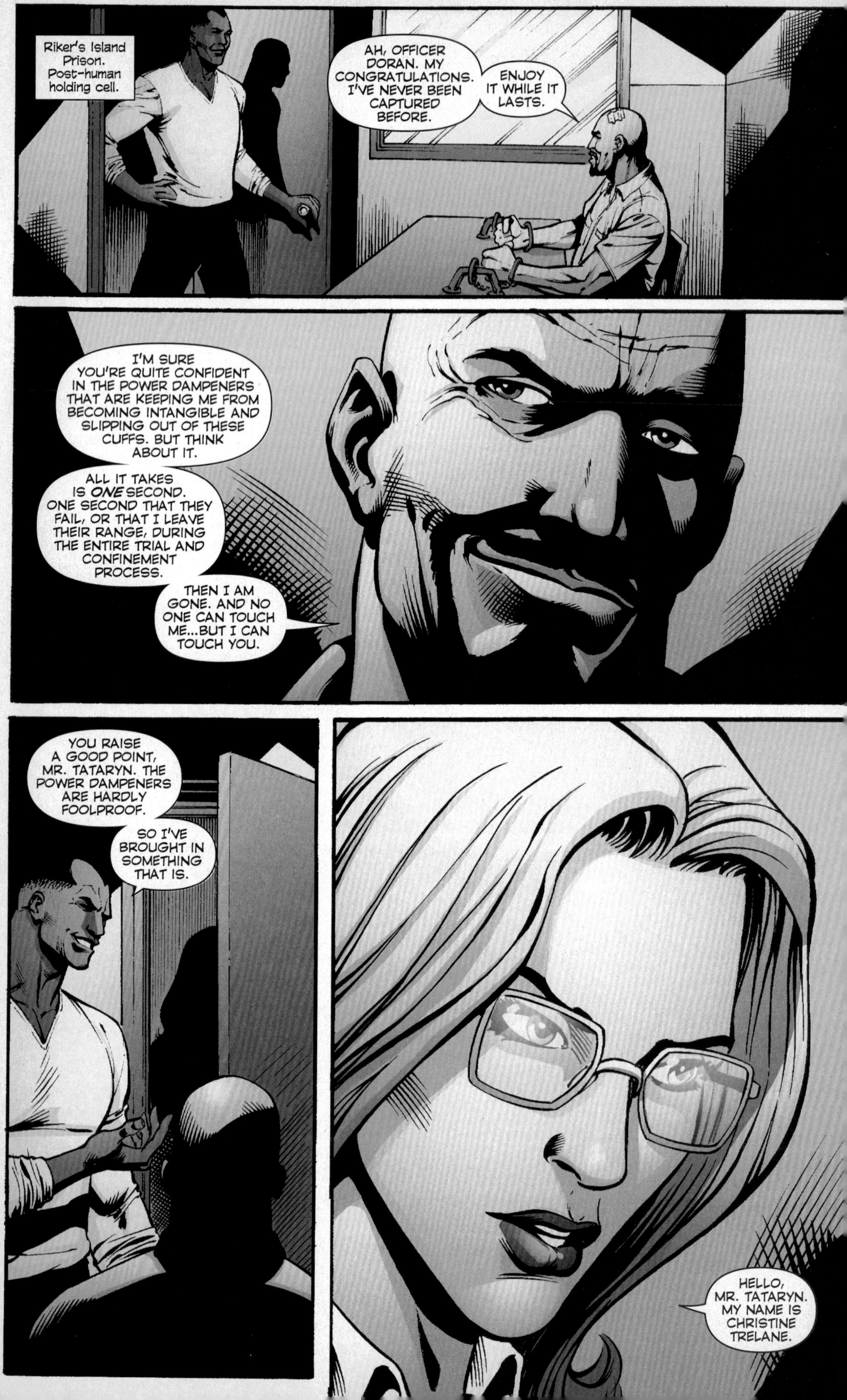
Riker's Island Prison. Post-human holding cell.
AH, OFFICER DORAN. MY CONGRATULATIONS. I'VE NEVER BEEN CAPTURED BEFORE.
ENJOY IT WHILE IT LASTS.
I'M SURE YOU'RE QUITE CONFIDENT IN THE POWER DAMPENERS THAT ARE KEEPING ME FROM BECOMING INTANGIBLE AND SLIPPING OUT OF THESE CUFFS. BUT THINK ABOUT IT.
ALL IT TAKES IS *ONE* SECOND. ONE SECOND THAT THEY FAIL, OR THAT I LEAVE THEIR RANGE, DURING THE ENTIRE TRIAL AND CONFINEMENT PROCESS.
THEN I AM GONE. AND NO ONE CAN TOUCH ME...BUT I CAN TOUCH YOU.
YOU RAISE A GOOD POINT, MR. TATARYN. THE POWER DAMPENERS ARE HARDLY FOOLPROOF.
SO I'VE BROUGHT IN SOMETHING THAT IS.
HELLO, MR. TATARYN. MY NAME IS CHRISTINE TRELANE.

YOU MAY HAVE HEARD OF ME. I'M WHAT'S CALLED AN *ACTIVATOR*...MEANING I CAN ACTIVATE LATENT SUPERHUMAN ABILITIES IN PEOPLE.

A LITTLE-KNOWN COROLLARY OF THAT TALENT IS THAT I CAN ALSO TAKE THEM *AWAY*.

WAIT. YOU CAN'T DO THIS. I HAVE *RIGHTS!*

AMERICAN CITIZENS HAVE RIGHTS, MR. TATARYN. YOU'RE A RUSSIAN NATIONAL, IN THIS COUNTRY ILLEGALLY.

NOW SIT STILL BEFORE YOU HURT YOUR-SELF.

IT'S DONE.

THANK YOU, CHRISTINE. COME ALONG, MR. TATARYN. IT'S TIME TO GO TO YOUR HOLDING CELL.

WAIT! YOU CAN'T PUT ME IN GENERAL POPULATION. THESE MEN ARE FROM RIVAL ORGANIZATIONS! THEY'LL KILL ME!

I'M SORRY, BUT WE HAVE A RATHER SERIOUS PRISON OVER-CROWDING PROBLEM. WE HAVE TO MAKE DO AS BEST WE CAN.

COME ON, COP KILLER. LET'S GET YOU TO YOUR NEW HOME.

PAYBACK TIME, BIG SHOT. AND IT'S GONNA BE *SWEEET.*

...SEE HOW SOLID YOU ARE AT SHOWER TIME, PUNK...

NOoooo

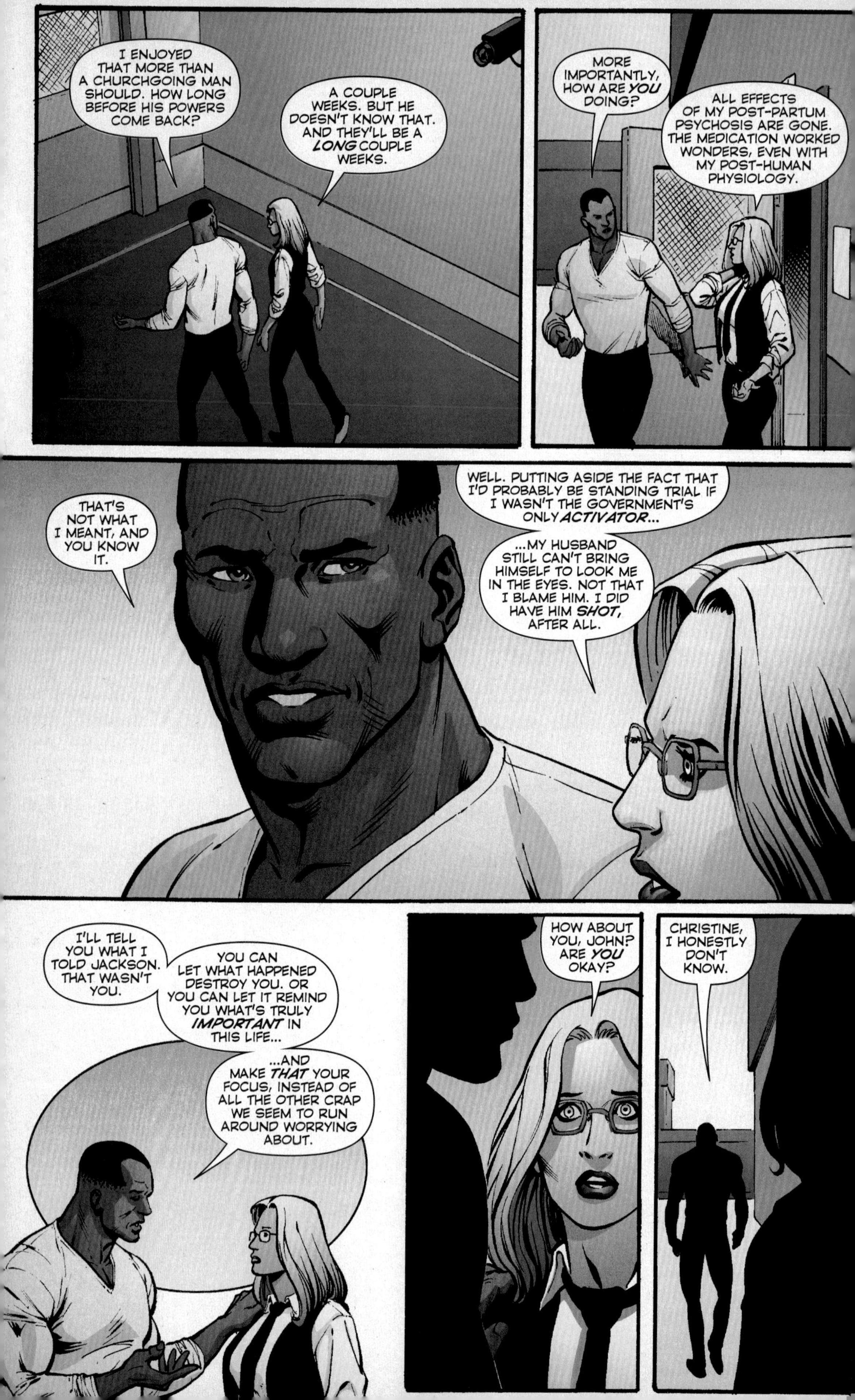
I ENJOYED THAT MORE THAN A CHURCHGOING MAN SHOULD. HOW LONG BEFORE HIS POWERS COME BACK?
A COUPLE WEEKS. BUT HE DOESN'T KNOW THAT. AND THEY'LL BE A *LONG* COUPLE WEEKS.
MORE IMPORTANTLY, HOW ARE *YOU* DOING?
ALL EFFECTS OF MY POST-PARTUM PSYCHOSIS ARE GONE. THE MEDICATION WORKED WONDERS, EVEN WITH MY POST-HUMAN PHYSIOLOGY.
THAT'S NOT WHAT I MEANT, AND YOU KNOW IT.
WELL. PUTTING ASIDE THE FACT THAT I'D PROBABLY BE STANDING TRIAL IF I WASN'T THE GOVERNMENT'S ONLY *ACTIVATOR*...
...MY HUSBAND STILL CAN'T BRING HIMSELF TO LOOK ME IN THE EYES. NOT THAT I BLAME HIM. I DID HAVE HIM *SHOT*, AFTER ALL.
I'LL TELL YOU WHAT I TOLD JACKSON. THAT WASN'T YOU.
YOU CAN LET WHAT HAPPENED DESTROY YOU. OR YOU CAN LET IT REMIND YOU WHAT'S TRULY *IMPORTANT* IN THIS LIFE...
...AND MAKE *THAT* YOUR FOCUS, INSTEAD OF ALL THE OTHER CRAP WE SEEM TO RUN AROUND WORRYING ABOUT.
HOW ABOUT YOU, JOHN? ARE *YOU* OKAY?
CHRISTINE, I HONESTLY DON'T KNOW.

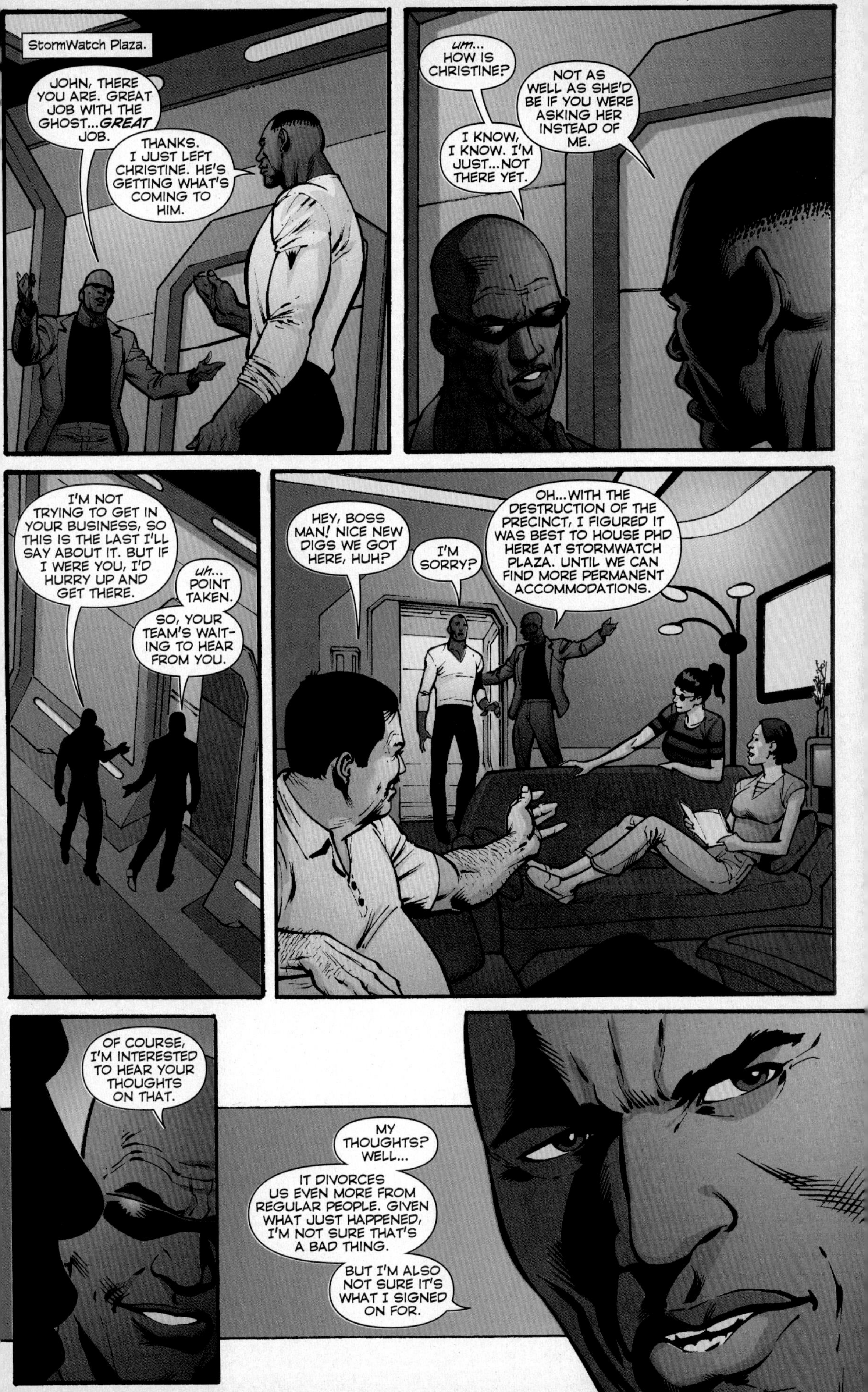
StormWatch Plaza.
JOHN, THERE YOU ARE. GREAT JOB WITH THE GHOST...*GREAT* JOB.
THANKS. I JUST LEFT CHRISTINE. HE'S GETTING WHAT'S COMING TO HIM.
um... HOW IS CHRISTINE?
NOT AS WELL AS SHE'D BE IF YOU WERE ASKING HER INSTEAD OF ME.
I KNOW, I KNOW. I'M JUST...NOT THERE YET.
I'M NOT TRYING TO GET IN YOUR BUSINESS, SO THIS IS THE LAST I'LL SAY ABOUT IT. BUT IF I WERE YOU, I'D HURRY UP AND GET THERE.
uh... POINT TAKEN.
SO, YOUR TEAM'S WAITING TO HEAR FROM YOU.
HEY, BOSS MAN! NICE NEW DIGS WE GOT HERE, HUH?
I'M SORRY?
OH...WITH THE DESTRUCTION OF THE PRECINCT, I FIGURED IT WAS BEST TO HOUSE PHD HERE AT STORMWATCH PLAZA. UNTIL WE CAN FIND MORE PERMANENT ACCOMMODATIONS.
OF COURSE, I'M INTERESTED TO HEAR YOUR THOUGHTS ON THAT.
MY THOUGHTS? WELL...
IT DIVORCES US EVEN MORE FROM REGULAR PEOPLE. GIVEN WHAT JUST HAPPENED, I'M NOT SURE THAT'S A BAD THING.
BUT I'M ALSO NOT SURE IT'S WHAT I SIGNED ON FOR.

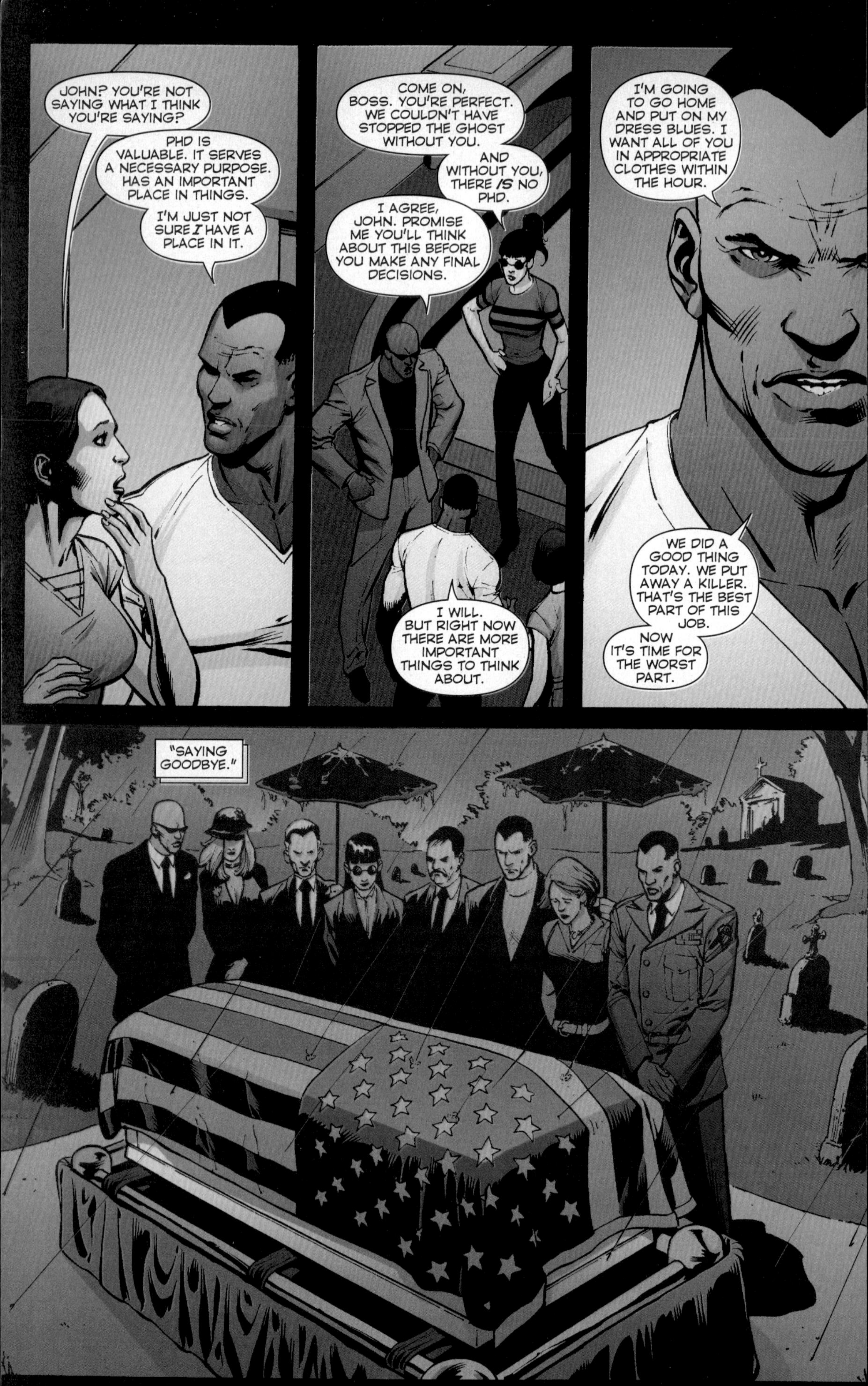
JOHN? YOU'RE NOT SAYING WHAT I THINK YOU'RE SAYING?
PHD IS VALUABLE. IT SERVES A NECESSARY PURPOSE. HAS AN IMPORTANT PLACE IN THINGS.
I'M JUST NOT SURE I HAVE A PLACE IN IT.
COME ON, BOSS. YOU'RE PERFECT. WE COULDN'T HAVE STOPPED THE GHOST WITHOUT YOU.
AND WITHOUT YOU, THERE IS NO PHD.
I AGREE, JOHN. PROMISE ME YOU'LL THINK ABOUT THIS BEFORE YOU MAKE ANY FINAL DECISIONS.
I WILL. BUT RIGHT NOW THERE ARE MORE IMPORTANT THINGS TO THINK ABOUT.
I'M GOING TO GO HOME AND PUT ON MY DRESS BLUES. I WANT ALL OF YOU IN APPROPRIATE CLOTHES WITHIN THE HOUR.
WE DID A GOOD THING TODAY. WE PUT AWAY A KILLER. THAT'S THE BEST PART OF THIS JOB.
NOW IT'S TIME FOR THE WORST PART.
"SAYING GOODBYE."

Sketches and Concept Art

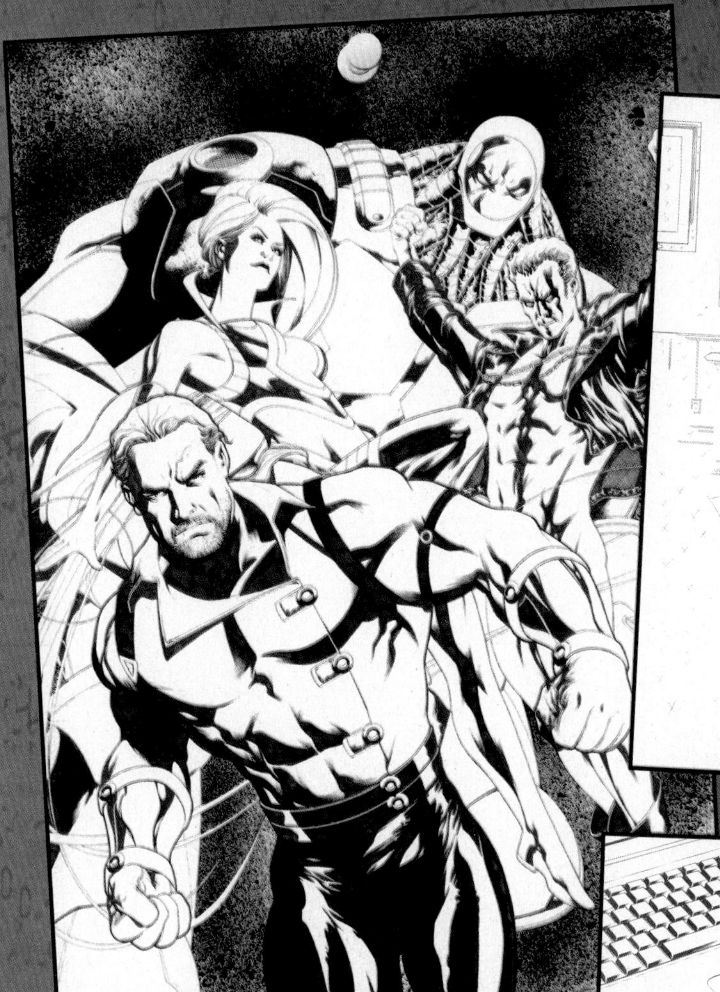

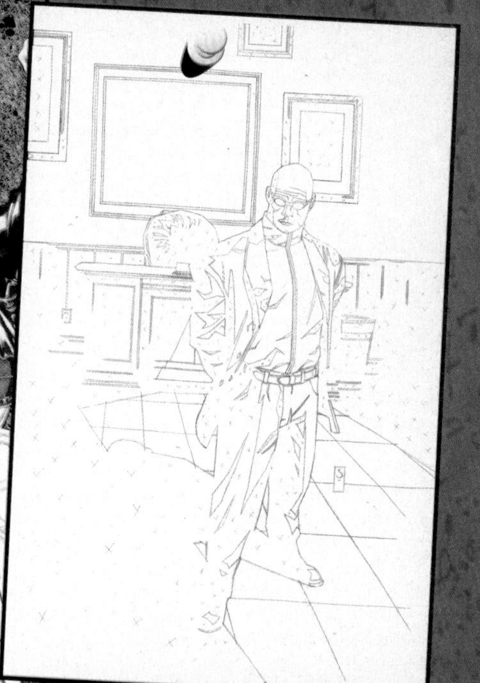

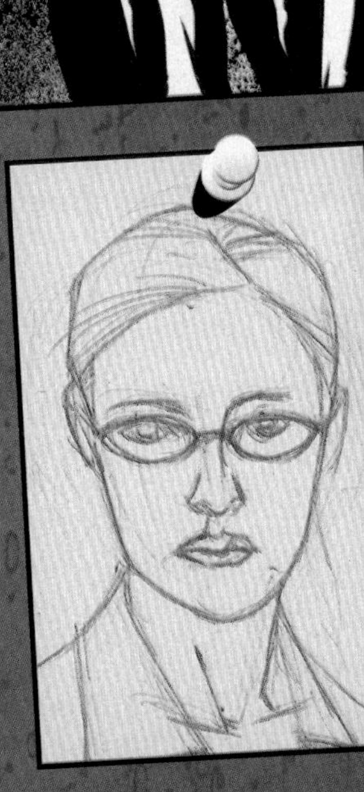

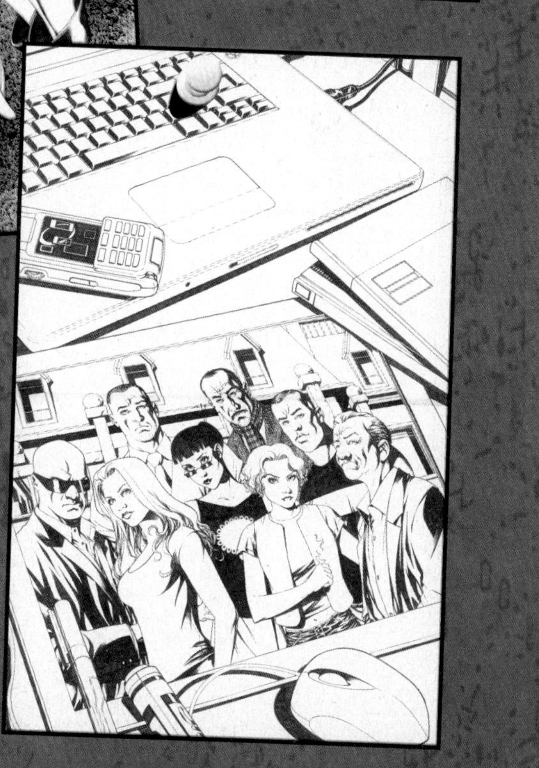

Cover Art by ▲
Mike McKone.

Conceptual art
by Matthew
Dow Smith.▶

These are 2 pinups by
Matthew Dow Smith.